Blackfoot Redemption

Spopee (or Turtle) at the time of his presidential pardon, 1914. Copyright © Underwood & Underwood/Corbis.

Blackfoot Redemption

A Blood Indian's Story of Murder, Confinement, and Imperfect Justice

William E. Farr

University of Oklahoma Press : Norman

This book is published with the generous assistance
of the Kerr Foundation, Inc.

Library of Congress Cataloging-in-Publication Data

Farr, William E., 1938–
  Blackfoot redemption : a Blood Indian's story of murder,
confinement, and imperfect justice / William E. Farr.
      p. cm.
  Includes bibliographical references and index.
  ISBN 978-0-8061-4287-6 (cloth)
  ISBN 978-0-8061-4464-1 (paper)
  1. Kainah Indians—History. 2. Kainah Indians—Crimes against.
3. Indian prisoners—Montana—History. 4. Kainah Indians—
Relocation—Montana—Blackfeet Indian Reservation. 5. Blackfeet
Indian Reservation (Mont.)—History. I. Title.
  E99.K15F37 2012
  978.6004'97352—dc23

                                                    2012011115

For Marianne

CONTENTS

List of Illustrations

MAPS

PHOTOGRAPHS

Preface and Acknowledgments

I have known of the intriguing if sketchy outlines of the Spopee story, as have others, for almost thirty years. I first learned of it in the early 1980s, when Spopee's name came up during a conversation with Joe Bear Medicine, an elder from the Starr School community on Cut Bank Creek, about aspects of the history of the Blackfeet Reservation. We were sitting at his kitchen table on a lovely spring morning; the coffee was hot and sweet, and Joe was in a talkative mood. He knew about Spopee, the Blood Indian from across the Medicine Line in Canada, because early in July 1914, Spopee had returned to Browning and the Blackfeet Reservation from Washington, D.C., to live out what remained of his life with Joe's people, the Southern Piegan, more commonly known as the American Blackfeet. Not that Joe had witnessed the event—he had not—but he had been told about it a good many times. It was a strange story if for no other reason than Spopee "was just like a white guy" when he returned to the world of the northern plains, according to Bear Medicine. Not only did he dress the part, which was easy, but "he could even write," which was not. In fact, the ability to write had long been the distinguishing feature of white culture in the eyes of Indian people. Whether factual or not, this was what Joe had been told, and the gist of this detail left its mark, popping to the surface of the conversation that morning. Sitting there with a yellow legal tablet and pencil at hand, I dutifully scribbled down what I could and then forgot about it. An old and popular story of making White Dog, the invincible Assiniboine, "cry" was far more interesting, and

Joe thought so too as he began to sing the well-known song that told the story, the side of his large finger thumping the drum beat against the edge of the table.

A number of Blackfeet historians have also stumbled across pieces of this strange case as they researched other topics, particularly after 1914, when for a second time Spopee enjoyed the unexpected benefits of executive clemency—a presidential pardon—this time on the part of Woodrow Wilson, President of the United States, for the killing of a white man in 1879.

Yet no one, not Bear Medicine, the historians, or myself, knew what to make of Spopee's story, or at least the limited portions of it that we encountered. Neither did the Blackfeet themselves. It was like the parable of blind men attempting to discern the shape of an elephant by running their hands over only a single part. Spopee's story had many parts—it was a story of personal loss, an unfair trial, imprisonment and confinement, and belated redemption. It was also a story of perseverance, a story of how translating from one language to another inevitably begot confusion and cultural misunderstanding, and a story with terrible consequences.

But the parts were fragmentary and inadequate, and thus the story was incomplete and thin; it had no legs. What did it mean? How could the fragments be sorted out? Could they lead to something more interesting? Could one part of the story be a loose end, like that of a double-knotted shoe lace that miraculously opens when you tug on one end? Could it be a point of entry, a pathway to understanding, a Rosetta stone giving critical clues to decipher Blackfeet situations otherwise flat or opaque and mysterious? Maybe Spopee's story too would open up, illustrate, or render understandable larger historical contexts: the continued relationships between the Blackfoot-speaking relatives—the Niitzitapi, or "Real People"—on both sides of the emerging American/Canadian border, be they Blood, Piegan, or Blackfoot proper, in the last days of the buffalo, for example, or maybe the myriad transformations necessitated by the creation of reservations there or here, following Treaty 7 in 1877. In other words, would telling Spopee's individual story inform a larger, tribal story, namely, that of the people's forced return to and confinement within their reservation in 1880, just after Spopee's capture and confinement?

Historians have often used the stories of individuals to throw into relief broader questions. So for example, Clare V. McKanna, hoping to illuminate the broader issues of race and justice in late nineteenth-century California, employed a double homicide case and the subsequent trial of "Indian Joe."[1] Reading McKanna, I remembered Spopee and thought his case might prove to be as rich and compelling for understanding issues relating to the Niitzitapi as a whole and the American Blackfeet in particular. After all, Spopee had witnessed and experienced the deadly starvation year of 1879, when the buffalo ranges of what would become Alberta had contracted and the once-teeming buffalo had miraculously disappeared. As had others there, including the period's most important political leader, the Siksika leader Crowfoot, Spopee had reluctantly left for Montana Territory and the still numerous buffalo populations south of the Missouri River in the United States. Would knowing Spopee's whole story, in detail, shed light on or make vivid these concurrent experiences?

I thought the chances or portents were pretty good if for no other reason than pieces of Spopee's broken narrative were intertwined with a number of governmental agencies that kept written records, sometimes meticulous ones, now accessible in archives to historical research. This evidentiary embrace happened as a result of Spopee having been tragically involved, along with a young Blood companion, Good Rider, in the death or murder of a white man. Where the event occurred is unknown. Fortunately for us, however, crimes, jurisdictions, arrests, and legal proceedings require prodigious documentation. Thus we know that either before or after the incident, the two Blood Indians had then fled across an emerging international border that was supposed to separate the United States from Canada, "their Indians from our Indians." In the grip of a particularly severe winter storm in 1879, Spopee was chased and arrested in an Indian camp by a famous whisky trader turned sheriff of Chouteau County, Montana. Encouraging too for the researcher were the detailed reports of Spopee's subsequent trial in the territorial capitol of Helena in the 1880s, when competing newspapers were already hungrily looking for information, gossip, political advantage, and stories of human interest, local and international. It also helped that Spopee was defended by Montana Territory's most prominent lawyer and national Republican political shaker, Wilbur Fisk Sanders, later to become one of Montana's first senators following statehood in November of 1889.

Webs of such personal entanglements and institutional attentions raised the probability that archival research might well give Spopee's story sufficient heft and telling detail to lift him out of the unfortunate anonymity most Blackfeet men and women of the time were consigned to. Blackfeet cultural differences, language barriers, and a tradition of oral transmission that had trouble communicating much beyond straightforward war exploits for more than three generations, left whites, then and now, blissfully ignorant of individual lives or behaviors on the Indian side of the territorial equation. Tribal census enumerations or ration rolls did little to fill in the blanks or rectify the situation. Agency officials wrote into the long vertical columns of their ledgers little more than the names of individuals coming to stand before them and an interpreter, along with perhaps the notation of gender, age, and maybe marital status.

The names officials transcribed were wonderfully descriptive Blackfoot names, in the best instances in both Blackfoot and English, although many times only in English. The Blackfoot names underwent multiple renderings into English, ranging from the easy, as with "Rides a Good Horse" becoming "Good Rider," to the less obvious, as with "Powder Bull" becoming "Dusty Bull." A father's heroic war exploits could result in multiple names for his various children, and thus personal names could become tribal reminders of individual bravery. In other cases, names that had once belonged to someone else, an ancestor or a relative, were bestowed again as an honor or a remembrance. And a single person could have multiple names throughout a lifetime, further complicating research.

The information in the ration lists and census data was precious information, to be sure, but could more be found? More importantly, would there be enough of an unadulterated Indian voice to give the emerging story, however asymmetrical, a semblance of shared involvement, so that in the end, after the laborious accretion of details, this salvaged and reconstructed record would return to public memory something of the Blackfeet experience? There needed to be a return on my investment. Or would Spopee's story remain broken and fragmented, little more in the end than at its beginning—a thin anecdotal story that simply petered out, that, for lack of evidence, went nowhere?

After all these years of knowing the beginning, I decided in 2001 that it was time to take the leap, to find out "the rest of the story," as the popular radio newscaster Paul Harvey used to say. But had I waited too long? Joe Bear Medicine and his generation were now gone, and all of the questions I should have asked, that could have been answered, somewhere in the reservation community, were now met with shaking heads, a suggestion that maybe so and so would know, or worse, blank faces and silence. I wished I had started earlier, before Joe Bear Medicine died in 1999. George and Molly Kickingwoman would have known, so too Mary Ground, or Grass Woman, or Percy Bullchild, Joe Bear Medicine's brother-in-law and author of *When the Sun Came Down*. Now, however crippled by these losses, I decided to belatedly capture what I still could of Spopee's story. Maybe there was some oral memory in Canada among the Bloods or the North Piegan. Maybe a Blackfoot-speaking elder, when asked about Spopee, would help out with the puzzle, like one of the elephant's blind men, remembering a missing and isolated piece of the fragmented story. Whatever was left, it would still be more than what I had, and already there was enough to encourage. With all this in mind, I set off on what would become a decade-long journey.

It is with real pleasure and some trepidation that I face the task of thanking people who have helped me in the research and writing of this book about the compelling trials of Spopee and the affiliated travails of the Southern Piegan, also known as the American Blackfeet. Research has always been a joint effort; books are not written alone or without help. Many individuals and institutions have lent a contributing hand in the attempt to find the muted voice of Spopee and to adequately describe the bewildering confusion that attended the confinement of the Blackfeet and their transition to the institutions of the early reservation period.

One of the first to provide guidance was Joe Bear Medicine, who patiently explained by story, song, and a quiet piety what it means to be an individual Piegan searching for historical direction and spiritual meaning. Eventually Bear Medicine gave me a name that he thought fitting, High Eagle, because I too, however inadequately, was searching for people, stories, and photographs, for experiences that give meaning and identity to the same reservation experience. Although I was the outsider and Joe the insider, we were fellow searchers. After Joe died, his nephew, Earl Old Person, hereditary chief of the Blackfeet and tribal chairman for many years, graciously continued to school me with detailed commentary, gentle correction, and the same quiet, self-contained religiosity expressed by his uncle. To both of these mentors I owe a great deal.

Another elder, this time in the Blood community, Charles Crow Chief, provided critical information through interviews about Spopee, particularly after he returned to the northern Plains in 1914. This information, as well as the origins of Spopee's name and his association with Good Rider, sparked questions regarding their "other" names and their identities that were essential for a better understanding of how Spopee was remembered north of the border among the Bloods.

Closer to home, here at the University of Montana, I have had the help of a number of dedicated and wonderful people, and I want to thank them. Gloria Phillip was a student of mine and then a research assistant at the O'Connor Center for the Rocky Mountain West. She meticulously researched microfilmed newspapers and rolls of microfilm from the National Archives, doing so with care, insight, and never a complaint. Jeannie Thompson, administrative secretary at the center, helped improve this effort in multiple ways, from helping me with my unfathomable computer to reading chapters and making certain that my sentences were short and my speculations grounded. The O'Connor Center for the Rocky Mountain West and its director, Larry Swanson, provided funding, time, and infusions of interest and encouragement as well as a welcome work environment and an office with curtains. I also want to thank two of my colleagues and friends in Missoula: first, historian David Emmons, who read and commented upon the Spopee project, chapter by chapter, with multiple suggestions and a historical imagination that prodded and provoked. And, of course, I want to thank philosopher Albert Borgmann, my running companion of decades, who listened patiently, run after run, as I tried to sort through Spopee's story and who periodically suggested avenues to deepen the analysis or to find meaning or grace.

Collaborations are critical and I have enjoyed the assistance of a number of dedicated professionals—archivists, historians, and librarians—who responded to my pleas for help without reservation, even eagerly. These include Eric Bittner, archivist, National Archives and Records Administration, Rocky Mountain Region, Denver, Colorado, who cheerfully responded to my many requests by telephone or e-mail; MaryFrances Ronan, archivist, Indian and Land Records at the National Archives in Washington, D.C., who helped tremendously in locating key documents and photographs; Brian Shovers, reference historian, Montana Historical Society Library, Helena, Montana, who went out of his way, repeatedly, to find references, corroborate details, and photocopy newspaper articles from their collection; Henry L. Armstrong and especially Ken Robinson of the Overholser Research Center in Fort Benton, who fielded inquiry after inquiry; Bonnie Moffet from the Writing-on-Stone Provincial Park, Alberta; Delores Morrow, in charge of the photograph archives at the Montana Historical Society in Helena, Montana; Harrison Red Crow, transcriber and translator with the Band Office on the Blood Reserve, who asked Blood elders about their knowledge of Spopee; Donna McCrea, archivist, K. Ross Toole Archives, Mansfield Library, University of Montana, who gave assistance in document recovery and citations associated with a University of Montana digital pilot program, Natives of Montana Archival Project (NOMAP); and Susanne Caro, government documents librarian, Mansfield Library, University of Montana, who helped me thread my way through the digital maze of government documents via databases.

I want to thank especially Dr. Jogues Prandoni, Health Systems Consultant, St. Elizabeths Hospital, Washington, D.C., whose time and expertise I came close to monopolizing as he researched, copied, and sent historical photographs of the hospital, researched physician records, and read with insight and care the critical chapter six dealing with Spopee's long incarceration at the Government Hospital for the Insane. In doing so, Dr. Prandoni not only provided essential information in terms of the historical and institutional record, but boosted my sense of confidence that Spopee's institutional record had been correctly described and understood.

Thanks also are in order for David Vecchioli, for sending me a copy of his 1997 presentation at the 29th Algonquian Conference in Thunder Bay, Ontario. Titled "'Where the Boundary Line Is:' Spopee and Blackfoot Borderlands," it had been written while he was a student at the University of Maryland. Although I have taken a significantly different tack on the significance of Spopee, Mr. Vecchioli's archival digging in the National Archives was impressive and extremely useful to me and my subsequent research.

Neal Wiegart, graphic artist with Printing Services at the University of Montana, did the wonderful maps for this book, and he graciously made numerous new additions and corrections with patience and a desire "to get it right."

This book is one historian's effort "to get it right" as well, and in that effort I have benefited immensely from the evaluations of two historians, Hugh A. Dempsey and Sherry L. Smith, who served as outside readers for the University of Oklahoma Press. No one knows the Blackfoot-speaking peoples of the northern Plains better than Dempsey does, and his numerous works and critical support much improved my efforts to give this bitter tale a Blood perspective. Sherry Smith urged a broader conception and challenged me to reorganize a good deal of the material in ways that were always helpful; she also alerted me to a number of parallel stories and bibliographic suggestions that jump-started new tangents and directions. Thanks to both of these scholars, this endeavor now has more coherence and more application than before.

Finally, I would like to thank my friend and colleague from Montana days, Chuck Rankin, now editor-in chief at the University of Oklahoma Press. From the very beginning he encouraged me to undertake the project and gave me a periodic boosts in order to persevere, to follow what was in the beginning but a simple story, with only a faint trail leading to it or away from it. Along the way Chuck offered sage analysis and kept steering the Spopee story forward. Thanks as well to Alice Stanton, special projects editor at OU Press, and to Patricia Heinicke, Jr., who spent an enormous amount of care in making the manuscript as consistent and readable as it could be, given what she had to work with. It was an enjoyable collaboration.

BLACKFOOT REDEMPTION

Introduction

The Tragedy of Spopee

In the early spring of 1914, as the cherry trees in Washington, D.C., blossomed and seasonal regeneration scented the warming air, the personal tragedy of a Blood Indian by the name of Spopee or Turtle unexpectedly surfaced. When taken up by government officials at the Office of Indian Affairs, the case of Spopee became a sensational media event across the nation. Then over sixty years old, Spopee had recently been discovered in St. Elizabeths Hospital, the Government Hospital for the Insane, not far from the U.S. capitol complex and the White House. The former buffalo hunter from the undulating short-grass plains of northern Montana had languished there within the generous confines of the mental asylum, vanished if not lost, for thirty-two long years.

His subsequent story as it was unearthed, piece by piece, was deemed newsworthy in terms of its human interest for dozens of newspapers, tragic for its enduring protagonist, and nostalgic for Americans, lamenting the loss of their enchanting frontier past, which included, they believed, the "vanishing Indian." Newspapers across the whole of the United States, now supplied by national syndicates and newswires, ran touching accounts of this former nomadic hunter from the picturesque tepee camps of the upper

3

Missouri River and his phoenix-like experience as he emerged into the hectic industrialized world of the urban and modern East.

It was not unlike the experience of another vanished "red man," the last member of the California Yahi, named Ishi. Near starvation, Ishi had unexpectedly walked out of a remote canyon near Chico in August of 1911 to end up in civilization and the city of San Francisco.[1] Ishi was celebrated as a "Stone-Age" man, and newspaper reporters investigated his astonishing ability to imitate the calls of coyotes and birds, to craft wooden bows, and to precisely flake arrowheads. He had walked unexpectedly out of the past into the present, delighting a romantic nation that had long searched for aboriginal survivors, mainly in books of ethnography and old photographs. Now instead of a fossilized image or artifact, here was a "real" individual, Ishi, who quickly became literally a living museum exhibit, under the supervision of Berkeley anthropologist Alfred Kroeber.

Spopee also attracted national attention—not because he had stepped out of the Stone Age as if from behind a tree, but because he appeared to have stepped off the pages of a fairy tale. Journalists likened Spopee's story to Washington Irving's popular short story of Rip van Winkle, who, after consorting with ne'er-do-wells and drinking a magic elixir, fell asleep; dead to the world, he woke up twenty years later to a profoundly changed world. Spopee had indeed "fallen asleep"; in 1880, at about the age of thirty, he had disappeared from his Blood homeland in what would become the southern part of the province of Alberta, as well as from the last big buffalo camps of the Judith Basin, south of the Missouri River, in the Territory of Montana. Taken away from his people for the alleged murder of a white man, Spopee had disappeared, swallowed first by a jail in Helena, Montana, then by a distant federal prison, the Detroit House of Correction. Nearly invisible and ghostlike in the official records, Spopee finally tumbled to rest in St. Elizabeths Hospital on the nation's east coast, in Washington, D.C., about as far away from home as he could possibly be.[2]

By 1883, Spopee had become physically mute, and his post-trial odyssey had gone all but unnoted in the drawn-out bureaucratic process. For most of his people, he had simply disappeared—they didn't know where. As for Spopee, he lost his bearings, his family,

Spopee in profile. (National Archives and
Records Administration, RG 418, St. Elizabeths
Hospital, case file 54465.)

his sense of self. He was unable or unwilling to communicate. Not
only did he not speak English, he did not speak at all. Unable to
communicate in his own Blackfoot language, misunderstood when
he attempted English, and humiliated by having had his long braids
chopped off, he lost his very identity as a band member, a relative, a
warrior in an age-grade society, a husband, and a father. All that he
had known he left behind, like a loved one on a port dock seen from
the stern of a departing ship.

Thirty-two years later, in 1914, as the spring days lengthened and
became brighter near the Potomac River in the District of Columbia, Spopee was jarred awake and asked to step into the present. It
was near the beginning of the twentieth century. Endless numbers

of electric lights now lit up America's burgeoning cities and towns. Coughing automobiles with strange names and even flying machines had become common sights and sounds in the shaded urban canyons of major U.S. cities.

The remembered knots and herds of black buffalo, heads down, grazing peacefully across a boundless swell of bunchgrass, were gone—as were the grey wolves that shadowed them. Their other close companions and predators, the Niitzitapi, or "Real People," the Blackfoot of Spopee's youth,[3] were still there, where they had always been, but like Spopee, they were no longer nomadic, free, or independent. Instead, they were confined to dismal reserves and reservations in what had become the United States and Canada, needing permission and written passes to leave even for occasional external visits. They were locked up perceptually as well as physically, because they were thought of as people confined to the past. Non-Indians on both sides of the international border would not allow the Niitzitapi into the changing present. They could exist perceptually only in a discontinued and romantic past, as if frozen in time. That past was where Indians belonged, and nowhere else.

In retrospect, these were parallel confinements—one for Spopee, following his personal flight to the Judith Basin and his subsequent abrupt arrest and removal for trial, and one for the Southern Piegan, also known as the American Blackfeet, who at the same time were about to collectively enter a long period of their own confinement, punctuated by unprecedented disruptions, economic trials, and prolonged psychic suffering. The Southern Piegan, like Spopee, could point to a common single event in 1879–80 that seemed to herald and cause their long time of troubles—in their case it began with their forced removal under their chief, White Calf, by the U.S. Army, from their traditional hunting grounds south of the Missouri and confinement to a reduced reservation whose boundaries they had not agreed to. Their treaty rights and legal standing had been ignored. Mercifully, both Spopee and the Southern Piegan under White Calf were unaware of the trials that awaited them. In Spopee's case, this would include capture, handcuffs, and a lengthy incarceration in Helena prior to a trial for murder and a last-minute presidential commutation of his death sentence to confinement for life in prison.

Subsequently, Spopee would be declared insane and transferred from a federal penitentiary in Detroit to custody in the government insane asylum, St. Elizabeths, in distant Washington, D.C.

Spopee's dismal circumstances coincided with and mirrored an emerging tribal tragedy. Collectively, the American Blackfeet would also experience arrest by U.S. authorities. They would be marched away, in the middle of a hunt, in the dead of winter, under blizzard conditions, and then unjustly, if not illegally, restricted to a reduced reservation void of game, large or small. It was only the beginning. There followed the bewildering disappearance of the buffalo by 1883, a winter of bureaucratic bungling that led to a staggering number of Piegan deaths due to a lack of owed rations, and the numbing loss of their former lives as "buffalo people." And as with Spopee's case, this confinement revealed the ease with which the legal rights of the Southern Piegan, which had been achieved via Lame Bull's treaty of 1855, could be ignored, dismissed, and violated.

While both stories have sometimes been alluded to, neither has been told before in any detail. And while the two confinements were, of course, separate, discrete events, occasioned by wholly different causes, I am struck by their similarity and resemblance. These were parallel situations. Spopee's fate meshed with that of his people. They were both subject to many of the same physical and mental stresses, and both shared the anxiety of having to wait behind their own restricting bars for an undetermined future. Both stories reveal as well the inherent racism that underlay the government policies of the day, and the growing white determination to contain and control Indian mobility and choice, as well as the American resolve to impose an all-encompassing system of what should pass as legal justice.

Asylums, be they hospitals or Indian reservations, come in various dimensions and with significant consequences. By 1914, both Spopee and the other Blackfoot-speakers in Canada and the United States had been confined for a long time. They were out of sight and out of mind—and while they had not yet become invisible, which over time would happen, both were remarkably silent and long-suffering. With the turn of the twentieth century, however, American Indians, including Plains Indians, erroneously believed to have essentially vanished, had again become the focus of popular interest among non-Indians. No longer seen as threatening, blood-thirsty enemies or "poor degenerates" without virtue, they became role models for Boy Scouts in search of outdoor and woodcraft skills and for business executives sitting behind desks, in need of physical exercise, anxious to recover a primitive vitality. Championed by sportsmen adventurers, old frontiersmen, and self-appointed Indian advocates, a popular literature extolling Indians, their cultures, and their humanity changed forever American perceptions.[4] Moreover, there was such an interest in the collecting of Indian images and artifacts, blankets, baskets, and pots that people referred to these activities as an "Indian craze."[5] Ishi's appearance and subsequent phenomenon brought further attention to what had been lost in the transition to modern America. "Past-tense Indians" were now, from a distance, remarkably interesting and inspiring, something to cele-brate as quintessentially American.

Spopee's unusual story came to light when two delegations of Southern Piegan leaders, from Browning in north-central Montana, visited the commissioner of Indian Affairs in Washington, D.C., in the spring of 1914. Such group visits from the Indian reservations of the American West, often initiated by government officials to im-press and overwhelm, had enjoyed a long history and were still quite common in the early twentieth century. Numerous delegations of American Indians made their way to the Great Father and the Office of Indian Affairs in Washington, seeking federal redress or support for promises made, as well as help with local projects ranging from irrigation to education. While in Washington, they would visit the various institutions of the federal government, bargaining for better conditions, for additional public support, for local political advan-tage.[6] There was a routine to these visits: a predictable round of con-gressional offices to visit, committees and subcommittees to lobby, and legal firms to see as the tribal representatives performed their intricate political minuet of nodding, handshaking, and convincing. Each delegation of Indian leaders arrived in Washington harbor-ing high expectations, but these were generally tamped down by bureaucratic delays and maneuverings. More often than not, reser-vation politics created a churn of inexperienced tribal leaders and many went home empty-handed, shaking their heads at what they had seen. In this instance, however unsuccessful they were politically, the Blackfeet leaders would find Spopee, alias Turtle.

Prior to the spring of 1914 very few Washington officials even knew that a peculiar American Indian by that name had grown old, heavy, and grey while confined in nearby St. Elizabeths Hospital. In Washington, then as now, a loud voice meant everything—even in an insane asylum. Spopee, however, was mute—either barely able or unwilling to speak—and he had been that way for a very long time. All that was known was that he was an American Indian convicted of a capital crime and that after first entering the jurisdictional maze of the federal justice system, he had been admitted to St. Elizabeths as case 5445, an "Indian, Indigent Convict."[7]

Much of the mystery surrounding Spopee stemmed from the inability of officials to communicate with him, or he with them. It was hard to know what to do with him. Unable to rely upon Spopee himself for testimony or information, baffled and busy officials relied upon the insufficient and incomplete official records that had been sent with him at the time of his admission. Because the officials were unable to confirm or learn anything new from the speechless and stoic patient, and were not even certain as to his tribal origins, Spopee languished quietly, even calmly, year after year—for over thirty-two years. Medical examiners at the Detroit House of Correction, where Spopee had been confined prior to his lockup at St. Elizabeths, had diagnosed his uncommon silence and lack of assertiveness as "severe melancholia," "chronic mania," or "depression," so much so that he was judged insane. The specific details of his malady or speculation as to its cause were either lost or hidden away in his medical records, ignored or at least not consulted, and slowly forgotten.

Spopee, only wanly present, became leaden and spiritless, if not invisible—a ghost of himself. And, of course, the Blackfeet believed in ghosts. After individuals died, their spirits often went to the Sand Hills on the edge of their territory to live as before in a spirit world. In other cases, however, ghosts who did not want to leave stayed close to home to protect their loved ones, or they were so irritated that their life had been violently taken that they wanted revenge and would not leave the living alone. This was particularly true of the ghosts killed by their enemies. Ghosts had different attitudes and different names. The general term was *stau-au*, meaning "fearing something unseen." A ghost that was well disposed or benign went by the name of "nothing," or a "fleshless person."[8] Spopee came close to being such a person. He had left the world of the living. He was a creature out of time, living where he did not belong. His past was gone, and there was no future. There was in its place a concrete, institutional present that gave no happiness; it came replete with white-coated authority, regimentation, and strictly enforced, if novel, regulations. Spopee's experience was all amazingly evocative of the Indian chief in Ken Kesey's modern novel *One Flew Over the Cuckoo's Nest* (1962), set in an Oregon mental asylum, who found it easier to negotiate his institutional world by pretending to be deaf and mute and who eventually escaped.

What had become of Spopee the skilled buffalo hunter, who had wildly raced, clamped to the back of a horse, into the dangerous melee of a stampeding herd, across uneven ground, riddled with prairie dog holes? Like Spopee himself, that world had become invisible if not extinct. Things could have been worse, of course. After all, St. Elizabeths was a hospital, an asylum, designed to protect and to heal the defenseless and the sick. It was not a prison focused on retribution or punishment. But that may not have mattered to a man who had become a ghost.

Once in a while, hoping to break through Spopee's invisible barrier of silence, a caring official would attempt to attract various visiting Indian delegations to come to St. Elizabeths Hospital. It was not an onerous journey from the capitol complex and the Washington law firms, and the hospital harbored a mysterious Indian detainee, maybe one of their own tribe. But these humanitarian efforts, however well-intentioned, came to nothing. Spopee generally viewed his few Indian visitors with a cold hostility. It was as if they had been tribal enemies, which, in fact, they may have been, and Spopee offered little more than silent disdain or a firm rejection. The asylum attendants would prod the Indian visitors to try and speak to Spopee in their own tongue—again, to no avail. Not a flicker of recognition crossed his frozen face. Rebuffed by the glaring older man, the Cree,

Cheyenne, or Arapahoe contingents inevitably gave up and went away to business or happier tourist pursuits, and Spopee returned to his silent and consoling routines, those guiding grooves, worn by him over the years into the surrounding institutional marble.

The first wobble out of these comfortable patterns and his equally protective wall of self-imposed silence came in the early years of the twentieth century, when some Sioux, visiting a member of their own tribe also confined in St. Elizabeths, wanted to learn about that other Indian patient, Spopee. Again, hospital officials encouraged the visitors to try to talk with Spopee, and this time, for whatever reason, he responded, deliberately attempting to formulate the difficult words that communication required. With lips loosened into unfamiliar shape, Spopee ineptly blurted out, in garbled fashion, that he was "Ba-fo." While this might have been unintelligible gibberish to his staff guardians, the Sioux understood his awkward efforts to speak English and knew he was attempting to say "Blackfoot." They carried word of this surprising revelation to two delegations of Blackfeet, as the Southern Piegan were now called, that were fortuitously visiting the capitol at the same time.[9]

In response, the Blackfeet from Browning, Montana, showed up at St. Elizabeths. One delegation was made up of progressive mixed-blood stockmen, including James Perrine, Charles W. Buck, and Mr. and Mrs. Malcolm Clark, who supported the proposed sale of surplus reservation lands following the breakup of the reservation known as allotment. The other was led by their outspoken opponent, Robert J. Hamilton, adopted mixed-blood son of A. B. Hamilton and the leader of a full-blood faction eager for agency reform and opposed to the proposed sale of Blackfeet Reservation land. (How bizarre that two of the children of A. B. Hamilton, who helped put Spopee away, would be part of the group that brought him out of his silence.) Both factions had come to Washington to represent their positions and were represented by local Washington attorneys in their struggle for recognition and political legitimacy.[10] Setting their differences aside for the moment, all did their best to engage Spopee. One question followed another. "First one, then the other . . . spoke to the old Indian. In the swinging, rolling, sonorous dialect of the tribe they questioned him." Spopee, at first hesitant and awkward, initially reverted to his old, tortured performance. Although his eyes registered attention and he painfully attempted to speak, his only replies were broken syllables and parts of words. It was as if he could not remember his own language. He struggled but could not form the necessary sounds.

Undeterred, the Blackfeet men tried sign language, an alternative means of communication between Indian tribes on the northern plains and one that elderly Blackfeet often used simultaneously when speaking. It was a parallel system that could either stand alone or reinforce and give color to speech. Although this practice was common at the time, sign-talk too failed to rouse Spopee—he merely shook his head.

At this juncture, Mrs. Ella Clark, who had accompanied her husband, became frustrated by the pitiful attempts of the reservation men and stepped forward. Although a mixed-blood and educated, she spoke fluent Blackfoot. Her father, Alfred B. Hamilton, had been a prominent white trader among the Blackfoot tribes on both sides of the border and would play an important, if negative, part in the Montana parts of Spopee's story. He spoke Blackfoot well and was known among the people as Inuispi, or "Long Hair." Like many early traders, Hamilton had married a Piegan woman. Her name was Lucy, a daughter of Iron Breast and Cut-a-est-t-ke-na, and with her Hamilton had fathered two daughters, Ella, born in 1874 and Gracie in 1880.[11]

Abandoning the more direct, if not inquisitorial, questioning of the men, Ella adopted the "little people's talk," the soft, encouraging baby talk employed universally by mothers, Blackfeet and otherwise. Speaking Blackfoot, she introduced herself in Indian style, telling the older Spopee her name and, of course, who she was related to, who her people were, who she was. Then, to the astonishment of the other members of the delegation, she began to softly croon an ancient lullaby. Periodically she interrupted this soothing refrain with descriptions of the grassy, well-watered Piegan country east of the Rocky Mountains or talked of the mountains, what the Blackfeet called Mistakis, or "the Backbone of the World." She described how the various bands had scattered up and down the creeks and rivers emerging from the mountains within sight of Ninastako, or Chief

Mountain, the lone sentinel that marks the boundary line between the United States and Canada. She explained how the black buffalo herds were now gone from the high prairies and river bottoms, no longer providing the Blackfeet with a solid and reliable living.[12]

These brief descriptions of home had to have resonated with the silent inmate as he struggled to understand. When she then casually asked his name, "he unhesitatingly spoke it: 'Spo-pee.'"[13] Startled with the breakthrough, the interviewers sucked in their breaths, Indian fashion, before impulsively asking other, more demanding queries. Bumping into each other, the questions quickly overwhelmed Spopee. He stopped responding, retreated, and only listened. Spopee surprised them again, however. He interrupted their questions and asked in Blackfoot, "Where is Three Bears?" Three Bears, it turned out, was his brother and had died twenty-six years earlier.

Although Spopee continued to have trouble forming words, now he relied on and understood the accompanying sign-talk as the expressive hands of the speakers spelled out their intentions. The scene caused quite a commotion. The hospital staff, led by a residing physician, Dr. Glickman, came to witness what was thought of as a psychological wonder. Dr. Glickman called it the "return of a human mind, the rebirth of memory, a restoration of the coordination of the faculties."[14] As the reassuring voice of Ella Clark continued and hospital interest mounted, Spopee reacted, responding more and more. Jumping the deep grooves of habit and silence, Spopee left behind the years of what proved to have been self-imposed silence. Words, in Blackfoot and broken English, silently absorbed over the years of incarceration, began to surface in a gurgle of sound. He was no longer speechless, no longer dead to the world, lost in the earlier limbo. Instead, he unsteadily pushed himself to retell, in his own inchoate words, the beginnings of his story.

Spopee related in fits and starts how, as a young Blood Indian, he came from across the 49th parallel in what was called by the whites in the 1870s and 1880s the "British possessions" or the North-West Territories, soon to become Canada. The Bloods, who also identified themselves as the Kainai people, were an independent division or part of the larger Niitzitapi, or Real People. Spopee belonged to the large and influential Fish Eater band of the Bloods, made up of just over nine hundred persons. Red Crow, or Mes-ka-to, had led this band since the spring of 1870 and would become the head chief of the Bloods, leading them until his death in 1900.[15] Spopee was a relative of Red Crow, probably a cousin, sharing with the chief a famous aunt, Natawista, or Holy Snake Woman, the sister of Seen from Afar, former leader of the Fish Eaters and the wife of Alexander Culbertson, fur trader extraordinaire of the American Fur Company and founder of Fort Benton on the upper Missouri River. Natawista's son, Joe Culbertson, would identify himself as a cousin of Spopee and also pointed out that both Crop Eared Wolf, Red Crow's adopted son, and his sister, identified only as Mrs. Red Crow, were also relatives.

Spopee was born about 1850, and little is known of his immediate family from his telling other than the name of his mother, Awakasiaki, or Antelope Woman, and the name of a brother, Three Bears. According to Catholic census files for 1874, Antelope Woman was listed as the wife of Siapiatow, or Comes in the Night. Comes in the Night, however, may or may not have been Spopee's father. In any case, Comes in the Night did not appear among the signatures affirming the 1877 Blackfoot Treaty, generally referred to as Treaty 7, and he may well have already died prior to its conclusion. In sum, most of what little is known about Spopee has to do with his belonging to a distinguished broader family of Blood leaders, specifically among the Fish Eater band, with whom he identified.[16]

As a young Blood, Spopee grew up in an era in which tribal populations had been devastated by repeated outbreaks of small pox, reducing their numbers by as much as one-third. Established political relationships were ineluctably altered or disintegrated; hunting territories, neutral zones, and homelands were invaded from every direction by buffalo-hunting enemies, who sensed an opportunity to capitalize on Niitzitapi weakness. Then, too, the gravitational pull of key trading centers had shifted or disappeared as illegal whiskey traders from Fort Benton on the Missouri River fanned out across the international border to build scruffy little trading posts in the British possessions, without any legal restrictions, hoping to capitalize on the lucrative bison-robe trade. The result for the Niitzitapi

Red Crow, chief
of the Bloods,
1895. (Glenbow
Archives, Calgary,
Alberta, NA-56-1.)

was devastating chaos. Missionary Father Constantine Scollen connected the two plagues, the pulsating outbreaks of small pox and
the ever-present whiskey, writing: "[S]urviving relatives went more
and more for the use of alcohol; they endeavored to drown their
grief in the poisonous beverage. They sold their robes and their
horses by the hundred for it, and now they began killing one another, so that in a short time they were divided into several small
parties, afraid to meet."[17] Red Crow and the Fish Eaters were no
exception, with Red Crow killing his youngest brother, Kit Fox, in
a drunken rage by repeatedly smashing his head with a rock. The
result for the Niitzitapi was a lawless, chaotic world where trading
posts brought unprecedented levels of violence, degradation, and
human misery.[18]

Hoping to address the deteriorating situation in Dominion
lands, the Canadian government had banned the "giving, selling,

and bartering to Indians of Spirituous Liquors" in 1870, and belatedly, in 1873–74, created and deployed a new institution called the
North-West Mounted Police (hereafter NWMP). Not only did the
new federal force take on illegal trafficking by the local whiskey
traders, it also came to play a significant role in pacifying, nego-
tiating with, and signing treaties with Indian tribes in an expanding Canada. One result was Treaty 7, signed at Blackfoot Crossing
with the Bloods, Northern Piegan, and Blackfoot in 1877.[19] Although
Spopee does not appear to have been present at the signing of the
treaty, according to the Blood annuity books he did show up for the
annuity payments the following year. At twenty-nine years of age,
Spopee had a wife and a daughter. He received annuity payment
under assignment to band number J16, led by the minor chief Bull
Turns Around.[20]

These were turbulent times. But no event was so immediate or so
debilitating as the contraction and then the virtual disappearance
of the Canadian buffalo in 1879 due to expanding population pressure of tribes migrating onto the northern Great Plains, increased
commercial demand in the form of the Indian and Métis bison-
robe trade, and the provisioning of meat or pemmican to Canadian
trading companies. This all resulted in overhunting that was not
sustainable. The problem was exacerbated by an increase among
natives and Métis in the practice of hunting cows, thereby impact-
ing the ability of the bison to reproduce.[21] The repercussions on the
economic foundation of the Plains Indian culture were decisive.
When it came time for the Blood leader Bad Head to record his winter count, the year's most important identifying event, the choice
in 1879 was simple—*Itsistsitsis/awenimiopi*, or "When first/no more
buffalo."[22]

Having been driven from the Canadian plains by overhunting,
the buffalo had moved south of the Canadian border and south
of the Missouri, never to return, and with them went many, if not
the majority, of the Blackfoot, the Piegan, and the Bloods, including Spopee. They had little choice if they wanted to eat, to clothe
themselves, to re-cover their worn-out lodges, to trade for ammunition, knives, or cooking pots, to say nothing of coffee, sugar, blankets, and liquor. Some of the Indians went to their newly created

reserves, expecting the Canadian government to feed them. Those expectations were out of the question. Canadian authorities at the time of Treaty 7 had disastrously miscalculated the disappearance of the buffalo north of the American border. They thought they had more time, at least another ten years, to transform the tribal buffalo hunters into dirt farmers or cattle ranchers, so they could "live in the future in some other way."[23] Unprepared and unable to ameliorate the dramatic changes, the Indians stood before the approaching famine bewildered and empty-handed. Proud warriors resorted to eating mice, gophers, and badgers.[24]

Some three thousand starving Indians, mainly Bloods, Northern Piegan, and Sarcee, were camped around Fort Macleod and its NWMP post in September of 1879, hoping to find some relief—if not for themselves, then for their crying and uncomprehending children. Unable to feed them indefinitely, Indian Commissioner of the North-West Territories Edgar B. Dewdney could do little other than to "strongly advise" those starving, whereever they may be, to follow the buffalo "further and further south" into the United States— which they did anyway, with or without his advice.[25]

The result was an immense exodus following the Blackfoot treaty payments at Fort Macleod, across prairies blackened by grass fires and empty of life. Previously fleeing bands had set fire to the country, hoping to drive before them whatever game it contained, not caring how difficult they made it for those who followed. After the treaty payments had been distributed, those who had waited—the majority—finally set out for the south on horses already weak from the overgrazed conditions near Fort Macleod. Those who were poor and without horses followed along—sometimes on foot, sometimes with their few possessions piled high on a dog travois. It would be a protracted struggle to reach the Missouri and its southern tributaries. They left in October in smaller groups led by a variety of band leaders. Individuals and single families also trickled away, soon becoming hungry again once the pitiful supplies issued by the government were gone. Their slow passage across the blackened prairies was cheerless and miserable.[26]

Spopee was a part of this exodus. In fact, he and his wife had made the trip the year before, trudging to the Blackfeet Agency on

Badger Creek, where they received weekly rations along with other Canadian Blackfoot speakers.[27] Like so many others, Spopee had decided in 1879 that he had nothing to lose and everything to gain by heading south once more—this time alone. On his way, however, instead of finding something to eat, Spopee found trouble and subsequent tragedy—he killed a white man, a *napikwan*, and it was this long-suppressed story that began to emerge in the visitor's facilities at St. Elizabeths. This time, however, the story would be told in Blackfoot, from Spopee's own perspective, without the limitations imposed by an alien territorial courtroom or the assaults of the disbelieving authorities, confident of their ability to convict an Indian in Montana Territory.

CHAPTER 1

"The *Napikwan* Was Dead"

Spopee's tragic story, at least the origin of it, began in November of 1879 in northern Montana Territory, amid the hysteria associated with the Sioux defeat of Custer's Seventh Cavalry at the bloody Battle of the Little Big Horn three years earlier. Even closer in time and place to Montana's population centers near the continental divide and in the western valleys was what would be later would be termed "the last Indian war," between the Nez Perce and the U.S. Army. Bands of the Nez Perce, who had been the friends and most trustworthy allies of the Americans since the days of the Lewis and Clark Expedition, had in their desperation at promises not kept and multiple threats to confine them to a much reduced reservation, turned on the U.S. government in 1877.[1] Lashing out, the Nez Perce had spilled civilian blood in Idaho and defeated U.S. Army troops under General Oliver O. Howard. About eight hundred Nez Perce had then fled in orderly fashion across the Bitterroot Mountains, into the settled Bitterroot Valley in Montana Territory. Peacefully, they slowly moved up the valley on their way to the Big Hole, a high, isolated valley surrounded by mountains. There, an array of pursuers, including U.S. Army troops led by Colonel John Gibbon and mounted volunteers from the town of Corvallis in the Bitterroot

19

Valley, attacked the unsuspecting Nez Perce, who thought they had left General Howard far behind.

Although the Nez Perce defeated their pursuers at the battle of the Big Hole, it was a costly victory. Limping away, the Nez Perce then won skirmishes in recently created Yellowstone National Park, terrorized tourists, and threaded their way out of its northern geographical maze before heading further north across central Montana and the Missouri River. They hoped for sanctuary in Canada. They did not make it. Instead, surprised and surrounded, the fleeing Nez Perce, cold, weary, and harried, were again forced to battle a many-pronged superior military force that against all odds had caught up with them. On the afternoon of October 5, 1877, they surrendered to Colonel Nelson A. Miles at snowy Snake Creek, near the Bear's Paw Mountains, some forty miles short of the Canadian border.[2]

For Americans in Idaho and Montana, whether government officials, townspeople, miners, cattlemen, or settlers, the Nez Perce rebellion was a threatening example of perfidy. Sioux hostility had been expected. But if the friendly Nez Perce could become disloyal and treacherous, all these years after Lewis and Clark, then there was little hope of redeeming any of the buffalo hunting Indians. It was in this charged atmosphere, when whites felt most vulnerable and hostile, that Spopee, or Turtle, a Blood Indian, unexpectedly became involved in the brutal murder of a white man along a stretch of what locally was called the Whoop-Up Trail.

This so-called road had been beaten into place over a short ten years. Caravans of versatile two-wheeled Métis carts, simple horse-drawn wagons, and heavily laden freight brigades had rolled their way into and out of the British possessions from Montana Territory south of the Canadian boundary, etching long lines of parallel ruts into the dense prairie sod. The freight wagons were pulled by teams of "bulls" (really oxen or cattle), and were spoken of as "bull trains" because spans of these animals, yoked in pairs, were hitched to three wagons "in train," which could be coupled together as were freight cars on a railroad track. Hauling as much as fifteen tons of freight between the three wagons, they lumbered along, making but twelve to fifteen miles in a long day's travel across the open, treeless, but periodically broken country. Moving in "their slow and regular way," from one water-crossing or spring to another, brigades of these broad-gauged wagons, each much larger than the "prairie schooners" of the Oregon Trail, were the most efficient freighters of the day. They carried goods and supplies out of Fort Benton, aptly named "Chicago of the Plains" because, like Chicago, it too had become a hub of trade and transshipment on the northern Plains. The spokes of this entrepôt ran in every direction, some to mining camps and settlements, but a number, especially to the north across the U.S. boundary, ended at colorfully named bison-robe–trading forts, established by Americans, whose principal stock in trade was whiskey.

In the early 1870s, the emerging trail passed through the immense Blackfeet Reservation and then across the international boundary, between Saint Mary Lake to the west and the Sweet Grass Hills to the east, into the rich buffalo-hunting grounds of the Kainai, or Bloods, Spopee's people, and the site of Fort Whoop-Up. This colorful settlement received its curious moniker when the traders, needing more whisky, sent a freighter, George Houk, back to Fort Benton. Asked how things were "up" there in the British possessions, Houk had responded "Oh, we're just whoopen-on-em-up." Deciding that this well-remembered phrase needed some explanation in 1913, the old freighter elaborated, saying that the expression meant that "they were whooping up the whiskey trade with the Indians and making good money at it."[3]

This hard-hearted, misery-inducing, but lucrative business enterprise, often disguised as boisterous merrymaking, had disastrous and murderous consequences for the peoples of the Blackfoot Nation, the Niitzitapi, be they Blood, Piegan, or Blackfoot proper. The fruits of this trade, as Crowfoot, head chief of the Blackfoot tribe, painfully described them in 1874, were deplorable: "If left to ourselves," he explained to Methodist missionary John McDougall, "we are gone. The whiskey brought among us by the Traders is fast killing us all off and we are powerless before the evil. [We are] totally unable to resist the temptation to drink when brought into contact with the white man's water." Crowfoot concluded on an even more dismal note, explaining his people's inability to escape the source of their poverty, the object of their trade, and their addiction. "We are

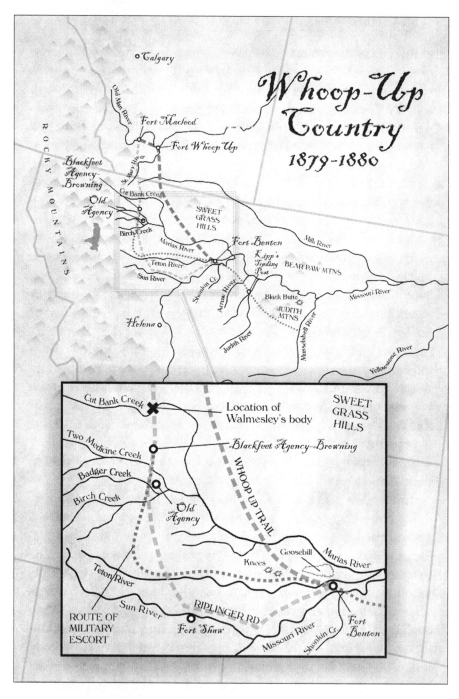

Whoop-Up Country, 1879–1880. (Map by Neal Wiegert.)

also unable to pitch anywhere that the Trader cannot follow us. Our horses, Buffalo robes, and other articles of trade go for whiskey, a large number of our people have killed one another and perished in various ways under the influence."[4]

American traders John J. Healy and Alfred B. Hamilton, both of whom will figure prominently in the Spopee narrative, had initiated the whiskey trade in the British possessions when they built the infamous Fort Whoop-Up and cashed out fifty thousand dollars' worth of robes and pelts for a short six months of trading. Other American traders, wanting to profit from the same opportunities, quickly followed their example. Like mushrooms following a soft rain, the whiskey forts popped up, sporting names equally vivid and memorable as the first; there was Standoff, north of Fort Whoop-Up on the Belly River, Slide Out to the west, up the Saint Mary River, and the short-lived Robbers' Roost at the mouth of the Little Bow River.

Voluminously supplied via the improved steamboats of the Missouri, the traders of Fort Benton sent wagon train after wagon train carrying whiskey, Indian trade goods, and supplies north, and then those same wagons were turned around and lumbered back by the same route, this time carrying bison robes, south to Fort Benton. Back and forth, up and down, between Fort Benton and Fort Whoop-Up and the numerous other trading posts between the Saint Mary and the Oldman River, the 245-mile trail became known far and wide as the Whoop-Up Trail; and the territory, as Whoop-Up Country. Since the Hudson's Bay Company had transferred legal and political authority in the former Rupert's Land to the distant and absent Dominion of Canada, Whoop-Up Country also became a place beyond enforcement and essentially outside any law.[5]

In this environment the whiskey trade, which centered on a beverage that was not really whiskey but an awful local concoction deceptively called "firewater," became particularly brazen and pernicious.[6] In 1873, for example, in a senseless act of violence, Montana wolfers attacked a drunken and defenseless camp of Assiniboine north of the border in the low-lying Cypress Hills, south and east of the junction of the South Saskatchewan River with its parent. Known thereafter as the "Cypress Hills massacre," this international

Fort Whoop-Up. (Glenbow Archives, Calgary, Alberta, NA-550-18.)

incident became a cause célèbre, exasperating relations between the
United States and Canada.[7]

Only in the aftermath of this tragedy did the Canadian government in Ottawa finally realize that it had to do something to ef-
fectively administer its western territory. In the spring of 1873, the
Canadian Parliament addressed the pressing problem of the illegal
U.S. whiskey trade by creating a mounted constabulary, the NWMP,
with the purpose of bringing law and justice to the region. It was
not, however, until October of 1874 that the NWMP arrived in the
Northwest Territories of southern Alberta and the Cypress Hills,
following an epic eight-hundred-mile journey across western Canada in what became known as the "Great March." Building a series
of forts encompassing barracks, barns, stables, supply depots, and
officers' quarters, the police force received a clutch of governmental
powers designed to stabilize the deteriorating situation. There were

multiple purposes to this activity, including, as one historian puts it, "pulling the West firmly into the nation's orbit."[8]

One NWMP contingent, under Commissioner George A. French, zeroed in on Fort Whoop-Up, but finding no whiskey there, the men moved north about twenty-five miles. There, under Assistant Commissioner Colonel James F. Macleod, the police began to construct their first buildings on the Oldman River in October of 1874, just in time for winter. They named their creation Fort Macleod, after their leader. Its purpose was to suppress, if not eradicate, the lucrative whiskey trade out of Fort Benton on the Missouri. Ironically enough, in order to provision their large force of 150 men, Commissioner French had previously contacted one of the Fort Benton traders, the I. G. Baker & Company, to supply its need for clothing, hardware, and groceries, already amounting to forty thousand pounds of supplies.[9]

The Blackfeet referred to the boundary between the United States and Canada (or Montana Territory and what would become Alberta) as the Medicine Line or the Iron Line for its magical, transformational, or even sacramental properties, including its ability to stop mounted, superior-armed American soldiers, as well as American legal authorities in the form of federal and territorial officials, dead in their tracks in the middle of nowhere and with no one in sight. This imaginary line exercised much less power over Indian people, especially the tribes of the Niitzitapi.

In 1870, Lt. Colonel Alfred Sully, superintendent of Indians for the Territory of Montana, described the Blackfoot collectively as "one of the largest nations of Indians at present in our country." He was quick to point out, however, that "they do not all properly belong to the United States," for they "claim in common a section of the country from the British line south some miles to the city of Helena, and north of the line to the Saskatchewan River."[10] Sully also felt obliged to remind his superiors in Washington, D.C., that "[b]eing a wild, uncivilized set, they of course do not take into consideration any treaties we have with Great Britain in regard to our boundary line, but look upon the whole of the country both north and south of the line as theirs."[11] Yet while the Indians hardly saw or paid much attention to the boundary line, they knew full well where it was, understood its significance among whites, and acknowledged that the Southern Piegan collected around their newly established agency on Badger Creek, a tributary of the Marias River.

Under U.S. Blackfeet Agent John Young (1876–1884), the first agency at Badger Creek, the so-called Running Crane agency, had been moved a dozen miles downstream to where, it was argued by some, there was better arable and grazing land. It was at this agency, still looking remarkably like a military fort with its wooden palisades, large gate, and commanding watch tower, that Spopee's perplexing story begins to take shape.

On November 18, 1879, Agent Young reported to Montana Territorial Governor Benjamin F. Potts that ten days earlier an Indian woman, while gathering firewood alone beneath the now leafless cottonwood and aspen trees along Cut Bank Creek, had discovered the body of a white man, a *napikwan*. The location was near the crossing of the Whoop-Up Trail with one of the other trails associated with it, west of the Whoop-Up and twenty miles north of the agency. The day of the body's discovery was bright, but cold and windy. The acrid smell of moldering leaves hung in the crisp air. The dead man's head was bashed in and covered in blood, and the blood, the woman could tell by the color, was fresh.[12] She was frightened, Young wrote, and "did not touch the body and moved Camp at once."[13]

The following Sunday, Young sent the agency physician and chief of its newly established Indian Police, Dr. Arthur C. Hill, as well as the agency blacksmith and some Blackfeet policemen, north to investigate the grisly death, to gather all possible information, and to "bring the remains on return."[14] Following clear directions provided by the woman who discovered the corpse, the group had no trouble finding it. Wolves had destroyed a large portion of the man's body; nonetheless, it was intact enough to determine that the unknown white man was "not much over thirty years, about six feet in height, high forehead, light complexion and light hair, cut short and very roughly."[15] The agent's report, relying on the information gathered on the spot by Dr. Hill, went on to say that the death was the result of a gunshot wound to the body and that the head "was beaten in and the skull broken by a blunt instrument." Nothing of value was found on the body. The victim was dressed for the coming season, wearing three shirts, "one a red flannel, next to the skin, over that a checked shirt, an outside one of blanket." In addition, the body had on it "two pair of overalls, one blue and the other brown, and a pair of coarse, heavy No. 9 boots."[16]

Curiously, the report, so specific and so detailed with respect to the deceased, contained no description of the exact location along Cut Bank Creek or of the larger scene. Nor was there any speculation as to why the body was so easily discovered, which contrasted dramatically with the efforts that had been made to hide the wagon the murdered man evidently had been driving. Seeing wagon tracks near the body, the agency employees had followed the tracks about two miles upstream, zigzagging back and forth across the leaf-strewn gravel streambed until they discovered "an old horse lynch-pin wagon, painted lead color." The wagon, they noted, "had been taken apart and sunk in the creek, excepting the bed and one wheel, which were hidden in the brush."[17] The investigating team also found a double set of English-made harness that had been wadded up in a makeshift bundle. Given its provenance, they speculated that it probably belonged to the NWMP stationed at Fort Macleod, across the boundary, on Oldman River near the terminus of the Whoop-Up Trail. The remains of a bison skin lodge or tepee were also found nearby.

Agent Young, relying on these investigations by Dr. Hill, concluded his report with the comment that all "the circumstances point to a murder committed by some white man, or men, traveling this way from the North."[18] Upon receipt of the news of the white man's murder in late November and knowing the effect the news would have among his already nervous constituents, Montana Governor Potts decided, as was his right according to the laws of the territory, to offer a thousand-dollar reward for the apprehension and conviction of the guilty party or parties.[19] This was not that unusual. Governor Potts offered another territorial reward of one thousand dollars the following year for a murder in Lewis and Clark County. However, the reason behind the territorial governor's offer of a reward for a murder on an Indian reservation that was under direct federal jurisdiction and not territorial authority went unexplained. Many years later Potts's decision in this instance was challenged as inappropriate.[20]

Agent Young, carefully following protocol, was not content to limit the recipients of his communications to Governor Potts. On the same day, he sent his report to other law enforcement officials, including the notorious whiskey trader and founder of Fort Whoop-Up, John J. Healy, who had become the sheriff in Fort Benton, Montana. Although Healy had remained involved in trading at Fort Whoop-Up after the NWMP arrived in 1874, by 1876 he had decided to sell out. The bloom was off the apple. Out of the trading business, Healy moved to Fort Benton in 1877. He became a partner, business manager, and reporter for the Fort Benton newspaper, the *Benton Record*, and published a remarkable number of firsthand accounts and personal reminiscences under the title "Frontier Sketches."[21] At the same time, Healy purchased an interest in the Overland Hotel and ran for and was appointed sheriff of Chouteau County in 1877 by the local Democrats. He won election as sheriff in 1878 and secured re-election in 1880.[22]

Young also sent his report to Major William Winder, the commanding officer of the NWMP at Fort Macleod, north across the border.[23] On November 28, after mounting a quick inquiry, Major Winder replied. A man named Charles Walmesley had been working in the neighborhood of Fort Macleod during the past summer and had left the area about the twelfth of October with the stated intention of going south to the Yellowstone country. Before leaving Fort Macleod, however, he had changed his mind and had decided instead to go to the Judith Basin to spend the winter poisoning prairie wolves for their skins. The wolves followed the bison herds in large numbers, preying on the old, sick, and the weak. Where there were buffalo, there were wolves.

"Wolfing," as it was known, had become a big business. In the late 1870s, it was nearly as lucrative a skin trade as the bison-robe trade—with both flourishing during the winter season when pelts were at their best. Generally the "wolfers" were a tough but scruffy lot who worked alone or with other unattached men. They did not need much of an initial investment, getting by with little more than

Superintendent William Winder, Northwest Mounted Police, Fort Macleod. (Glenbow Archives, Calgary, Alberta, NA-1385-2.)

a light wagon, ammunition, a frying pan, supplies, and, above all, an adequate supply of strychnine. Some combined their efforts with occasional whiskey trading for buffalo robes, and alcohol was often found in their camps.[24]

Walmesley's decision to go "wolfing" for the winter south of the Missouri fit his circumstances. Whether it fit his character is a different matter. He had a wagon, a team of four horses, and supplies. He had with him at least two hundred dollars in cash (later estimates went as high as four hundred dollars), a fact well known by a number of people in the vicinity of Standoff, another famous former whiskey and trading post not far away. "From the description you give of the body found," wrote Major Winder, "there is no doubt but it is that of the man Chas. Walmesley, for instance you say the man's hair was roughly cut. I find that he cut his own hair immediately before leaving for Mont. This will account for your description and combined with the color of hair and wearing apparel, etc., viz., blue army overcoat lined with flannel, the overalls, the description of the wagon, all goes to show that the body found is that of Chas. Walmesley; so far I am unable to ascertain his nationality or home."[25]

Three days earlier, in the course of his investigation, Winder had forwarded to Agent Young the description of a horse thief who went by the name of Byron Howell.[26] At the time the NWMP officer thought that Howell might well be implicated in the death of Walmesley. Two men, James Cobourn and James Armstrong, had encountered Howell on the prairie near the Waterton River, then known as the Kootenay River, wrote Winder. When interviewed, Cobourn told Winder that at the time they met, Walmesley was with Howell and that the two were on their way to the home of Fred Kanouse, a notorious former whiskey trader who became an early rancher as well as a trader around Fort Macleod. Strangely, Cobourn noted, the two men were heading in the opposite direction. Howell was described as "riding a roan paint horse and leading a small black horse on which was a pack covered with a Buffalo robe. He had a needle gun, Revolver & Belt full of cartridges and was riding a new California saddle."[27]

Howell was young, twenty-four or twenty-five, about five feet eleven inches tall, with a light complexion, brown hair, and a moustache. He had, according to Winder, "very square shoulders and walks with quite an important gait. In conversation has a decided way of expressing himself . . . and was quite addicted to telling stories when in company with great emphasis." Howell allegedly had stolen his equally distinctive horse from Jefferson City, Montana Territory, and Major Winder had heard that he "had passed the Blackfeet Agency, in company with another, named Charles Laxton (alias Tennessee)," whom Winder believed was known to Young and needed no further description. Winder was highly suspicious. He thought both of these men "should be detained where ever they may be found, to give any information or answer any charge that may be brought against them in this matter."[28]

By December 1 the Fort Macleod correspondent for the *Saskatchewan Herald* informed his readers that "[a]bout two weeks ago the authorities here [Fort Macleod] received a letter from the Blackfoot Agency (American), to the effect that a white man supposed to hail from this country had been found near that place, with a bullet through his chest and a crushed head. Appearances were suggestive of murder. From the description the deceased was identified as one Charles Wormsley, who had been working for different ranch-men here and who had left for Benton some time previous with a conservable sum of money in his possession. "[29] The correspondent went on to say that suspicion "was directed towards a certain party who left Belly River about the same time." This is the first Canadian response outside of the NWMP records, but it indicated that word of the murder was common at Fort Macleod.

Two days after this correspondence, the *Helena Daily Independent*, quoting the *Fort Benton Record*, informed its readers that Sheriff John J. Healy of Fort Benton also believed the young victim found on Cut Bank Creek to be "Charles Wamsbly,"[30] whom the sheriff de-scribed as "a hard working and peaceable citizen." Sheriff Healy's information may have come from Fort Macleod, where he was well-connected, or it may have come from Agent Young, who had continued to keep Healy informed and had reported on the new in-formation received from the NWMP. The Fort Macleod newspaper correspondent had cast suspicion on a certain party who had disap-peared from there as well. Still, there was no further information implicating the young, square-shouldered horse thief, Howell, or any indication that he and "Tennessee" had been found or ques-tioned. The *Fort Benton Record*, however, had expressed its opinion that since this suspected murder had taken place on an American Indian reservation, the case should be placed in the hands of fed-eral authorities, which meant the U.S. marshal in Helena, Montana Territory.[31]

On December 9 Agent Young responded to Major Winder at Fort McLeod and to Governor Potts, informing both that there "was no doubt that the murdered man was the missing Chas. Walmesley."[32] He also notified both recipients that "'Tennessee' alias Chas. or James Laxton" and Byron Howell, "known north by the name of Phillips," had passed near the Blackfeet Agency on their way south, without stopping, about October 15. At the Teton River, "Tennes-see had sold a horse to Thain T. Dennis, who resold it to a freighter going north." But that was not all. Young also noted that a "tall good looking buck of about 30 years," a Blood Indian named "Spo-pe (Turtle)," had also passed through about the same time and that he had "purchased a horse here, paying for it in greenbacks, and having over $50.00 left." Spopee had not only bought the horse from one Thomas Davis, he had also "traded a saddle, and gave away a dog, both of which articles have been identified as the property of Walmesley."[33]

Additionally, Young reported that he had ordered fragments of the murdered man's wagon found at Cut Bank Creek to be put together, and that they too had been deemed by a passing freighter as belonging to the victim, along with Walmesley's dog, which Spopee had given away before leaving the Blackfeet Agency. In his letter to Major Winder, Young stated that Spopee claimed to have received his money and his horse, saddle, and dog from Fred Kanouse, "for whom he had been working, and who is, I believe, known to you. Can you supply any information as to his character?"[34] If this was an alibi it was a reasonable one; after all, in the early 1870s Kanouse had married Spopee's aunt, the famed Natawista, formerly Mrs. Alexander Culbertson, whose husband had led the American Fur Company at Fort Union and Fort Benton and who had been labeled the "king of the high Missouri." Settled near Fort Macleod, Natawista stayed with Kanouse until 1878 or 1879 and may well have intervened on Spopee's behalf.[35]

Young's decision was to request from Potts the arrest and examination of all three suspects, who were all "supposed to be with the Indians in the Judith country, the Indian 'Spo-pe' belonging to 'Running Crane's' band of Piegans." Then, in a final aside, Young informed the governor that "[a]ll reports agree as to Walmesley's having been a quiet, inoffensive, industrious man, without a known enemy. He was unmarried."[36]

Although the clues were beginning to add up, there were still surprises. Young reported the most important one the following day, December 10. Writing almost breathlessly to Major Winder, Young forwarded new, conclusive information implicating Spopee in the crime. Young had extracted this data from a young Blood boy by the name of "O-ne-to-ches or Good Rider," who along with Spopee had crossed the Medicine Line in the hope of finding buffalo and who had been suspiciously using "greenbacks" to buy things around the Blackfeet Agency from those who were still waiting to go to the Judith Basin to hunt.[37] The agent felt the evidence to be strong enough that he wanted to move ahead, and he wrote to Sheriff Healy with a warrant "to follow [Spopee] to the camp [on the Judith River] and arrest on suspicion."[38] He also was glad, he wrote, that the white men suspected were innocent, "and disappointed that any Indian was bad enough to do the deed," adding that he had known for a long time that "Spo-pe" was "turbulent, and not a good Indian." This information rested probably on the basis of Spopee's earlier history of securing rations at the Blackfeet Agency while with Running Crane and his band of South Piegan.[39]

Spopee and Good Rider, as we have seen, were part of the pitiful diaspora of Canadian tribespeople moving south in an attempt to find whatever was left of the overhunted and long-contracting buffalo herds north of the Medicine Line. The Blackfoot-speaking tribes were under great distress and were suffering from extreme hunger. There was widespread famine. Drought, as was often the case, had only compounded the problem, driving the buffalo farther south to other ranges, and their Indian predators had followed. Following years of enormous hunting pressure on the part of the Métis and competing tribes, several thousand refugee Sioux from the United States exacerbated the difficulty by hunting in the region after the Little Big Horn, as did some 3,600 Cree who had left their northern Canadian reserves, established by treaty, for the south.[40]

James Macleod, now NWMP commissioner, wrote in the spring of 1878 that the bison hunt for that winter among the Blackfoot tribes "was a complete failure" and that many groups had to travel "as far as 100 miles from their usual winter locations to find remnant herds." In Macleod's opinion, most "were in starving condition."[41] The following year brought no relief. In his annual report for 1879, Major Winder informed his NWMP superiors that during the summer there were "1,200 to 1,500 Indians, Bloods, Piegans and Sarcees, encamped around the Fort," and later on as "many as 7,000 men, women and children, all in a destitute condition, applied for relief."[42] This dire situation was well known and had been reported by others. Father Constantine Scollen, a missionary with the Oblates of Mary Immaculate who knew the Blackfoot and Bloods well, had written a scathing letter in April relating that "[m]any sustained life by eating the flesh of poisoned wolves. Some lived on dogs; and

I have known others to live several days on nothing else but old bones which they gathered and broke up, where with to make a kind of soup."[43]

These dreadful conditions continued at Fort Macleod despite the fact that the Mounted Police issued rations and "paid treaty" on the first days of October in fulfillment of the provisions of Treaty 7, concluded in 1877. Canadian Indian Commissioner Edgar Dewdney, as already noted, was there for the payment that year and remarked in his daily diary that the Bloods appeared "anxious to be off to the Buffalo," then reported to be plentiful in Montana, south of the Missouri River.[44] And it was Dewdney who famously had "advised them strongly to go," to leave the Dominion and to ignore the political boundary of the 49th parallel in order to continue to hunt. To enable the Indians to do so, he said, he had given them "some provisions." He then described how "[t]hey continued to follow the Buffalo further and further south until they reached the main herd and there they remained. . . . I consider their remaining away saved the Govt. $100,000 at least."

The situation was so bad, reported the *Saskatchewan Herald,* using a December 1 correspondence from Fort Macleod, that "[m]ost of the Indians—Bloods, Blackfeet and Piegans—have gone South and are now in the Judith Basin and about the Bear-paw and Little Rocky Mountains. Before going they set the prairie on fire in several places, with the avowed intention of keeping the buffalo out of the country and confining them to the district to which they are bound."[45] These fires had run unchecked in every direction so that the whole country was "nothing but a blackened waste." Then, confirming Commissioner Dewdney's economic assessment, the correspondent concluded there was a benefit to this desperate migration, for it was "generally believed that the Indians have gone so far away that they will not be able to return until June at least, and thus an immense saving of trouble and money will be secured to the Government."[46] By early October, "the majority of the Indians left for the Milk River country, south of the boundary line, in quest of buffalo"—if they still had horses and had not pawned them off for food and if their horses were not too weak to follow. The recently appointed Indian agent for Treaty 7, Norman T. Macleod, wrote in December that "only the old and helpless" remained in the camps near Fort Macleod and that all the others were gone.[47]

Thus Good Rider and Spopee were by no means alone or unusual in their desperate drift south. Whole bands, such as those of the Blood war chiefs White Calf (Onista-poka) and Medicine Calf, had mobilized themselves and gone south into Montana Territory in 1879 as well.[48] There was little choice. It was move or starve.

The migration was by no means limited to the Blackfoot-speaking peoples but included Cree, Assiniboine, Gros Ventre, Métis, and Lakota people in numbers that attracted the interest and attention on the part of government officials, who estimated that between seven and eight thousand left for the United States.[49] With all of these various peoples desperately looking for food, all of the old animosities and feuds shouldered their way to the fore and were exacerbated by the narrowed buffalo ranges of the Musselshell and Judith Basin. Inevitably there was more horse stealing, more fighting, and more contact.[50]

Across the line, Southern Piegan had abandoned their new Blackfeet Agency on Badger Creek as well, and for the same reason—to go to the buffalo. Agent Young reported that most of his Indians had "left earlier than usual to the winter hunt, the Buffalo being reported . . . in large numbers, leaving near the Agency only the infirm and aged, with their families."[51] In such a desperate environment Young had quickly learned about the "greenbacks" that were being spent on the part of the two Bloods, Spopee and Good Rider. Spopee, the older of the two, had already left for the bison hunting on the Judith River. According to his letter to Major Winder at Fort McLeod, Young sent out word that he wanted to see Good Rider, who had lingered behind and was hanging around Badger Creek.[52] He did so without letting the teenager know of his suspicions or what the audience was about. Surprisingly, Good Rider appeared at the agent's office as requested, with, however, a small number of friends. He was noticeably disturbed by the unwanted attention. According to Agent Young, Good Rider was sweating profusely. "When I questioned him about his Canadian friends and experiences on his way south," wrote Young, Good Rider responded by abruptly standing up and offering to shake the agent's hand, "as their custom is when about to make a relation or statement." The young man said that "he would tell a straight story."[53] With that Good Rider blurted out what amounted to a detailed confession.

Good Rider began by relating to Melinda Wren, the agency interpreter, then thirty years of age and the wife of the agency farmer, John Wren, how he had for a short time been working for a white man by the name of McFarland near Fort Whoop-Up when he decided to go to the Blackfeet Agency in Montana. Perhaps, he reasoned, there would be rations there. Others had signed up there for food; perhaps he could, too. North of the border was only starvation. Good Rider was hungry, had no prospects, no horse to ride, no shelter, little clothing, and had simply started out, alone and on foot. The route he decided to take is unclear, but probably it was not south via the Whoop-Up Trail. More likely Good Rider struck out for Fort Macleod to the west before heading toward the Blackfeet Agency on the Riplinger Road. The two roads paralleled each, with a good many shortcuts across the open prairie to connect to one another. Before the end of the first day, perhaps near Kipp's or Middle Coulee, while still well north of the 49th parallel, Good Rider encountered Spopee, who, with at least two ponies in his possession, had overtaken him and generously offered him one to ride. Before long, according to Good Rider, "they saw fresh wagon tracks and Spopee said there must be a white man ahead, and he proposed that they try and catch him, as he would probably give them something to eat."[54] The two young Indians soon overtook the wagon and its sole white occupant, and the driver agreed to let Good Rider save his horse and join him on the wagon seat as they made their way south.

Although Spopee had initiated the encounter, so far their intentions were innocuous enough and by no means exceptional or noteworthy. They were simply two hungry and restless young men, with few possessions, hoping to break out of their desperate reservation straits—with its pitiful handouts, its demoralizing emptiness, and its gnawing hunger. Things had to be better elsewhere. Of course, this was nothing like those heroic forays of their immediate predecessors, who had eagerly thrown a string of extra moccasins over their shoulders and joined in exciting war parties or small horse-stealing expeditions away to the south. Nonetheless, there remained enticing reports of buffalo east of the Sweet Grass Hills, the area the Blackfeet referred to as "Across," or Ah-po-mokes, and along the Musselshell or further south across the Missouri River.[55]

It is unclear how far the threesome traveled together or where they stopped for the night. If it was on the Whoop-Up Trail, perhaps they went only as far as the Red River, just before crossing the international boundary, or perhaps across it to Rocky Springs, with the Sweet Grass Hills and the West Butte in clear sight. Then again, they may have made it as far south as a series of four coulees north of the Marias River prior to veering off from the Whoop-Up Trail, angling west, and heading along Riplinger Road toward Cut Bank Creek and the Blackfeet Agency.[56] This road had been developed by John Riplinger to transport goods from Fort Shaw and the Sun River area in Montana toward Standoff and Fort Macleod in a more direct north-south route than the Whoop-Up Trail, and it skirted the eastern edge of the Rocky Mountain front, which rose up so abruptly off the adjacent prairies that in Blackfoot the wall of mountains was called the "tipi liners."[57] Whether in Canada or the United States, it was here, on the Riplinger Road, that Good Rider said they stopped for the night, making camp on a little creek that he did not identify.

While Spopee and the white man unpacked the wagon and got a fire started, Good Rider went for water. Returning after a short time, he said he saw Spopee alone, hunched up on the ground with his blanket pulled over his head. Good Rider immediately asked what had happened, and "Spopee said the white man had knocked him down and struck him with a shovel, and that he [Spopee], would kill the white man."[58] Good Rider objected strenuously, saying that they would be discovered and that they would be certain to get into trouble. Spopee said nothing, and the matter was dropped. There is no indication as to why Walmesley might have done this, nor was there any evidence that alcohol was involved, although that was always a possibility in this transitional world where "wagon traders" had replaced whiskey forts and where alcohol was so available and so sought after by the various tribes and bands. The next day, as if nothing had happened, the three set off down the broad trail with

Good Rider again sharing the wagon seat. Unable to keep quiet, Good Rider warned Walmesley that Spopee was very angry and that he had threatened to shoot him. Unconcerned, the white man blithely waved the threat away, saying that no, Spopee would not shoot him.

In the course of the day's travel south, Spopee rode ahead. According to Good Rider's account, Spopee reported to the others that he had seen some antelope moving over the horizon and asked to borrow Walmesley's rifle and some ammunition. Evidently Walmesley discounted any danger from Spopee, for he readily complied, handing over the rifle, an old .45 caliber army weapon.[59] Spopee returned without any game and, at least to Good Rider, continued the threats he had made the night before. When Good Rider again objected, Spopee threatened to kill him, too. "Spopee," wrote Agent Young, representing Good Rider's account, then made the boy get out of the wagon, mount a pony, and ride off a little way. Spopee then "got behind the whiteman and shot him in the back with his own gun as he sat driving the wagon." Where exactly this happened was never determined—it may have been in either the British possessions or the United States. Spopee then compelled Good Rider to get into the wagon and drive.[60]

Shooting Walmesley from behind, with his own gun, did not quite fit with the graduated scale of war honors normally celebrated by the Blackfoot. Granted, Spopee had taken his enemy's gun, generally considered a "coup of the first class" in the 1870s.[61] In these circumstances, however, the gun was acquired by guile and peacefully, and it is hard to believe that this would have been acknowledged as the act of a courageous warrior or a coup worthy of recounting. Nor is it easy to construe Spopee's action as necessary or in self-defense. It did, however, revenge the humiliation of the evening before, if Good Rider's account is accurate, and it suddenly provided Spopee with a gun, pieces of camp equipment, and an unimaginable amount of money.

Upon reaching the ford on Cut Bank Creek, a western tributary to the Marias River and well south of the boundary, the wagon eased its way down the bank to the willow-lined stream. There, Spopee and Good Rider unloaded the bloody body they had been carrying, "wrapped it up in a quilt, and part of a robe over all." Then, hoping to hide the wagon, the two men drove it farther up the creek, crossing back and forth a couple of times, looking for a suitable place to hide it, out of the way of traffic and prying eyes. "Then Spopee," with considerable calculation, "got out the wrench and took the wagon apart, sinking the greater portion in the river. The harness was tied in a bundle and sunk in deeper water." Instead of keeping the horses for themselves, which would have been particularly incriminating, Spopee and Good Rider decided to drive the team further upstream and shoot them.[62]

Finishing his report to Governor Potts, Young noted that Spopee and Good Rider kept Walmesley's rifle, a "needle gun," and carried it all the way to Badger Creek, near the new agency, before hiding it carefully in the brush. Spopee then gave Good Rider thirty dollars, keeping the rest, however much that might have been, for himself before he left sometime later for Hamilton and Hazlet's trading post at the settlement of Teton Crossing, fifty miles away.[63] Once there, Spopee continued east down the Teton River, attempting to follow or catch up with White Calf's Southern Piegan, who had preceded him during the first week of November. The goal was the Judith Basin or the Musselshell River, both south of the Missouri River and the reservation boundary, over two hundred miles distant from the Blackfeet Agency on Badger Creek.[64]

Unlike hunting prospects farther west or south, hunting on the Musselshell and in the Judith Basin was still good. There had been less hunting pressure in this buffer zone between the competing tribal hunters, and migrating bison herds had gravitated into this momentary haven. The *Helena Weekly Herald* had already reported that Major Young had received "recent and reliable advices from [Blackfeet Agency Indians], and is gratified that . . . they are in the midst of buffalo, are securing an abundance of meat, have fat ponies, and are making plenty of robes."[65] The route to this Promised Land on the Judith ran down the Marias or Teton River through Fort Benton, then crossed the river and meandered southeast across Arrow Creek, to join a bewildering array of bands and tribes that had converged for one of the last winter buffalo hunts. The Blackfeet bands were expected to remain off the reservation and south of the Missouri on the Musselshell and in the Judith Basin during the entire winter, returning to the reservation only when the prairie grasses greened up in the spring.

Nor were the Blackfeet the only ones "going to buffalo." The *Helena Weekly Herald* reported that "about 200 Flathead Indians from the Jocko passed through Helena to-day en route to the Judith Basin to hunt buffalo. . . . Our advise to these Flatheads," intoned the editor, "is to 'look a little out' or they may be scooped up by one of the war parties hunting in the Judith."[66] Not surprisingly, the Crows objected strenuously to these Blackfeet visitations, complaining in particular to the War Department that they wanted the Blackfeet returned to their reservation and out of their country.[67]

The day after his confession, on a very stormy December 16, 1879, Good Rider took Agent Young to where he had stashed Walmesley's gun, confirming at least that part of the story and lending credence to the rest. "I trust," Young wrote to all concerned, "that immediate steps may be taken for Spopee's arrest. He is supposed to be with Running Crane's camp, which, according to late advices, is still in the Judith Basin. As soon as the present storm is over, I will send O-ne-to-ches [Good Rider] as a prisoner to Fort Shaw, for such disposition as you think proper to make of him."[68]

Young, who had already written to John Healy "to follow" Spopee, also indicated that he thought Good Rider, because of his "youth and appearance," probably had been compelled to assist in the murder. In expressing this opinion, Young asserted that "Spopee has for a long time been known as a turbulent unruly character."[69] It is not at all clear how Spopee had acquired this reputation, whether or not it was warranted, and how Young knew of it. There certainly is no written record of Spopee's having been arrested or run into trouble with the NWMP or anyone else.

There is, however, some surprising and belated Kootenai oral testimony supporting such a reputation. In 1950 a Kootenai chief, when describing the last of his tribe's buffalo hunts and their changing relationship with the North Piegan and Bloods, told of how one "Spupe" had killed in cold blood a Kootenai man by the name of Simon from across the mountains. The text of the chief's comments is quite detailed and leaves little doubt that Spopee was the individual involved.

This murder had taken place the same day as treaty monies and supplies were distributed to the Bloods at Fort Macleod at the beginning of October in 1879. The Kootenai chief, Eustace, related that this was after "there were no more Black Game (Buffalo)" and "there was no more trouble from that time when they [Kootenai] went over the mountains. They always met the Piegans, the Bloods, and the Blackfeet on good terms." He attributed this amity to the arrival of the NWMP and to their determination to end intertribal warfare and "to put an end to the killings. If anyone killed somebody he would be hanged at once if it were proven that he did it . . . and so it was achieved that the Indians would no longer kill each other."[70]

There was one notable exception to this situation, and that was the murder victim, Simon, who had friends among the Piegan and Bloods and was evidently well known. He had been "shopping" at Fort Macleod and had forgotten to take with him the bullets he had purchased from the white trader. He returned the following morning, retrieved the bullets, and was on his way back to camp when he was overtaken by two Piegan youth, one of whom he considered an old friend. The two were cousins. They "traded a few things with him" and in the course of the trading decided to exchange their blanket coats. Then, "exactly as Simon was going to put his belt around the blanket," in other words, when he was preoccupied with buckling his belt, "the other young Piegan fellow [not the friend] shot him and killed him." The killer justified his action by relating how "in the old time when the Kootenais were fighting each other, Simon had killed his father. He was always thinking that when he grew up, he would kill Simon." The man then offered Simon's horse to his cousin, who evidently had given Simon the horse some time back. Simon's friend said, "I won't take it back, I gave it to my friend. . . . Why did you do such a thing? He has been my friend for a long time and I loved him and look what you've done." Eustace closed by remarking, "It seems the name of the young Piegan fellow who had killed Simon, his name was Spupe."[71]

Later on that same day, the two cousins joined the other Bloods and Piegan on their way across the buff, treeless landscape to the confusion and crowds gathering for the treaty distributions of rations and payment at Fort Macleod. Although the proceedings were slow and tedious because of the weighing, counting, checking off of names, and associated paperwork, all went off without a hitch.[72] Spopee and other Bloods, after being paid, returned to their earlier camp near the mountains, but they were followed by a detachment of the NWMP who suspected "that they might have gotten a hold of whiskey." Upon arriving in camp at night and dismounting from their horses, the police came across a lodge where a Piegan was talking inside. Chief Eustace was of the opinion that "[o]ne of the Mounties must have been in that country a long time, it seems he understood Piegan. Wait he told his friends. Wait. I am going to listen to his talking. He listened and he told his friend. Go in there and arrest Spupe. He is talking, he says he killed someone. He says he killed a Kootenai this morning. They went in and he was arrested." After a pause, Eustace concluded, "That was the last time that the Piegans had killed someone. Now it is only done on the sly."[73]

There is no record of any such arrest. Of course, the NWMP arrested many Indians but let them go when there was insufficient evidence. Whether the body of Simon could not be found or witnesses could not be provided, the result was the same. There is no record.

Agent John Young, however, knew nothing of this earlier incident. Spopee's unsavory reputation at the Badger Creek agency may have stemmed from the year before, during the winter months of January, February, and March, when Spopee and his wife had drawn weekly food rations at the Blackfeet Agency, passing themselves off as Southern Piegan. Agency officials had dutifully recorded their names in their own distinctive hand. Given the situation to the north, they likely expected the Bloods to be back. Moreover, as any agent worth his salt, Young paid a good deal of attention to the eddying swirls of gossip, always such a delicious and instructive part of agency life.[74] He had certainly heard something.

Young had learned something else from his interrogation of Good Rider: when Spopee had told the youngster that he wanted to kill the white man for striking him with the shovel, Good Rider had said, "[T]hat would not do now—such things might have been done in the old times, but not now, it would be discovered."[75] In other words, this was a different world. The NWMP were forcing change. The old warrior ways on the warpath had to be abandoned; they would no longer be tolerated. The white man's law appeared to Blackfoot speakers and others to be clear-cut, black and white. As far as they were concerned there were few distinctions and little or no difference between how or why a killing took place. Killing was killing, and for such you too would be killed. Murder was murder. There would be no discussion. There was only hanging.

Such a draconian interpretation was not uncommon among Indians. Neither Spopee nor Good Rider understood that the white man's law provided for "extenuating circumstances," that the provocative actions of Walmesley and the striking of Spopee with the shovel constituted a special category of the law called "self-defense." Consequently, when Spopee heedlessly ignored Good Rider's warnings and shot Walmesley, both he and Good Rider believed themselves to be in serious trouble—this time Spopee had killed a white man and it would not be forgotten. There would be retribution if they were caught. There was nothing to do now but to hide the evidence and put the event behind them. Perhaps, as with Spopee's alleged first murder, he could again avoid the consequences. He had escaped then; maybe he could do so a second time.

After Treaty 7, however, the NWMP were more entrenched at Fort Macleod and elsewhere. Already the reputation of the Mounties for strict enforcement of the law was such that the best thing to do was to get away, to escape their jurisdiction—to leave for Montana, where the legal authorities were fewer and not so intent or so relentless. Spopee and Good Rider, in other words, would use the international border and its magical properties to their own advantage—if the murder took place north of the Medicine Line or close to it, subject to the NWMP, they would escape by moving Walmesley's body and all of the incriminating evidence. Superintendent L. F. N. Crozier of the NWMP fully understood the impulse, writing in his 1880 annual report, "Now [the Indians] call the boundary the 'Medicine Line,' because no matter what they have done upon one side they feel perfectly secure after having arrived upon the other."[76] Whether there would be sanctuary in Montana Territory for Spopee and Good Rider remained an open question—but not for long.

CHAPTER 2

THE CHRISTMAS CAPTURE
IN THE JUDITH BASIN

The severe December storm that delayed Agent Young's plan to send Spopee's companion, Good Rider, to Fort Shaw did not abate, but grew worse. Fort Shaw, on the Sun River, reported that by December 23, the mercury had fallen to thirty-seven degrees below zero, the lowest ever registered there. Not only was it bitter cold, but nearly three feet of snow covered the ground on the Bird Tail Divide, on the road between Helena and Fort Benton. A large number of enlisted men from Fort Shaw, out on patrol, were reported to "have been frozen more or less severely."[1] In an obvious reference to Good Rider, the *Helena Daily Herald* also noted that "[a] young Indian has been placed in confinement here, being it seems, an accomplice in the murder of a white man near the Blackfeet Agency and he has turned States evidence."[2]

Alfred B. Hamilton, former partner of John J. Healy and a whiskey trader at Fort Whoop-Up and now licensed Indian trader at the old Blackfeet Agency on the Teton River, was the local correspondent to the *Helena Weekly Herald*. He confirmed the massive cold front east of the Continental Divide, reporting on December 17 that the temperature was seventeen degrees below zero and that it was difficult to get back and forth between the Teton River and the new Blackfeet Agency on Badger Creek. He also alerted readers to Good Rider's

44

Alfred B. Hamilton, who with his partner John J. Healy established Fort Hamilton, or Whoop-Up, in 1869. Hamilton later became a licensed Indian trader at the Blackfeet Agency on the Teton River and the father of two of the major participants in Spopee's story, Ella Clark and Robert J. Hamilton. (Overholser Historical Research Center, Fort Benton, Montana, 1995-RP-624-C.)

agency confession and the killing of a man named "Wombsley" on Cut Bank Creek about November 1.[3] By December 23, Fort Shaw reported 37 below zero, with twenty-four inches of snow on the level and stage coaches stranded.[4] Farther east, at Fort Benton, it was even colder. There "the thermometer . . . registered 55 degrees below zero, the coldest weather known in the locality for many years."[5]

Given this weather and the blizzard conditions accompanying it, there was little expectation that the warrant for Spopee's arrest would be served. After all, there was not only the extended storm and temperatures as low as anyone could remember, but Spopee was over 120 miles away from Fort Benton—by horse, somewhere along one of the many tributaries of the Judith River in the broad expanse of the Judith Basin, most of it surrounded by mountains.[6] It was also possible that he had left the area for the Musselshell Country. Supposedly, he was still either with Running Crane's Piegan band or riding with a variety of resentful Bloods and Blackfoot proper from north of the border.

The previous summer Running Crane, on his way east through Fort Benton, had told a pitiful story of starvation at the agency on Badger Creek. Lack of game and subsequent starvation was by no

means limited to Canada. His Southern Piegan band had "been sub-
sisting during the summer upon dogs and a few prairie chickens,"
he reported.[7] Fort Benton residents were already aware of their
condition, as well as that of the neighboring Assiniboine and Gros
Ventre, for it was reported that the Sioux had pushed all of Montana's Indians west of the Bear's Paw Mountains, "where game of
almost every kind is nearly exterminated."[8] It was not just that there
was no buffalo west of the Bear's Paw—there was no game at all
on the reduced Blackfeet Indian reservation designated by President Ulysses S. Grant in 1873 and 1874. As a result, "within the last
two weeks many hundreds of them [Blackfeet and other Indians]
have crossed the Missouri, above and below Fort Clagett towards
the Muscleshell to hunt buffalo for food."[9] The operative word was
"food." Just when Indians were being urged to remain on reservations in order to learn how to "make food," the buffalo disappeared
in all but a few areas.[10]

Why had this happened? The Piegan chief Middle Bull offered
one answer: "The Great Spirit is angry with us. He has driven the
buffalo away and has given our country to our enemies."[11] Whatever the reason, the Niitzitapi—all of them, Bloods, Piegan, and
Blackfoot—felt aggrieved. Already irritated at the encroachments
and at having to leave their reservations, by the time they arrived
in the Judith Basin in the late fall, the Blackfeet and Bloods were
touchy. They would not look kindly upon the seizure of Spopee,
whom they considered one of their own, even if he was guilty and
the warrant for his arrest properly served.

Governor Potts did not know what to do. He had made public
his thousand-dollar reward, but he had to have begun to wonder
if anyone would attempt to claim it. Writing to John Young on December 20, Potts promised to lay the whole difficult situation before
the then absent U.S. marshal, Alexander Botkin, in Helena. Among
other things, Potts said, "I am afraid we cannot arrest the Indian
Spo-pe for he will learn of the confession of the other Indian [Good
Rider]." Why this should matter was left unsaid, as was the question of why this particular murder was so important other than that
an Indian had murdered a white man. Still probing, the governor
asked Young, "What will you suggest about the matter? Should the

officer go at once to the Judith—do you think the Indians will sur-
render him?" Then, mindful of subsequent legal needs, Governor
Potts remarked, "I trust you will preserve the confession in writing
so we can go to the Department with the subject if necessary."[12]

Potts was not alone in recognizing the importance of Good Rider's confession. Marshal Botkin, when finally responding to the
letters Young had written Potts, was of the opinion that he would
arrest Good Rider as an "accessory, and then use him as a witness,
of necessity," a possibility in Montana, which allowed Indian testimony in a court of law. What the marshal termed "the examination" of Spopee would take place as soon as he was arrested. At that
time, he stated, "it will be necessary for the interpreter to be present through whom One-to-chez [Good Rider] made his statement
to you. . . . If as I suppose, he [the interpreter] is in the employment
of the Government I will be able to reimburse him for his actual expenses." In fact, the interpreter was Melinda Wren of the Blackfeet
Agency, and she would figure prominently in subsequent develop-
ments. Botkin closed by asking Agent Young if he thought Running
Crane would "deliver Spo-pe to my deputy without a request from
you to do so."[13]

Improbably, Sheriff Healy and Deputy Sheriff Jefferson Talbert
had started from Fort Benton five days earlier on the chilly morning
of December 15 to cross the Missouri and to attempt the arrest of
Spopee. The warrant for the arrest had been "placed in the Sheriff's
hands" only that morning, and the small party had started at once.[14]
They were followed the next morning by Deputy U.S. Marshal Basil
M. Boyle, who had arrived in Fort Benton with his family only
shortly before. He set out on this arduous trip across the frozen Missouri with the wind blowing, the temperature in the thirty-below-
zero range, and in, of all things, a buggy.[15] Their joint mission, at the
time, was unknown, but as the *Benton Record* observed, "[I]t is safe
to say that only important business could have taken them away
at a time when the hardiest prairie men prefer not to venture upon
long journeys through the unsettled portion of the Territory."[16] In
Agent Young's opinion, "The Sheriff acted with promptness and
vigor. The weather was very severe enough so to have made a man
less courageous hold back for a time."[17]

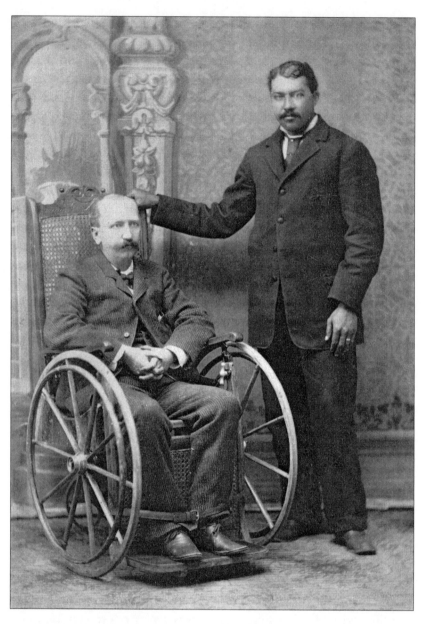

Alexander C. Botkin, U.S. marshal, Montana Territory (seated), "with his faithful servant, William Woodcock." (Montana Historical Society Research Center, Helena, Montana, 941-193.)

Why the two Chouteau County lawmen were so eagerly involved in the action under such challenging conditions later became the subject of considerable speculation. Why such dedication? Had Healy and Talbert been deputized as federal officials by Marshal Botkin to assist on this occasion because of their extensive experience with criminals and Indians? Not likely, for later Marshal Botkin referred to them as a *posse comitatus*. Did the warrant for Spopee's arrest stem from the governor's office, or were the men essentially bounty hunters responding to Governor Potts's offer of a thousand-dollar reward? Perhaps they were enlisted because there was no one else who could enforce the warrant.

Marshal Botkin was absent in what he called "another case of like character:" serving an arrest warrant in a murder case on the same immense reservation, near Wolf Point on the Missouri River. This time it involved the murder of a white by members of the Mountain Crows. One suspect had confessed his complicity at the Crow Agency, many miles away, and had implicated others who were still camped on the Big Porcupine Creek, north of where the Bighorn River joins the Yellowstone.

Botkin confronted a real problem. First, the fugitives, both Spopee and the Crows, were in Indian hunting camps, far away and off their reservations, and both reportedly had enough immediate support that an arrest would not be easy. Hostilities were, in fact, likely. Secondly, the costs of serving the federal warrants were prohibitive, for the fugitives were a very long way from Helena and the route led through unsettled territory. Simply getting to where they were would be hard, dangerous, and costly. Marshal Botkin had written the attorney general in Washington, D.C., asking if this difficult work could not be turned over to other federal offices. "Would not the War Department undertake the investigation?" The War Department had military authorities and troops in place in Montana, Botkin speculated, "who were probably in possession of more recent and more authentic information." Another suggestion of his was to have "the officers of the Indian Bureau . . . perform the duty."[18]

Clearly, Botkin did not want to go, either to the Judith Basin or to the Big Porcupine. The fact that Botkin was confined to a wheelchair and had to be accompanied by a deputy marshal was not the only problem. As he explained, even if he sent the deputy marshal alone, the fees allowed would pay only two dollars for the deputy's horseback ride, no matter what the distance—in this case, eight or twelve hundred miles round trip, and in severe winter weather. In addition, the deputy would only "be reimbursed for his actual expenses, itemized and sworn to."[19] Moreover, the paltry amount of money available for compensation to witnesses for travel and expenses, he complained, "is little less than a paralysis of the administration of justice in this territory."[20] Without witnesses in federal court, serving arrest warrants was often an exercise in futility. Little wonder that there was no enthusiasm on Marshal Botkin's part. The best he could offer was to "send a deputy to arrest him [Spopee]; but it is doubtful, on the one hand whether the officer can make the arrest with a *posse comitatus* of three citizens, and, on the other hand, whether the military authorities will make a detail of troops to assist in the execution of the warrant."[21] Enter Sheriff John J. Healy.

Given Botkin's characterization of the group as a *posse comitatus* and with Potts's reward money as motivation, Healy may have been the governor's choice from the beginning. In all events, he was perfect for the job. Healy loved an adventure and loved his own reputation as a hard case. The argument for the reward as the principal inducement for Healy is buttressed by a later case, similar to Spopee's, described by Cecil Denny, inspector with the NWMP. He related how during the winter of 1879 and spring of 1880, probably following news that Spopee had been arrested south of the Missouri, his superior had instructed Denny to proceed to Fort Benton "and try indirectly, with the sheriff of Fort Benton," John Healy, to have the alleged killer of a North-West Mounted policeman, another Blood Indian, by the name of Star Child, captured. The dead policeman, Marmaduke Graburn, had been stationed at Fort Walsh, where he had been killed—with a shot through the head—on November 16, 1879, only six days after Charles Walmesley had been killed in his wagon, moving south on the Whoop-Up trail.[22] Word had been received that the supposed killer was in one of the Indian camps south of Fort Benton, hunting buffalo.

"Extradition," wrote Denny, "was out of the question, as our evidence was very slight, and I endeavored by the offer of a reward to have this Indian captured, but the terms asked [by the sheriff] were out of my power to give, according to the instructions I had received."[23] Evidently Sheriff Healy, who would make hauling Indians out of hostile camps a hallmark, thought the reward in the Graburn case was too little. Sheriff Healy reportedly said that the Mounted Police "would have to put up five thousand dollars before he would try and make the arrest."[24] Or then again, maybe the legal risk of acting without a warrant was too great. In any event, Healy turned down the formal request from the Canadian north. In Spopee's case, however, the Blackfeet Indian Agent John Young and Governor Potts, with their written requests and their warrant, had put the sheriff on safer legal ground.

Whatever the situation, the attempt to arrest Spopee was a daring escapade made all the more dramatic because of the treacherous winter weather that only seemed to worsen. A further uncertainty was that Healy and the other two lawmen did not know where the various Indian hunting camps were in the snow-covered expanses of the Judith Basin. It was also possible that the severe wind and weather had forced the Indians to move for lack of wood or better shelter—to where could only be guessed at. The combined camps of Piegan and Bloods were large, and there was a chance, however unlikely, that they may have been forced to break up into smaller camps as winter set in and firewood and feed for their horses became scarce or the buffalo drifted with the ground storms. Moreover, arrests of this kind, as Marshal Botkin indicated, were usually left to the military units operating out of Fort Shaw or Fort Ellis. Despite the conditions, Sheriff Healy was undeterred. As the Helena newspaper, *The Independent*, described him, Healy was an "old frontiersman, thoroughly acquainted with the Indian and his peculiar habits," and being a "prairie man," it "mattered little to him whether a blizzard was blowing or the daisies were nodding their heads on the plains."[25]

But on December 19 blizzard conditions and sinking temperatures first slowed and then stopped the small party. Blowing snow, driven by extreme wind, swallowed and blurred every sign as it swept the surface of the open plains in pulsating clouds of thick swirling snow. It was a whiteout. All horizons had disappeared.

Blessedly already in camp, the party had no choice but to stay put
and hunker down. Soon they exhausted their wood, and as the
storm intensified, they simply wrapped themselves in their thick
buffalo robes and lay on the ground, offering as small a silhouette
as possible, and determined to wait out the storm. It was forty hours
before the storm blew itself out. No mention was made of the horses
or how they fared during this time. Having weathered the worst of
the storm, Healy and company stomped themselves warm, found
the drifted horses well beyond camp, and struggled on—with, of
course, the buggy driven by Deputy Marshal Boyle.[26]

The Judith Basin and adjacent regions were chock full of Indian
bands from a welter of tribes, pulled there since the late summer by
numerous sightings of buffalo in significant numbers, unlike anywhere else. Magnetic reports of plentiful game had spread rapidly
through many camps—Indian, Métis, and white. Prominent Piegan
chiefs, White Calf, Little Dog, Running Crane, and Little Plume,
had not only decided to winter there the previous summer, hoping
once again to be able to "make meat and put up robes,"[27] but they
had also discussed those plans with their favorite trader, Joe Kipp,
then operating out of Fort Conrad on the Marias River. He agreed
to establish a satellite post on the Judith River, not far from Warm
Springs Creek, the following winter if they would agree to trade
only with him. Kipp suggested further—ironically enough, given
his history as a whiskey trader—that in this case whiskey would
not be used for trading.[28] This proposal was agreed to by the Piegan.
The trading post on the Judith would be "dry."

After stocking up in August at the I. G. Baker & Company store
in Fort Benton, Joe Kipp, his employees James Willard Schultz and
Frank Pearson, and others, including Kipp's adopted son, Dick
Kipp, and a smattering of Indian wives, had taken their five wagons and four-horse teams across the Missouri and into the last bas-
tion of the northern buffalo, the bountiful Judith Basin. By October
they had located their operations among the cottonwoods near the
confluence of the Judith River and Sage Creek, had cut the necessary logs, and had constructed a main cabin, which would serve
as a trade room and storehouse, and a second, smaller one, which

Joe Kipp. (Photograph by Charles Spenser Francis, 1889. Overholser Historical Research Center, Fort Benton, Montana, 2005-KGR-142.)

would function as living quarters. By the middle of the month, almost all of the Piegan with adequate horses, as planned, had left the agency at Badger Creek. Eli Guardipee left his government employment with the Blackfeet Agency and with his wife tagged along with White Calf's band down the Teton River, ablaze with cottonwoods, through Fort Benton, and across the Missouri. Once on the north-flowing Judith River, the Southern Piegan were joined by Bloods and others from across the line, and all settled into a huge camp not far from Kipp's newly constructed trading post.[29] Serious robe-hunting did not begin until November, when the onset of cold weather made the buffalo hides glossy and thick. By December, as reported by Schultz, enough fresh robes had been tanned that "we had a good trade for buffalo robes."[30] By March, said Schultz, "we had taken 1,800 buffalo robes; 3,000 elk, deer, antelope hides; and a few fox and beaver skins."[31]

By the end of December, White Calf's band of Southern Piegan, numbering over eight hundred people, was camped on the Judith River above the mouth of Warm Springs Creek along with Running Crane's band and a collection of others.[32] These included a band of Fox Head's Piegan, as well as "Bad Boy" and some Northern

Piegan, who had arrived from Canada. All were on their way east toward Armell's Creek in the hopes of finding buffalo. As for the Sioux, rumored to be found in strong numbers between the Judith Mountains and the mouth of the Musselshell River, they remained a threatening presence, forcing the Piegan to "hunt in large parties, numbering over three hundred men, and all armed and mounted in the best manner in arms" in order to protect themselves.[33] There were also more Piegan under Big Nose, Black Weasel, and Double Runner on the Musselshell. All of them traded at Kipp's post.

As the winter progressed, hunting conditions changed. The buffalo, for example, drifted further east and the hunters had to follow them out of the Judith Basin. The *Benton Weekly Record*, the source of the above locations, described the Canadian Indians, reporting that while the "hungry hordes of the north have taken possession of the Judith country . . . [t]he Judith Basin is destitute of buffalo, and the Indians were obliged to live on small game, which is plenty."[34]

Finding just the right Piegan camp in such a bewildering array of options in the middle of a December storm was not going to be easy, even for one such as Healy. It helped, however, to know that Kipp's trading post was on the Judith River and served as a kind of catbird's seat, into which flowed a steady stream of information regarding the various buffalo hunting camps: their inhabitants, their locations, and their successes. Healy and Joe Kipp were old friends; both having been involved in the whiskey trade in southern Alberta and in Fort Benton. It did not take much imagination to know that when seeking a fugitive among the camps, the best place to learn the local scuttlebutt was to go to Kipp's. And that is what Healy did.[35]

Finally, after twelve days in harsh, trying conditions, with deep snow forcing the horses to plow their way forward with each step, Healy, Talbert, and Boyle felt their way into the targeted hunting camp, located between the north and south Moccasin Mountains. They had traveled over 150 miles in the severest of weather and in intense cold. It was Christmas Eve.[36] The hunting camp of Northern and Southern Piegan and Bloods had holed up there out of the open, near firewood and water. The Piegan and Blood winter counts had referred to the previous winter as *Itsistsitsis/awenimiopi*, "When first/no more buffalo"; this year the description was just as trenchant—the entire year was characterized as the winter of "Deep Snow."[37]

Although the gathered Indians were by and large friendly, they were surprised at the sight of Sheriff Healy, whom many of them knew either by sight, dealings, or reputation. Spopee, however, was not there, having left with a large hunting party a few days before. Once again the sheriff and party swung back up on their worn-out horses, and in time they finally succeeded in locating the second camp and their quarry. Reports differ regarding their reception. The *Helena Herald* papers, both daily and weekly, noted that surprisingly, neither Spopee nor the other members of the camp offered any resistance to the three lawmen.[38] Other contemporary reports, however, and the account of James Willard Schultz, a great number of years later, told a different story, with many of the tribesmen provoked and in an agitated state. "The Bloods swore that they would not allow him [Spopee] to be taken from them," wrote Schultz, and he noted that while the Piegan were noncommittal, they were inclined to side with the Bloods. Mounted Indians excitedly charged around in different directions, and tribal elders wanted to know the reason for this intrusion and for the arrest of Spopee. In Schultz's mind there was real doubt as to whether the arrest could be successfully concluded.[39]

Schultz was at Kipp's trading post at the time and was a witness to some of what happened. He reported that both he and Kipp had been convinced that there would be trouble. Kipp, in fact, told Sheriff Healy, "These Bloods are pretty mean, and Turtle has a whole lot of relatives and friends among them. I believe they'll fight. Old man, you'd better go back and get some of the soldiers at the fort to help you."[40] While not oblivious to the danger, Healy strenuously objected, saying, "I don't give a continental damn if he has a thousand friends and relatives!"[41] Kipp, while not liking the situation, nonetheless offered to help out.

Healy's first step was to ask to see Running Rabbit, the Blood chief who had spent considerable time among the Southern Piegan and at their agency on Badger Creek. When shown into Running Rabbit's lodge, Healy quickly explained the situation. Running Rabbit, said Schultz, agreed that he would send for Spopee and that Healy could

James Willard Schultz and his son, Lone Wolf (Hart Merriam Schultz), 1884, at Kipp's Trading Post, Robare, Montana. (Montana State University, Special Collections, James Willard Schultz Collection, 303.)

John J. Healy, whiskey trader, publisher and reporter for the *Benton Record*, and sheriff of Chouteau County, 1877–85. (Overholser Historical Research Center, Fort Benton, Montana, 1995-RP-624D.)

talk with him, but that he would not be responsible for whatever happened if the lawmen tried to take him away. "My young men are wild. I can't control them"[42] When Spopee, surrounded by a curious group of onlookers who wanted to know what the sheriff wanted, appeared and heard the charges, he said in Blackfoot, "I don't know anything about it . . . and I am not going with you. . . . I'll not go; I'll fight; I've got lots of friends here who will help me."[43]

Without the least hesitation and quicker than anyone could imagine, Healy "snapped a pair of handcuffs on his wrists" and relying on his well-known reputation as a hard case and for his coolness under fire, Healy defied the malcontents in the camp and walked out—with his prisoner. They returned to Kipp's trading post, where, according to Schultz, "he chained him [Spopee] to a big, log roof support. A crowd of Bloods and some young Piegans surged in after him and right there we all came near passing in our checks, for Healy was obdurate and would not release his man."[44] Schultz's final comment was revealing. "None of us slept much that night."[45] The *Helena Daily Herald* reinforced this description by reporting that Sheriff Healy, "being well known to them for many years, and knowing the people he had to deal with, was enabled to make satisfactory explanations and bring the prisoner away."[46]

Healy, called Ahkopikini or "Scar Nose," was helped immensely by his ability to speak "good Blackfoot" because of his earlier marriage to a daughter of Many Spotted Horses, the leader of the Many Fat Horses band of the Bloods, and because of his famous run-in with a Blood named The Weasel Head.[47] In this last encounter Healy had unexpectedly turned the tables on The Weasel Head, who had returned to Fort Whoop-Up and who had hoped, through the ruse of shaking hands with Healy in front of a war party, to recover from an earlier humiliation. He would count coup on Healy, an enemy, by first visibly touching him and then killing him in the sight of all. This would bring The Weasel Head great honor. Healy, with his own honor at stake, had left the safety of his whiskey fort on foot to stand in the open air before the mounted warrior, unafraid, ready to shake hands. Then, suddenly recognizing The Weasel Head's real intentions, Healy reacted. As the Indian smiled and reached down from his horse to shake Healy's hand, Healy suddenly "gave him a sling and a twist as quick as a cat and with all my force. He hit the ground head on, he was riding bareback, and I caught the gun as it fell. The next instant he was calling out 'kimokit, nappi' meaning 'Have pity on me, O God!'" Now it was Healy who had counted "grand coup" and had done so in front of a war party of sixty.

The Blackfoot never forgot that event or Healy's bravery.[48] Not only did The Weasel Head become his best friend, but the Blackfeet also adopted Healy. In Healy's words, they "made me a member of their tribe. I was taken in as a member of the Black Elk Band of warriors. They made an Injun of me!"[49] It seemed to the Bloods as if a great spiritual force were in play, as if Healy had been aided and protected by an unknown spirit helper whose power was irresistible. As a result, when Healy showed up in the Judith Basin, with trouble over Spopee looming, the Indians knew things would not be easy. "Take off those iron things, or we will do you harm," they said. Healy responded by saying "Listen! . . . You know me; I guess you know I am not afraid. . . . If any of you interfere, I will not be the only one to die." That did it. They remembered all too well his "power." Without pulling his gun, he stared them down and claimed his man.[50]

Although not mentioned in written accounts of the arrest, another law enforcement body was present in the buffalo camps of the Piegan—the so-called Soldiers Band, an organization of thirty-six Indians from the different bands who in 1877 were charged with "the maintaining of order in camps, making arrests and enforcing the orders of the head-chiefs." They were led by Double Runner, often called "The General," and represented the traditional enforcement body.[51] In June of 1878 Agent Young had been instructed to organize an Indian Police Force at the agency, but in August he acknowledged difficulty because of the "absence of our present rude police at the hunting grounds with the great camp." The "rude police" were the Soldiers Band, and the election from among them would have to wait until they returned.[52]

Development of an Indian Police Force was one of the general reforms initiated by Secretary of the Interior Carl Schurz that was being applied to all U.S. reservations. The *Helena Weekly Herald* was not impressed. Instead of creating an Indian Police, the editors stated, the government should follow the example of "the English across our borders in which a few Mounted Policemen keep the peace among tribes in that vast country. It is because the Indians of the various tribes look up to these policemen as disinterested and without prejudice. An offender would more readily yield to one of a superior race and would be able to count less upon sympathy from his own tribe."[53]

Complying with Washington's orders, Young had not only expanded the numbers of the Indian Police to thirty by July of 1879, but he also requested uniforms, horses, and saddles, arguing, "[T]his reservation is of such great extent that unless mounted, the Police are of little service."[54] The police organization included prominent Blackfeet, including a number of band leaders. "The General," meaning Double Runner of the Soldiers Band, held the rank of captain; Fast Buffalo Horse was a lieutenant; and Running Crane was the first sergeant; Brave Man, the second sergeant; and Wolf Coming Uphill, the third sergeant. There were ten privates, including White Grass, Crowfoot, Mad Plume, and Mountain Chief. These men, Young suggested, should be furnished with carbines of the same caliber and pattern as that used by the U.S. Army Cavalry.[55] The General's band, for example, numbered 124 individuals at the spring issue of annuities, while Fast Buffalo Horse led 188 and Running Crane, 191.[56] There were, of course, important leaders who had nothing to do the Indian Police, men such as Big Nose-Bear Chief, White Calf, Tearing the Lodge, and others. Nonetheless, the officers of the Indian Police were selected because they were already in positions of authority and were used to maintaining order through coercion. They had long been in charge of the hunting camps, usually while on the reservation but also when the camps left the actual reservation and crossed over south of the Missouri to what the Blackfeet termed "Tat-tsi-kyoo-hss" or "the land of the middle."[57]

The Blackfeet agency physician and chief of police, Arthur C. Hill, reported that it was these policemen who maintained order "in the large hunting camp in the vicinity of the Buffalo. In the latter they have prevented the sale of whiskey which some unprincipled white men have attempted to barter. Constant reports is made to me, from the Hunting Camp as to the state of affairs there."[58]

Members of the Blackfeet Indian Police Force, Blackfeet Agency on Badger Creek, ca. 1880. (Photograph by Charles Spencer Francis, 1889. Author's collection, no. 183.)

Back at the agency on Badger Creek, Agent Young also reported on a steady trickle of individuals who went back and forth during the long winter's hunting season. He told the *Helena Daily Herald* that he had "recent and reliable advices from them, and is gratified with the reports sent that they are in the midst of buffalo, are securing an abundance of meat, have fat ponies, and are making plenty of robes."[59] In other words, agency officials were in regular contact, apprised of the general situation, and confident that their Indian Police Force, now expanded, exercised a significant authority.

Unfortunately, the police reports do not include the last quarter of 1879, when the Spopee affair took place, but it is inconceivable that they were not involved in Spopee's arrest in some immediate fashion. Their stature and presence would have made them unavoidable, although, in the end, given the extant agency records, they received no credit. It was easier to attribute success to the three intrepid white lawmen.

For Spopee and the lawmen it would be a long, cold journey back to Fort Benton. The storm had blown itself out, but the country was still plastered with deep, fresh snow, and the going would be tough. First, however, the law enforcement officers had to secure a horse for Spopee to ride. While he waited, graphically described by one newspaper account as "ironed in a lodge," the lawmen spent one whole day bargaining for a horse before they could begin the difficult route to Fort Benton with their prey in hand. However difficult the snowy return to Fort Benton, we hear nothing of it from any of the lawmen personally, although the *Benton Weekly Record* did report that Deputy U.S. Marshal Boyle had "the misfortune to break a costly buggy on the trip."[60] Nor did Spopee remember any of the details. Later, during his sentencing, he indicated why. Asked about his confession, he said, "I don't know what I told Healy: he gave me all the whisky I could drink, both going to Fort Benton and coming here [Helena]."[61]

Only with the arrival of the New Year did the public learn that the three lawmen and their prisoner were safely back in Fort Benton. On January 2, the *Benton Weekly Record* announced that "Sheriff Healy and Under-Sheriff Talbert returned from the Moccasin mountains with Spo-pee (Turtle), the Blood Indian who killed Charles Walmsbury, on Cut Bank river, in October [*sic*] last."[62] There was no presumption of innocence. The newspaper also revealed that once Spopee was in Fort Benton, Probate Judge John J. Donnelly had conducted "an examination" of the prisoner, through an unknown interpreter, and that Spopee had stated that despite being drunk on the way back to Fort Benton, "he told the Sheriff the truth, and that he did not hide anything." According to the newspaper, Spopee acknowledged to the judge "the killing of Walmsbury, but stated that he was urged to commit the crime by Good Rider. The judge ordered the prisoner to be held to await the action of the U.S. authorities."[63] Three days later Sheriff Healy wrote to Agent Young that not only had he arrested Spopee, but that Spopee had "confessed to the murder before Judge Donnely—and is held here to await instructions from the Governor."[64]

Spopee's statement at the examination amounted to a compelling confession. The circumstances, however, also attested to Sheriff

Healy's Indian savvy. Not only had Healy pacified the prisoner with firewater, but five days after Spopee's arrest in the Judith Basin, upon their return to Fort Benton, Sheriff Healy "found" a copy of the *Helena Independent*, dated December 23, in which Agent Young had reported the lengthy confession of Good Rider. "The Sheriff took the paper to Spopee, and said he had a 'medicine paper' which told all about how he killed the white man, and that he wanted him to talk and tell him all about how it was done, and show whether the 'medicine paper' talked right."[65] Spopee was dumbfounded. How did it happen that the "medicine paper" knew what had transpired? How could it have possibly seen or learned of the secret details that only he and Good Rider had been a part of? Were the spirits talking? Confused and scared, Spopee did not know what to do. Slowly comprehending that Good Rider had to have talked, Spopee decided to tell what happened from his perspective. Good Rider's confession had to be countered. The result was his confession to Sheriff Healy, again either through an unknown interpreter or directly to Healy with the sheriff doing his own interpreting.

This new disclosure began in true Indian fashion. Spopee wanted his listeners to know something of his identity, and to do so he needed to tell who he was related to. "I am," he said, "a Blood Indian and my friends belong to Me-kas-toe's [Red Crow's] band."[66] Having dispensed with this necessary preliminary, he went on. "After my people had gone away to South in search of buffalo, I was around Fort Macleod and the Blood Whiteman's [Fred Kanouse, or Kainaikwan (Blood Indian Man)] at the Kootenai Lake [Waterton Lake]: but I determined to follow after my people."[67] In order to do so he stopped at the I. G. Baker store in Fort Macleod, where he asked Donald W. Davis, whom the Bloods called Spi-ta, or Tall Man, for credit. Davis had been a close friend of Sheriff Healy when the whiskey trade was at its peak. Spopee relied on the fact that Davis's wife, Revenge Walker, was a sister of Red Crow and thus a relative of his, and he thought, correctly, that Tall Man would give him provisions.

Spopee's version differs almost immediately from that of Good Rider. According to Spopee, he did not overtake Good Rider walking along the trail south, but rather had met him in Macleod, where "the boy" had been "working for the whites [McFarland]." Leaving together, the two later stopped at "Crazy Whiteman's Place" [Dutch Fred's] at Standoff just north of the Belly River, and he gave them some bread.[68] From there they followed what Spopee called "the white man's road that runs along the foot of the mountains," meaning the Riplinger Road. It veered off from the Whoop-Up Trail, angling west and south to the Blackfeet Agency, and the two kept to it until they came to the North Fork of the Milk River.[69] By this time they were so tired and hungry that they even resorted to eating "some old wolf bait, which we found, but it was so nasty that we could not swallow it."[70] After leaving the North Fork of the Milk, as Good Rider had also confessed, they discovered fresh wagon tracks; the two desperate travelers quickly decided to catch what had to have been a white man in order to get something to eat. "We overtook the white man and camped with him on the South Fork of the Milk river," related Spopee, "and got plenty to eat from him."[71]

Spopee also noted that the man had a "needle gun [a breech-loading Springfield] and four mares with their tails cut off square." Shifting the blame to Good Rider, he related how "Good Rider told me that the man had plenty of money, and if I would kill him we could buy many things: but I said that I was afraid to kill a white man; that the soldiers were strong and would follow and kill us." In this telling it was Spopee who is concerned with being discovered, not Good Rider. Not only that, but Spopee acknowledged that "the Catcher at Fort Benton," meaning Sheriff Healy, "knew all the Indians, and that he would follow on the trail like a wolf, if he wished to catch a man, and that he would be sure to find us out."[72] While this description was perhaps self-serving on Spopee's part, Healy's reputation among Indian and white alike was already legendary.

Then, perhaps hoping to add a personal dimension to his story, Spopee divulged discursively that he had been at Heavy Runner's camp on the Marias River at the end of January in 1870, when U.S. soldiers out of Fort Shaw, under the command of Colonel E. M. Baker and led by the then young Joe Kipp, had mistakenly attacked a friendly camp of Piegan recovering from smallpox. They had killed 173, mostly women and children.[73] One of the soldiers, "riding a large grey horse[,] had shot me," he confided. Spopee then showed Healy the scar where the ball had passed through both hips and said, "and as I went down, I begged him for my life; the soldier taking pity on me told me to get away and hide and I managed to crawl up a coolie and hide myself. Since that time I have been running with the whites. This story I told to Good Rider to show him that the whites are strong."[74]

Unimpressed, Good Rider had only laughed at him, said Spopee. In two other departures from Good Rider's confession, there was no account of a shovel-wielding Walmesley having knocked Spopee to the ground, and Spopee described Good Rider, not himself, borrowing the gun from the white man, not the other way around, in order to chase after the band of antelope they all had seen from the road. Spopee went on to say that Good Rider, after firing a number of shots unsuccessfully, returned and "urged me to take the gun and shoot the man, but I refused and said I knew nothing about the gun and was afraid. Good Rider took a cartridge, opened the gun, and placed it in the barrel, and then he kissed me [not unusual for a near relative or men's society brother] and begged me to do the deed, and I should keep all of the money for myself. Then I shot that white man."[75]

Having confessed to the killing, Spopee, according to the newspaper account, fell suddenly silent before the sheriff. He refused to say anything more or to acknowledge that he had spent any of the stolen "greenbacks" other than for a few supplies at the traders on the Teton River. While Spopee's confession was not exactly fingerpointing, for he did admit to the actual killing, much of the initiative in Spopee's account rested with Good Rider; he constantly egged Spopee on and it is Good Rider, said Spopee, who got the money, "of which there was quite a lot."[76]

Writing from Fort Benton on January 5, 1880, Sheriff Healy notified Agent Young of his success in arresting Spopee and of his subsequent confession. Healy then awaited instructions from Governor Potts. As for Young, on January 20 he tendered his "sincere thanks" to Healy for "his prompt and vigorous action in the matter" and also notified Major Winder of the NWMP that Spopee had been arrested by Sheriff Healy and was currently in custody. As Young understood it, Spopee "has made a full confession . . . claiming that he was urged on by O-ne-to-ches [Good Rider]. His trial will take place in March."[77] On January 14, Healy and Deputy Marshal John X. Beidler transported Spopee to the territorial capital in Helena, detouring along the way to Fort Shaw on the Sun River to pick up Good Rider. He had been in custody there since his confession before John Young at the Blackfeet Agency a month before. The two Kainai now were to be quartered in the Lewis and Clark County Jail in Helena to await trial in the March term of the federal district court.[78]

As early as January 3, before he knew of Spopee's arrest, U.S. Marshal Botkin had determined to arrest Good Rider as an accessory and to use him as a witness. To do so he would need the deposition of the person who had translated Good Rider's confession to Agent Young. Less than a week later Botkin sent a blank subpoena to Young, asking him to insert the name of the government interpreter and "to serve it on him by reading, sign the return on the back and forward to me." He wanted this done as soon as possible as "both the Indians will be awaiting examination by the 14th."[79]

The schedule was much too tight. Young responded on January 14 that the interpreter in question was a woman who was of the opinion that in the "present state of the weather and roads it is utterly impossible for her to make the journey." As soon as possible, he promised, "I will send her to Helena to make a deposition." In addition, he would send Walmesley's gun to Helena with her; he added in a postscript that he too would endeavor to be on hand.[80] The woman in question was Melinda Wren.

By the end of January, Agent Young had returned the subpoena that had, he said, been served "on Mrs. Wren." He further reported, "She leaves in the morning for Helena, where if the weather permits she hopes to reach before Monday, February 2. I sent the gun by Mr. Wren who will deliver it to you." Young also wanted to know from Marshal Botkin the names of other witnesses from the agency that he might want for the forthcoming trial. Young then mentioned that Thomas Davis, the agency herder, had "bought a saddle—the murdered man's—from Spo-pe and sold him a horse for which he was paid in greenbacks of which Spo-pe paid," and that Dr. Hill had examined the body and the "nature of his wounds and assisted in the discovery of the wagon." Young concluded by noting that "some harness, portions of clothing, two blankets and some small articles are in my possession."[81] It is remarkable how thorough and how legalistic the officials' preparations were. Arrangements, including subpoenas for these additional witnesses, were pursued with a bureaucratic and professional exactitude seemingly anxious about its legal standards. This appears to have been typical of Montana Territory, however, and in no way suggests that concerns were heightened or procedures were tightened because Spopee was an Indian, and a Canadian or "foreign" one at that. Nor was the jurisdiction of the court debated.

Meanwhile, in Helena, the two jailed Indians, who had arrived on January 14, underwent a "preliminary examination," this time on the afternoon of January 15 before U.S. Commissioner Isaac R. Alden, who was also the clerk of the Montana Territorial Supreme Court.[82] This examination was similar to a preliminary hearing, where instead of using a grand jury, a U.S. commissioner determined probable cause on the basis of witness testimony prior to actual court proceedings. According to the *Helena Daily Herald,* the only witness called was Sheriff Healy, "who made the arrest" and whose testimony "as to the confession made to him by Spo-pee a few days after his capture was essentially the same as the report furnished by the *Benton Weekly Record* of the 9th [January 9, 1880]."[83] Having heard the testimony of Sheriff Healy, the commissioner adjourned the preliminary examination until the following Saturday, "to await the other witnesses. The Indians in the mean time are safely quartered in the county jail."[84]

The other witnesses from the Blackfeet Agency, Dr. Hill, Thomas Davis, and especially Melinda Wren, were unable to make it before February 2. Unfortunately, there is no extant record or newspaper report of their appearance or their testimony before Commissioner Alden. The only evidence of its having taken place is a short notice in the *Benton Weekly Record.* Written from Helena, dateline February 3, it reported that "Spopee and Good Rider, the Indians who murdered Charles Walmsbury . . . had their examination before U.S. Commissioner Alden today. Both Indians confessed to having murdered Walmsbury."[85]

Despite the careful proceedings, Spopee and Good Rider were not tried during the March term of 1880. Instead they languished in

Spopee at the Blackfeet Reservation, ca. 1880. *Minneapolis Journal,* July 9, 1914, p. 1. This photograph accompanied an interview with Captain Arthur C. Hill, one of the witnesses for the prosecution at Spopee's trial in Helena. Spopee's photograph was taken at the time of the trial, and the presumption is that Dr. Hill provided the *Minneapolis Journal* with the photograph.

custody in Helena for the rest of the year. The reason for the delay, explained the U.S. attorney, was that Congress, for some inexplicable reason, had made no appropriations for the execution of process, so that all United States business had to wait until late the following fall. The legal machinery in the territory ground to a sudden halt.[86] As a result, James W. Andrews, Jr., the federal attorney in Helena, informed Agent Young: "It will be impossible therefore to indict or try 'Spo-pe or Good Rider' during the spring term of court as planned. You will therefore please notify all witnesses, whom you were to subpoena against the above named Indians, not to come to Helena at present."[87]

While waiting behind bars, Spopee and Good Rider did their best to keep themselves occupied. There were some breaks in the monotony, often reported by the local papers. They were, for example, escorted to the photographic gallery of O. C. Bundy and had their pictures taken. Unfortunately, these are no longer extant.[88] Spopee also tried to remain in contact with his wife, who was on the Blackfeet Reservation, by having letters written in English on his behalf, which were then sent to Agent Young on Badger Creek. On October 10, 1880, for example, Spopee sent a letter from the Helena jail. It addressed the agent as "Father," and asked: "Will you please tell my wife to send me a sack of Kinnikinnick" and noted, "I received the moccasins she [his wife] sent. They are very good. I am well and in good spirits. Your son [Agent Young's] came and saw me the other day. He kindly brought me some tobacco and told me that you would be here when I am tried. I shall be glad to see you and the other friends who come with you." It is hard to believe that Spopee understood the judicial role his "Father" would play in the forthcoming days. Innocently, Spopee also pointed out that Good Rider was doing well. "The officers here treat us very kindly and do everything they can for us," he wrote, and then in closing he added, "I should like very much to see my family and hope they are well," and signed his name, "Spopee, Piegan."[89] There was no answer. A week later Spopee dictated another letter to Young, this time more cognizant of the gravity of the situation. "Please write me and let me know how my folks are. I do not know but that I may have to die and I would like to hear from my family and how they are. Your friend, Spopee, Piegan."[90]

CHAPTER 3

AN AURA OF LEGITIMACY

The Helena Trial of Spopee
and Good Rider

By the year 1880 the judicial machinery in Montana Territory was surprisingly well developed. The territory's criminal justice system included elected county sheriffs, deputy sheriffs, county judges, and clerks of court. There was also a federally appointed U.S. marshal, deputy marshals, federal district courts and their judges, territorial and federal grand juries, probate judges, district attorneys, a Supreme Court with its clerk, and, since 1871, a territorial prison at Deer Lodge. This was not a lawless West. And while there were numerous problems in Montana Territory with federal funding, court facilities, and a lack of printed laws and decisions, perhaps the greatest obstacle was the geographical size of the judicial districts and the daunting hardships of travel by coach or on horseback. County seats were few and far apart. Much of the territory was only beginning to be settled. Associate Judge Everton J. Conger, who came to preside over the Spopee case in the territory's Third District, wrote three years later, in 1883, that his district "was fully one half of the area of the territory" and that he had to travel, regardless of the season, over three thousand miles a year to hold court.[1]

Montana Territory in 1880 was not only subject to the rule of law and possessor of a flourishing judicial apparatus, it was also, not surprisingly, already home to a good many lawyers, including the twenty-one members of the Helena Bar Association, which met the first Monday evening of each month.[2] Many of these attorneys, like those who followed, had come onto the territory with excellent legal training and practice. They had been former state bar members and either had migrated into the territory in the wake of multiple mining rushes and settlement opportunities or had arrived as a result of federal appointment to territorial positions. Among the latter was the territorial governor, Benjamin F. Potts, and Decius Wade, appointed chief justice of the Montana Supreme Court by President Ulysses S. Grant in 1871. Most of these carpetbag attorneys insisted upon a defined and well-organized set of legal procedures and judicial practices similar to what they had learned and practiced elsewhere. They brought these models with them, and together, the lawyers and their legal models constituted what some scholars have termed a "carried legal culture." This imported legal culture reflected critical institutional elements and procedures of the assembled lawyers who had cut their teeth in the bar associations of the older states in the Midwest, California, and the East. It was a professional culture that the newcomers were determined to replicate. In tandem, this shared legal culture and the reality of federal appointment gave the territorial courts a robust legal confidence.[3]

In Spopee's case, this anxious concern for proper legal procedures in a frontier setting meant that even though Spopee was an Indian and without any means—he was, in fact, indigent—he was going to be surprisingly well represented by experienced counsel. In effect since 1872, the "Laws, Memorials, and Resolutions of the Territory of Montana" provided that if any person upon indictment for felony was "without counsel to conduct his defense and he be unable to employ any, it shall be the duty of the court to assign him counsel."[4] The issue of whether Indians in Montana were legally "persons" remained unclear, but they certainly could offer testimony in court. Prior to Spopee's trial, in 1879, Standing Bear, a Ponca chief, famously and successfully argued in U.S. district court in Omaha that Indians were legal persons. Spopee certainly could not vote or serve on a jury, but Indians in both Montana and Dakota Territories—unlike elsewhere in the United States—were called as witnesses and did give testimony in Montana territorial courts, both civil and criminal.[5] Legal historian John Wunder termed this "a unique development in legal doctrine in terms of time and place in the United States" and "a fundamental divergence from precedent."[6] These evidentiary questions, however, were moot because, as everyone agreed, Spopee was a Blood Indian from the British possessions, where in 1876 the Dominion of Canada had passed the Indian Act, making all "Indian" inhabitants of the plains legal wards of the Canadian state.[7] In any event, there was no definition of his rights as an Indian alien by the Americans, who were concerned only with the location of the murder, and neither the NWMP nor Canadian authorities demanded, or perhaps even wanted, legal extradition.

Extradition, however initially appealing, was a difficult path both politically and practically because of recent experiences, and officials on both sides of the emerging international border were hesitant to employ the legal process.[8] Moving ahead, the Montana justice system provided Spopee with court-appointed legal counsel, and it can only be assumed that the expenses were to be borne by the court, as they were in Nebraska and elsewhere across the west, or to be essentially "pro bono."[9] Not only was legal counsel, one prerequisite for a fair trial, available to Spopee, "the foreign Indian," but his court-appointed team of defense attorneys took their task seriously as a professional obligation. Although hardly blind to issues such as his race or his origin "on the other side of the line," the team was interested in protecting Spopee's legal rights as best they could; he was treated humanely, if not always fairly, and benefited from or enjoyed a court experience that remained relatively speedy even though it was postponed because of fiscal shortfalls. The legal proceedings were procedurally practiced and predictable, and although Spopee's defense counsel was inadequately funded (adequate funding being a second prerequisite for a fair trial), the judicial system's public goal was to demonstrate an admirable standard of due process.

But although Spopee's case was by most appearances procedurally correct, its fairness and substantive justice were dubious. Procedural implementation depended upon and reflected territorial beliefs, and when it came to American Indians, territorial beliefs were anything but fair or impartial. To begin with, most citizens of the territory believed that Indians were not equal to whites, perhaps not even "persons" before the federal law, in spite of the recent federal decision regarding Standing Bear.[10] Negative or pejorative views of Native people, especially the Blackfeet, reigned supreme among fur traders, settlers, miners, and politicians. Hostile to the tribal cultures, settlers, stockmen, and city-dwellers saw buffalo-hunting Indians as armed and roaming vagabonds who needed to be unhorsed, disarmed, and confined to reservations, where they should be forced to work, or perish.[11] These attitudes and the territorial conviction of white supremacy shrouded most Indian–white encounters, and they were not left at the courthouse door, whether in Fort Benton or in Helena.

Spopee, moreover, did not understand English, let alone the legal language of the court, and he had no idea of the laws to which he was to be held accountable or how those same laws could provide him with protection. Simply put, he did not understand that he had legal rights. It mattered greatly that the victim of the 1879 crime was a white man, and this fact alone created within the criminal justice system a unique dynamic. The ghastly crime along a well-traveled trail, assumed to be in Montana Territory, and against a lone white man had been committed, it was alleged, by one or two Indians. Something had to be done. The territory had to set an example—a show trial for the instruction of all, but especially for other Indians. This was the reason for the trial, even though, as it turned out, the facts in Spopee's case were less than persuasive, the motive contested, and the jurisdiction questionable. As long as the citizens themselves were not free of bias or prejudice, there is no way the legal proceedings could be, no matter how far those involved strove in that direction.[12]

Spopee's court case, postponed because of congressional dithering, began on Monday, November 29, 1880, in the thriving city of Helena, which then numbered a population of just over 3,600 people. The federal grand jury of the Third Judicial District of Montana Territory charged that on the October 14, 1879, Spopee "feloniously, unlawfully and of his malice aforethought, did make an assault . . . in and upon the body of one Charles Walmesley in the peace of God and of the United States."[13] The indictment went on to state that he

Helena, Montana Territory, ca. 1880. (Montana Historical Society Research Center, Helena, Montana, 945-181.)

did so with a so-called needle gun that belonged to the victim, and that he shot Walmesley, wounding him "in and upon the left breast, in and upon the left shoulder and in and upon the back and body" with the result that Walmesley "instantly did die."[14] As James L. Dryden, United States Attorney, District of Montana Territory, filed the grand jury's indictment, he also had begun the process of notifying a number of witnesses, including Blackfeet Agent John Young, who arrived in Helena for this purpose on November 28. Young subsequently used this obligation to excuse his tardiness in submitting his monthly agency report, writing, "I have the honor to forward the monthly report of this agency for November delayed until now, by the absence of the agent in Helena under subpoena to give evidence in a murder trial."[15]

On December 10 the U.S. attorney submitted the indictment for murder in the case and listed the witnesses to be called. These included Dr. Arthur C. Hill, the physician at the Blackfeet Agency;

the agency farmer, John Wren, and his wife, Melinda Wren, agency interpreter; and a clutch of others—Clark Tingley, Sheriff John J. Healy, Samuel Alexander, Deputy U.S. Marshal John X. Beidler, and I. R. Alden, who as U.S. commissioner had conducted a preliminary hearing.[16]

The grand jury had determined that there were two cases or actions, one against Spopee alone, and one against Spopee *and* O-ne-to-ches, alias Mats-o-ke-to-pe, alias Good Rider, in which Good Rider was charged as being "present, aiding, helping abetting, assisting and maintaining the said Spo-pe in the felony and murder aforesaid."[17]

The Third District Court in the November Term, with Associate Judge Everton J. Conger presiding, heard the charges on December 11, 1880, and on the basis of the territorial law of Montana regarding indigents accused of felonies, he appointed and assigned "Col. Wilbur Fisk Sanders and Judge William Chumasero as counsels for the defense and ordered to plead Monday next."[18] How the defense counsels were to be paid for their services was not covered. Later, during a plea for clemency, Sanders asserted that their entire service was "without "pecuniary consideration, expected or promised."[19]

These two Helena attorneys were staunch Republicans in an overwhelmingly Democratic territory and were more than competent lawyers. They were not legal opportunists, inexperienced at trial, or in any way unequal to the task. Quite the opposite was the case. Sanders was probably the most prominent and gifted attorney in Helena and across the territory. Called a Montana "Pericles," after the fifth-century B.C. Athenian orator and general, for his role in establishing democratic practices in Montana and assessed as the "keenest blade" around, Sanders was well regarded even by his many enemies.[20]

Sanders had studied law in Ohio and was admitted to its bar in 1856. In 1863 he and his family went west to Virginia City and Alder Gulch, then in Idaho Territory, in the tow of his uncle, Sidney Edgerton, who had been federally appointed chief justice of Idaho Territory. Once there, both Edgerton and Sanders founded and led a political movement urging Congress to carve out of Idaho Territory a new federal creation, Montana Territory, with Virginia City as its

Wilbur F. Sanders, ca. 1890.
(Archives & Special Collections,
Mansfield Library, University of
Montana, 81-369.)

capital. It was a clumsy process, taking place during a fevered gold
rush in which there only makeshift laws. Whatever little government
there may have been was the result of miner's courts and informally
elected officials. When a spate of robberies by "road agents" broke
out as wealthy miners and merchants attempted to transport their
gold "outside," vigilante committees were formed to correct the situation. Sanders, noted historian Frederick Allen, was "a party to the
discussions."[21] When the case came to trial, the young Sanders took
on the role of prosecuting attorney, successfully trying and convict-
ing George Ives for murder before a miner's court in Virginia City
in 1863. Afterward he helped to organize a vigilance committee on a
more formal basis, with rules, officers, and goals.[22] In 1864, Sanders
agitated for the creation of Montana Territory, and when the movement succeeded, he then campaigned unsuccessfully as Republican
for the office of Delegate to Congress. Following statehood in 1889
and a controversial political struggle, he would eventually become
one of Montana's first two U.S. senators.[23]

So at the time of his appointment by the court to defend Spopee,
in 1880, not only was Sanders a seasoned trial attorney whose clients
included the Northern Pacific Railroad, but he was also a powerful
Republican voice in the nation's capital and in the general elections

of 1880. In the months following Spopee's trial, Sanders would run against Martin Maginnis for the position of territorial delegate in Washington, D.C.[24] Politics were a part of Sanders's being, and they were undoubtedly involved in his willingness to defend Spopee.

Born in Nottingham, England, William Chumasero had immigrated in 1829 to Rochester, New York. He studied law in Rochester and Buffalo and was admitted to practice in New York in 1838 and in Illinois in 1839, before moving west in 1864 to Virginia City, where he was appointed district attorney for that judicial district. In 1866, Chumasero moved to Helena, soon to be active not only as a lawyer but also as an involved businessman, with considerable holdings in mining companies and mineral claims.

Both attorneys appointed to defend Spopee were respected and, in the case of Sanders, often feared in the rough political tumble of the capital city. Again, they were not legal or political lightweights, and why they took the case remains unknown, as does whether they had any choice and whether they were selected from a pool of competent lawyers then in Helena and available to the court. The decision may have even been occasioned by political spite. In 1875 Wilbur Fisk Sanders had represented the Canadians in Helena during their efforts to extradite the Fort Benton Americans arrested for the Cypress Hills killing of Assiniboine men, women, and children. Attorney Sanders had denounced the accused as "Belly River wolfers, outlaws, smugglers, cutthroats, horse thieves and squaw-men." His opponents, both politically and at the extradition hearing, were the powerful Fort Benton Democrats, led by the Irish contingent, whose spokesman was the Fenian stalwart John J. Donnelly. A colorful man who had led abortive invasions into the Dominion, a lawyer, justice of the peace, and agitator, Donnelly despised the Canadian efforts and was taken aback at the effectiveness of Sanders's charges, although U.S. Commissioner W. E. Cullen ultimately freed the "wolfers" for lack of sufficient evidence. But the phrase stuck in the public mind, and five years later, during the heated political debates of the 1880 general elections, the Fort Benton Democrats were still derisively referred to as the "Belly River wolfers."[25] When the Fort Benton Democrats, led by Sheriff Healy and Justice of the Peace Donnelly, became intimately involved in the arrest and early judicial examination of Spopee, a Canadian Indian, in 1879–80, it cannot

Everton J. Conger, territorial judge, Third District Court, Helena, Montana. (Montana Historical Society Research Center, Helena, Montana, 952-569.)

have been mere chance that Spopee's legal defender was Wilbur Fisk Sanders, even if he was appointed by the Helena federal court.

The presiding judge of the Third District Court was Everton J. Conger. He had been appointed associate justice by his old friend President Rutherford B. Hayes in 1880 and arrived in March of that same year. Judge Conger, a Republican appointee, was not at all familiar with territorial circumstances, and Spopee would be one of his first cases. A Civil War Union officer, severely wounded in combat, Conger had in 1865 also played a significant role in capturing the assassin of President Abraham Lincoln, John Wilkes Booth. In 1869 he was admitted to the Illinois bar and later practiced law there. The recommendations for his federal appointment as territorial judge, in the opinion of historian John D. W. Guice, emphasized his "war record, wounds, and Republican loyalty," but at the same time the recommendations were "average to better than average for the period.[26]

Not long after the Spopee case was over, in 1883, Judge Conger was suspended under a barrage of criticism and investigated on charges of incompetence, gambling habits that were decried as "unbecoming, unseemingly [sic], and indecorous," drunkenness, and "keeping companionship of low, vile people." Members of the bar of the Territory of Montana, including many Republicans, wanted his removal. They charged that he was "utterly destitute of the learning or the ability to qualify himself for the discharge of the duties of his high office." And after a long bill of attainders, he was deemed unfit.[27] Wilbur Fisk Sanders, whom Judge Conger had supported for territorial delegate, was among Conger's many detractors. Although a special examiner eventually lifted Conger's suspension, he was not reappointed at the end of his four-year term. In retrospect, and given the nagging concerns and questions at the time of Spopee's trial, the charges of incompetency seem germane.[28]

On Monday morning, December 13, Spopee and Good Rider, having presumably met with their defense attorneys, pleaded not guilty to the charge of murder. Sanders motioned to quash the grand jury indictment on a variety of grounds, including the fact that "the place, point or country where said offense was committed is not sufficiently set forth or described in the indictment" and that the wounds were not sufficiently described.[29] Both claims, but especially the first, were critical, for the first implied that the murder may have taken place outside the United States. On December 16 Judge Conger overruled the motion to quash, called the jury, empanelled it, and swore it in. Attorneys for the defense, Chumasero and Sanders, recognizing how difficult it would be to secure a fair trial for their Indian defendant, had "only enquired of the jury as to their ability to try the defendants with the same care and solicitude they would white men."[30] This was the right question.

The racial issue was present from the outset, in spite of the fact that Montana Territory, unlike many states and western territories, allowed for Indian testimony as competent witnesses.[31] And while the jury and the court professed their determination to provide equal treatment for the Indian, the question of race, equity, and bias remained for Spopee front and center. The trial failed to be fair. Moreover, the failure to impose this standard of equal treatment became a principal reason for the counsel for the defense's subsequent plea for clemency, following the expected and unfavorable verdict.

On December 17 attorney James L. Dryden opened the trial by presenting his case against Spopee to the jury. Then he surprised one and all by asking to have the two Indians, Spopee and Good Rider, as well as a witness for the prosecution, "separated," that is excluded, from the court room while the other witnesses were testifying, a violation of the defendants' right to face their accuser. The motion was held under advisement.[32] On a related matter, Alfred B. Hamilton, former whiskey trader at Fort Whoop-Up and business partner of Sheriff Healy, himself a witness for the prosecution, became the official court interpreter.[33] This court appointment was crucial given the individual confessions of the two Blackfoot-speakers and the likelihood of confusion and mutual misunderstandings, on both the part of the defendants and the court, be such misunderstandings cultural or factual or both. There was no discussion of the matter, however.

Dryden's request to separate the Indians from court sparked an immediate objection, fueling the only controversy in the early stages of the trial. Defense attorney Sanders vigorously protested the petition, saying such a segregation of witnesses "for fear of collusion was unheard of; that a party vouched for the integrity of his own witnesses and could not ask for such action."[34] As far as Sanders was concerned the motion amounted to judicial novelty. Spopee was a British subject, he argued, and "if new methods of jurisprudence were to be invented they should not be first applied in cases liable to raise international questions."[35] In other words, this was no time to be creative. Sanders's argument must have been convincing, for without waiting for a ruling from the court, the U.S. district attorney withdrew his motion, and with that, reported the *Helena Daily Herald*, the trial of the case began.[36]

The first order of business involved presenting and swearing in the first prosecution witnesses, Sheriff John J. Healy, A. B. Hamilton, two others, and Good Rider, who was to testify on behalf of the government.[37] Oddly enough, the prosecution then "asked leave to withdraw a juror, saying the identification of the deceased was not possible with the witnesses present," and the case was adjourned until two o'clock. Once again, the legal jockeying pivoted on the presence of the witnesses, primarily, one may assume, Good Rider.[38]

As a prosecution witness, Good Rider presented a serious problem for the defense team. Sanders and Chumasero, without hesitation, moved to address a number of matters, including the important issue of interpretation. They requested via a writ of habeas corpus that a certain John V. Brown, "who understood the signs and speech of the said Indian to assist in the interpretation of the testimony of the said Good Rider." Clearly they did not want to rely upon Hamilton, who had been appointed interpreter for the court but was also being called as a witness for the prosecution and had a number of past associations with Sheriff Healy. Instead, the defense counsel was determined to secure an independent understanding of Good Rider's testimony, as well as to secure for themselves the services of an interpreter who could facilitate their communication with Spopee and the development of a trial strategy. Without this help, they would be at a decided disadvantage. Why they did not avail themselves of Melinda Wren, the Blackfeet Agency interpreter, remains unclear. Perhaps they thought she was already too involved in the case as a subpoenaed witness for the prosecution to be convincing. And, as we shall see, they had reason to be concerned about her impartiality.

The request for John V. Brown, who was white, was awkward. Brown was at the time in jail himself, awaiting trial on two charges, the first relating to forgery, and the second, to "the unlawful taking and carrying away papers relating to claims."[39] Moreover, there was no way for the court to verify Brown's facility with the Blackfoot language or to establish how he had learned it. Surprisingly, the court, in the interest of fairness, granted the unusual request and ordered the U.S. marshal to produce Brown for the examination, re-examination, and cross-examination of Good Rider during the day of December 16 and the morning of December 17. Brown duly appeared and interpreted as requested. During the morning session on December 17, the court heard the testimony of the prosecution, and after examination, the prosecution rested. At noon both sides announced that they had closed the prosecution examination and reexamination and the defense cross-examination and agreed "that said Indian [Good Rider] could not communicate his ideas except by signs and the Blackfoot language."

It was at this time that the prosecution asked if Good Rider might take the witness stand for a second time. They then "asked him if he had been shown by anyone how to make the line of where the alleged homicide had occurred with relation to the International boundary line between the United States and the Northwest territories of the Dominion of Canada."[40] This provocative question, as can be imagined, immediately brought objections on the part of the defense attorneys, "whereupon the District Attorney stated that the witness [Good Rider] wished to change his testimony and out of court had expressed his willingness to do so as to material fact thereof."

It is hard to explain what was going on here. When the court was about to adjourn on the evening of the sixteenth, the previous day, it had specifically warned and forbade "all persons not to converse with said Good Rider as to the evidence which he had or should give in said case, including the interpreter A. B. Hamilton." Hamilton, however, ignoring the injunction, had gone ahead and "conversed with Good Rider as to the evidence given and to be given." In spite of this egregious breech, the court ruled that Good Rider might now, a day later, answer the proposed question. This being the case, Sanders and Chumasero asked that "in as much as they did not understand the said signs and language," they should be able to have the "other" interpreter, Brown, returned to the court "to testify as to the correctness of the interpretation of the questions to and answers of said Good Rider because they could not."[41] The court denied this request. Brown did not appear in the courtroom. While the defense objected, there was little they could do other than demand that their objection be included, "signed, sealed and made a part of the record which is done accordingly."[42] Judge Conger, for his part, wrote into the bill of exceptions that he had "no knowledge of Brown's ability to translate or understand the signs or language and further he is in jail and convicted of a felony [December 9, 1880] and awaiting the sentence of this court."[43]

While this legal scuffling was going on, Spopee amused himself by "drawing a very faithful likeness of District Attorney Dryden on a scrap of paper. When finished, it was passed around among the attorneys and created much amusement."[44] This was not the only levity of the day. The *New North-West*, published in Deer Lodge, carried a story under the headline "Spopee Wants to Hunt Fat Buffalo." Deputy U.S. Marshal John X. Beidler had interviewed the two accused Indians, reporting that Spopee "fully expects and seems willing to be hung," but that he thought Good Rider ought to be set free. Having revealed that bit of speculation, Beidler went on to report that "the Indians express the modest desire to be allowed to go hunting, as the buffalo are now fat. It is probable that their next hunt will be taken on the Happy Hunting Grounds."[45]

When court resumed on Saturday, December 18, the damage to the prosecution's case seemed to have been contained. Good Rider's testimony, if changed, was neither officially nor unofficially noted. The issue vanished. Nothing more was said regarding the issues of unbiased interpretation and the impropriety of Hamilton, the court interpreter, coaching the state's witness. Evidently this was a technicality that now could be overlooked.

The courtroom awaited the case for the defense as presented by Sanders and Chumasero. According to the court's Journal of Proceedings, Spopee was "duly sworn and examined as witness on the part of the defendant upon which testimony he rests." That is it. There is nothing further—no extant testimony and no record of exactly what Spopee said, how he said it, or how he conveyed this interpreted information. There are no details as to the length of Spopee's testimony. This is puzzling. The *Helena Daily Herald,* although present, had nothing to say other than to engage in a bit of territorial racist humor. "While Col. Sanders was making the closing argument for the defense, [Spopee] remarked to the interpreter; 'Too much talk no good, heap dam fool. Injun talk little, smoke heap, then go out and kill a man.'" The newspaper's conclusion was that Spopee was not at all impressed with the "white man's method of trial." However, seen in the light of what subsequently occurred with Spopee, the *Helena Daily Herald* did reveal a tantalizing bit of information disguised as humor. When told that his jail mate, Peter Pelkey, also charged with murder and tried by the same court at the same time, "would plead insanity, a broad grin spread over his [Spopee] face and he remarked," presumably through an interpreter, "'Tell them I am crazy too.'"[46]

The next line in the Journal of Proceedings began "I. R. Alden, John Young and A. B. Hamilton appeared as prosecution witnesses in rebuttal[,] and after the evidence the argument of counsel and the instruction of the court, the Jury retired to their room to consider their verdict."[47] There is no record of their testimony, either. The *Helena Weekly Independent*, however, corroborated this condensed information, reporting: "[D]efense introduced testimony and rested; arguments of counsel presented; jury having been charged and instructed by the court retired in charge of sworn officer."[48] Returning to court at ten o'clock in the evening, the members of the jury each answered to their names, and Thomas B. Smiley, foreman of the jury, presented the verdict. "We the jury in the above entitled cause find the defendant, Spo-pe alias Turtle guilty of murder in the first degree as charged in the indictment."[49] Then the U.S. attorney moved for a *nolle prosequi*, Latin for "we shall no longer prosecute"—in effect, a declaration to the judge that the case against Good Rider could not be proved and should be dropped. Obviously, this was in fulfillment of a previous arrangement, or else a new deal had been cut. The motion was sustained and Good Rider was discharged from custody.[50] Newspapers within the territory widely reported aspects of the trial and the verdict, including news that the United States' case against Good Rider was dismissed and the prisoner discharged.[51]

Sentencing did not occur until after the Christmas holidays. The weather was cold and Helena lay deep in snow cover. The court had scheduled sentencing for the morning of Monday, December 27. But the holidays and the inclement winter weather had not dampened public interest in the legal proceedings of the court. According to the *Helena Daily Herald*, "the court house was thronged this morning by a large crowd attracted by curiosity to hear sentence passed upon the various criminals convicted at the present term of court." The attorneys, on the other hand, were slow in showing up, "straggling in by ones and twos" and then gathering in little groups around the burning pot-bellied stoves, where they "cracked jokes together and seemed, despite the storm and altercations which have existed between them during the trial of various causes, to feel a high regard for one another as men and citizens."[52] These included Spopee's court-appointed attorneys, Sanders and Chumasero, as well as District Attorney Dryden.

In the first order of business, Judge Conger sentenced a number of men for grand or petit larceny to the penitentiary and to the

Lewis and Clark County Jail. Among these men was John V. Brown, who had been specially selected to interpret in addition to the official interpreter in the Spopee case. As noted, the charges were forgery and "two other indictments." District Attorney Dryden declared that Brown was to be sentenced for forgery "by imprisonment in the Territorial Prison of the Territory of Montana" for a term of one year and "that he did not urge sentence on the other two indictments."[53] These charges included "unlawfully taking and carrying away papers relating to claims." Dryden did not disclose his reason for recommending that sentencing for these charges be dropped, nor did the newspapers speculate.[54] Perhaps his lenient approach had to do with the interpreting service Brown had rendered the proceedings. Judge Conger, however, did not agree. He added to the first sentence "a fine of one dollar."[55] Brown was remanded to the custody of the U.S. marshal, to be delivered into the custody of the warden of the territory prison at Deer Lodge.

The next matter on the docket had to do with sentencing the two murder cases, that of Spopee, of course, and that of his jail mate, Peter Pelkey, a twenty-four-year-old French-Canadian convicted by the jury for the murder of Charles Tacke. Like Spopee, Pelkey also had been captured by three men—woodcutters, who as a result of Governor B. F. Potts's decision to offer a territorial reward of one thousand dollars, tracked Pelkey down and captured him, oddly enough, in the same Judith Basin where Spopee was arrested. Later, just prior to Spopee's trial, Pelkey's counsel had attempted to argue to the court that Pelkey had gone mad at the sight of blood, and while the jury did not buy the insanity defense, Pelkey's appearance and behavior gave it credence—enough so that Spopee, as noted, could not resist blurting out, "Tell them that I am crazy too."[56]

On the wintry morning of December 27, both Spopee and Pelkey were escorted "in irons" into the Third District Court to receive their respective death sentences.[57] Spopee was first. He seemed in good spirits, said the *Helena Weekly Herald*—not the least depressed. He was dressed for the occasion in what was termed "civilized costume," but Spopee had augmented his store-bought clothing with "a white 'choker,' which had evidently been arranged with much care."[58] Before sentence was passed, Sanders and Chumasero motioned the court to set aside the verdict and to grant a new trial, arguing that the verdict was contrary to the law and that "material errors" existed.[59] Judge Conger overruled the motion. The case was closed. Except that it wasn't at all closed—and in fact, Spopee's trial would now take a totally unexpected turn.

In a final effort to stave off the sentencing, Sanders then read a statement—or perhaps more accurately given its original dictated nature, a narrative or telling. It was Spopee's. He had dictated it to be read to Judge Conger at this moment. Spopee's statement had been translated from Blackfoot into English and carefully written down by John V. Brown, prisoner and backup interpreter. Spopee and Brown, working together, had done this some time over the Christmas break, while both were in jail. How closely the translation followed or resembled what Spopee actually said—and in what sequence or order—is open to question. The two men did have sufficient time to check and recheck the telling for a correct rendering, and the accounting certainly appears to be a close approximation of what Spopee had said.

Interpreting from one language to another, however, is terribly subjective, and usually the interpreter's skills on either side of the linguistic divide are decidedly uneven or asymmetrical. One language is native, the other learned and thus subject to opportunity, interest, and practice. Competencies varied immensely among Blackfoot interpreters, depending upon their background and whether they translated from English to Blackfoot or vice versa. Examples of interpretive shortcomings ranged from the elaborate, ornate, orotund English imaginings, intoned by well-intentioned Victorians who were lucky to have anything that approached a working knowledge of Native languages, to the famed laconic three- or four-word summations of lengthy Blood or Piegan orations by Jerry Potts, the mixed-blood scout and interpreter for the NWMP. While Potts certainly knew Blackfoot, he preferred not to waste words. So, for example, when asked to interpret the long, detailed pleadings of a band chief whose followers—men, women, and children—were destitute and starving, Jerry Potts grunted succinctly in English, "He wants grub."[60] Clearly, there was lots of latitude!

There is now no way of knowing the extent of Brown's competence. What is known, however, is that once Brown had translated Spopee's words, had set them down on paper, in a sense had fashioned them into chronology, sequence, and arguments, they became more than Spopee's speech. Now transformed into questions, challenges, and disagreements, these renderings acquired greater organization and became a recorded account, a document that possessed structure and authority and aspired for even more. Brown had carried this written document into the courtroom prior to his own sentencing, but when and under what conditions it was transferred to Sanders is unknown. What is known is that, instead of being dismissed following the imposition of his sentence, Brown was allowed to stay—evidently at the court's insistence or agreement, in case further translation or interpretation was necessary.

Procedurally, Spopee's statement was awkward at best, if not unwelcome. It raised, of course, any number of questions having to do with origin, motivation, and issues of a factual nature. Lurking behind these matters was the involvement of the defense team, especially Sanders. Had the defense attorneys orchestrated this posttrial effort, or were they as surprised as everyone else when John Brown reached over the table to hand them Spopee's statement? Secondly, even if Sanders, as the lead attorney, had put the idea into play with Spopee, Brown, or both, did he already know the details of what was, essentially, Spopee's new confession? In effect, this was the statement Spopee should have made earlier, when he was a witness for his own defense. But he hadn't made it then. Why now?

Sanders seemed to have been as surprised as anyone. It seems reasonable to assume that had he known about these new revelations and their potential to have impacted the jury's verdict, he would have used them during the trial. He did, however, use Spopee's disclosures in subsequent pleas for clemency, upon deciding that he would not seek to appeal the court's decision to the Montana Supreme Court. Unlike the court and Judge Conger, the local newspapers, the *Helena Daily Herald* and the *Helena Weekly Herald*, recognized full well the import of Spopee's new statement. On the basis of popular demand, the editors of the *Herald* decided to publish the complete statement, verbatim, in the *Daily* on Tuesday, December 28, and the *Weekly* on January 6, 1881.

Spopee's personal statement began by responding to Judge Conger's question, "Can you give us any reason why you should not
die?" This was clearly a query that had stirred Spopee emotionally.
It took him back to another life-and-death situation ten years earlier, when he had been shot through both hips by a U.S. soldier at
the Baker massacre, referred to above, and had been remarkably
spared.[61]

This horrendous blunder had happened in 1870, when four companies of U.S. cavalry and fifty-five mounted infantrymen, under
the command of Colonel E. M. Baker, plunged and plowed their way
on horseback to the Marias River in one of the worst January storms
Montana had seen in years. The purpose was to capture or kill the
Piegan murderers of Malcolm Clark, a prominent white citizen of
Montana Territory. The perpetrators were supposedly with Mountain Chief's band, then locked in place in a frozen camp along the
cottonwood bottoms of the Marias River. With temperatures around
twenty degrees below zero and ground blizzards sweeping uneven
swaths across the high plains, Baker attacked the wrong camp of
thirty-seven lodges, their occupants sick with small pox and huddled together below the bluffs on both sides of the river. Through
one of those misunderstandings so common between whites and
Natives, the Blackfeet thought they were momentarily at peace with
the whites and had nothing to fear.[62] They had posted no outlooks or
scouts. Most of the men, except for Heavy Runner, the band leader,
were away hunting and unable to defend those left behind. It was
a sickening disaster in which the troops killed 173 Indians, 140 of
which were women and children under the age of twelve. These in-
nocents included Spopee's mother. In addition, the soldiers took 140
women and children prisoner and captured the horse herd of over
300 horses. The mistake was further exacerbated when the troops,
in the extreme conditions, burned the Indian lodges, camp gear, and
supplies and set the now homeless refugees loose and on foot to
find shelter as best they could.[63]

Spopee was among those wounded, shot through the hips by a
cavalryman on a grey horse. He had not forgotten. "Ten years ago,"
he said, "the Great Father's soldiers came to my people's homes
and killed a great many young men and women, old men and little
children. I myself was shot. The soldier chief did not ask us if we

wanted to die. But you," said Spopee to Judge Conger, returning to the issue at hand, his sentencing, "are a great chief; you ask me to say why I should not die."

With that important preamble, Spopee then confessed to killing Charles Walmesley. But, for the first time, he confided that he had thought "if I did not kill him, he would kill me; he told me that he would do so." His statement then disclosed a new perspective on his former testimony. From the very first encounter along the trail, there had been tension, if not outright hostility. As was customary, Spopee had wanted to shake hands, the sign for which was to raise the forearms up straight with the fingers touching, but Walmesley had refused to do so.[64] Didn't he know what was being asked? When they eventually camped that night, Spopee said he told Good Rider to go to the creek to get some water. While he was gone, Spopee went over to where Walmesley was sitting. "I told him I was poor: that I had no gun with which to kill anything to eat, and asked him to give me something to eat: he told me he would not, and for me to go away quick; he then got his gun and loaded it. I went up to him and took hold of the gun: I told him not to kill me." Walmesley put the gun down and again told Spopee, probably in English and with gestures but in no uncertain terms, to leave. Spopee did not leave but went to get a drink from a pail near the wagon, only to have Walmesley throw the water in his face and again demand that he, according to Spopee, "go away or he would kill me." Uncertain as to how to respond, Spopee went over and sat down by his saddle, which was lying on the ground, and pulled the hood of his capote or blanket coat over his head. Spopee said the white man swore at him while he sat there and became so incensed that he struck him with a shovel. "When I could see again, Good Rider, who had come back . . . was washing the blood from my face and neck." Then, fearing for his life, he determined to leave before things got worse and told Good Rider to get the horses.

After Good Rider left, Spopee went up to his assailant and asked him, "Why did you try and kill me?" Spopee's account continues: "He began swearing at me and told me he would kill me. I ran to where the gun lay and took it: when the white man saw me with the gun he picked up an ax and ran towards me: I ran away, but he ran after me; I nearly turned around: the white man was quite near me, with the ax raised over his head: the gun lay on my left shoulder: I quickly cocked the gun and fired it: the ball hit him in the Breast and he fell on the ground."[65]

This was new. The issue of self-defense in the individual confessions of the two Indians had never come up before. Everyone seemed surprised, as if self-defense was a plea reserved for whites, not Indians. Unfortunately, there was already a verdict, as well as a history of inadequate or insufficient confessions, that already had muddied the water. How had this happened? Why didn't Spopee's attorneys know of this critical legal consideration? In retrospect, this failure to communicate should not be that surprising. Spopee's defense team had frequently complained that they had not had an opportunity to adequately communicate with Spopee, or vice versa. They had been left in the dark, neither able to ask questions nor to get the whole story. All of this was compounded by the fact that Spopee had not realized how critically important it was to tell the whole story, convincingly—and now it was too late.

Judge Conger undoubtedly thought that Spopee had been coached—a last-ditch effort, following the verdict—for only now was he exercising his right to confront his accusers and to offer an alternative motivation, self-defense. Moreover, if the earlier versions of the story had been so fabricated and incomplete, why would this version be any more truthful?

A second disclosure surfaced, raising equally serious questions. This time it had to do with the question of jurisdiction. Spopee now averred that Walmesley had been killed "near a little creek just beyond the Milk river ridge, and a mile or two north of the boundary line." The convicted murderer went on to inform the court that he knew full well where the international boundary was, for, as he said, "I saw the white men and the soldiers when they were making it." Then, to further reinforce his assertion of knowledge about the location of what the Indians called the "Iron Line," he pointed out that he knew a white man, identified as Fred Kanouse, "who killed a white man at Benton and ran away to Macleod; Healy could not come there and take him. If the boundary line is nothing, why don't you send Healy after this man and hang him?"[66]

While this was not exactly the case, it was close to true, and Spopee made his point. Eight years earlier, in 1871, the power of the international boundary had manifested itself to inhabitants on both its Canadian and American sides. Deputy U.S. Deputy Marshal Charles Hard had been stopped cold as he attempted to arrest Joe Kipp's whiskey outfit, with some six hundred gallons of alcohol, near the border. Kipp, according to his later employee James Willard Schultz, had defied the marshal, arguing that the U.S. official was no longer in the United States. Instead the marshal was in the British possessions, and here, he was transformed: he was no longer an officer, argued Kipp, no longer within his jurisdiction. Surrounded by Kipp's armed men and uncertain as to the location of the border, Charles Hard turned around. Not only was this a standoff, giving rise to the naming of a subsequent whiskey fort clearly across the border, but it was also a powerful reminder, to both Indian and white alike, that the border mattered.[67]

Spopee also recognized the importance of determining the exact location of the murder. "Good Rider tells me that Healy told him that if he would say that I killed the white man this side of the line, that he [Good Rider] could go home, but Good Rider said 'no,' that he would not tell that lie." Spopee had a final question. "If it is good to hang me, why don't you let Macleod do it? I killed the man in his [Macleod's] country."

The man in question was Colonel James F. Macleod, commander of the NWMP, who had trekked west in 1874 and built Fort Macleod on an island in the middle of the Oldman River in the newly acquired North-West Territories. Bull Head, the Northern Piegan chief, had been impressed enough to give permission for the police to erect their fort, to use the trees necessary for construction and firewood, and to give Macleod his own name, Stamixotokan.[68] Quickly establishing close ties with other Native leaders, Macleod proved to be resourceful and was amazingly successful in combating the whiskey trade and in giving the Indians the impression that they would be fairly treated under the law. By 1875 the NWMP had made enough progress that the Blood chief Bad Head, alias Father of Many Children, had characterized that year in his winter count as "When it was finished/whiskey."[69]

In the summer of 1876, such was Colonel Macleod's reputation that he, along with Lieutenant-Governor David Laird, was appointed commissioner to negotiate a treaty with the Blackfeet, Bloods, Northern Piegan, Sarcee, and Stonies, later known as Treaty 7. As far as Spopee was concerned, it was Macleod's law that was in place north of the Canadian boundary, and he did not understand why this was not acknowledged now, in the outcome of his murder trial.

As for the reason Spopee had not mentioned this critical piece of information earlier in his confession, especially the one elicited by Sheriff Healy—that was simple: he had no idea what he had said because he was drunk. "He [Healy] gave me all the whisky I could drink, both going to Fort Benton and coming here." And he chastised the court, "Why do you let Healy get me drunk, and then tell you what I say?"[70] It seemed a reasonable question.

Spopee's third query dealt with the paucity of witnesses on his behalf at the trial. These included three people whom Spopee and Good Rider had turned to in desperate need of advice after the murder—Good Rider's unnamed father, who was near the Blackfeet Agency, a white man called simply "Tom," also in the vicinity of the agency, and White Calf, the Southern Piegan chief, whom Spopee termed the "head chief of my tribe." They had all recommended that Spopee "go at once to a Judge and tell him all about it, and that nothing could be done with me." Tom had even said that he knew Walmesley and "that he was a bad man and had a bad heart."

None of these men had been called to testify, although they knew, in Spopee's words, "the straight story of the killing." Without knowing how to say it, Spopee strongly implied that the district attorney was in effect withholding exculpatory evidence. This kind of manipulation of evidence, the withholding of information, was further addressed when Spopee openly acknowledged that he had no idea what he had told Sheriff Healy. Healy had drunked him up, not once, but a number of times, while Spopee was transferred from the Judith Basin to Fort Benton, from Fort Benton to Fort Shaw, and finally, from Fort Shaw to Helena. "I do not know what I told Healy."[71]

Whether Spopee had told this to his own defense counsel is unclear; he probably had not, as Sanders and Chumasero's frequent complaints that they had no interpreter assigned to their effort

would attest. On the other hand, whenever Spopee did communicate, no one could be sure of the fidelity of the interpretation.
Spopee revealed an example of this as well. There had been, it
turns out, a previously unmentioned examination or preliminary
hearing. It had taken place in Helena, before what Spopee or his
translator, Brown, called a "Commissioner," soon after Spopee and
Good Rider's arrival. The examination was conducted through the
commission's interpreter, an unidentified woman. Spopee believed
that this woman deliberately mistranslated his responses during the
examination, and he thought of her mistranslations as toxic, taint-
ing the process. Spopee learned about this only afterward, when
he was returned to the jail. This revelation happened, Spopee said,
when "[a] white man came in [to my cell] and gave me a can of
molasses. I had known him at Macleod. He spoke good Piegan."
Then, continuing, Spopee said that upon arriving in Helena from
Fort Benton he had been taken to a shoe store for a pair of shoes.
The same man he knew in Macleod was working there. "His name
was Stum-mich-sena [Bull Chief]; . . . he was present when I talked
to the Commissioner; when he came to the jail, he told me that the
squaw interpreter had lied about my talk, that she had not told what
I said; this is the reason I would not [later in court] talk before the
squaw; why was not this man before you when I talked? He knew
what I had told the Commissioners [commission] and would have
told you."[72]

The commission in question appears to have been formed under
Isaac R. Alden.[73] The commission had been appointed to establish
a preliminary hearing on behalf of the court, as the grand jury and
the actual court would not meet before the November term because
there had been no federal appropriation. Considering, however,
the rarity of a woman Blackfoot interpreter and given the list of
witnesses called when Spopee's case came around, the "squaw interpreter" had to have been Melinda Wren, Blackfeet Agency interpreter. She and her husband, John Wren, the agency farmer, were
among the list of prosecution witnesses and incurred expenses "at
the examinations of Spo-pe and Good Rider."[74] As for Alden, he too
was listed among the prosecution witnesses and, as noted above,
had given testimony at Spopee's trial, rebutting the testimony of the
defense even though he had conducted a preliminary hearing.

Melinda Choquette Wren, interpreter,
Blackfeet Agency, Badger Creek.
(Author's collection, no. 1460.)

Spopee's objections were telling. He had not been able to tell his side of the story, and with so much manipulation, so much suppressed or tainted evidence, and so much disagreement over interpretation, he had been deprived of his constitutional right to due process of law. The legal process, on the surface so procedurally correct, had been hollow, stacked against him with a predetermined outcome. His story was that he had been provoked and attacked, with the scars to prove it; that he had killed in self-defense; that the incident occurred across the international boundary and not in the United States; that the prosecution witnesses, including Good Rider, had been tampered with or promised rewards; and that reputable defense witnesses, including White Calf, had not been called. Eloquently, if obliquely, Spopee summed up the proceedings of the court by relating how he had followed his people's standard of behavior when dealing with enemies: "When I saw the Sioux I killed them; I stole their horses; my heart is brave. You are a great chief and can hang me, but you have no right to do so. I have spoken straight, and am done."[75]

Spopee had signed the statement with his mark. Curiously, he did not identify himself as Spopee, or Turtle; rather the inscription at the bottom of the statement read, "The Big Snake or O-much-sixXsic–a-nach–gaon." How this had happened was never addressed, much less explained. Why he identified himself in this way was never explained. Subsequently, especially when writing to his wife, Spopee used this identical name or its abbreviation—in English, simply "Snake."[76] On the other hand, it was not culturally unusual for Blackfoot speakers to change their names, in some cases multiple times. They did so depending upon their age, upon individuals who had named them or transferred names to them, according to battles or war records of their own or their fathers, or upon the occasion of spirit intervention at different times in their lives. Sometimes significant names or those of their ancestors became available through transfers or death, creating naming opportunities; sometimes a new name came with entry into an honor society. And there were always what we would think of as "nicknames" that "stuck," as the Blackfeet put it, because of physical attributes, habits, practices, or associations.[77]

Thus there was a wide spectrum of possibility. Spopee may have been given this name as a result of the way he walked, in a crabbed, turtle-like fashion, following his injuries at that snowy tragedy, the Baker massacre. He was certainly listed under this name in 1878 as having accepted annuities along with the other Southern Piegan. On the other hand, he may have taken on or been given the new name, "Big Snake." There was nothing to have prevented him from using simultaneously either name, or others, at any given time. After all, Good Rider had two Blackfeet names, Mats-o-ke-topi and On-e-to-ches, as did any number of others—Mountain Chief or Big Brave, for example.[78]

Having finished delivering Spopee's statement, Sanders sat down. There is no record of any immediate reaction—either by the court, the attorneys on both sides, or Spopee. There was silence on all fronts. Nothing in the subsequent official court record documents the court's response; the newspaper accounts are void of any response other than the printing of the statement, and there are no extant personal recollections. It was as if the historical slate had been wiped clean. In any case, it was too late. The statement had not been sworn, was not acknowledged by the court, and was not made a part of the formal record, although a clipping from the Helena newspaper was subsequently included in the case file.

Without acknowledgement and without addressing any of the issues that Spopee had raised, the court then asked Spopee if he had any legal cause to show why the judgment of the court should not be pronounced against him. This was the question he had sought to answer. Incredibly, this question was conveyed not through the court interpreter, A. B. Hamilton, but through Spopee's informal interpreter, John Brown, who was still in the courtroom. When Spopee replied that he had none, Judge Conger then asked the convicted man to stand up. He "ordered, adjudged and decreed" that Spopee be removed from the court room and kept in close custody in the jail of Lewis and Clark County until Friday, the fourth day of February, when he was to be taken "to the place fixed by law for execution and then and there between the hours of eleven o'clock am and three o'clock pm of said day be hanged by the neck until you are dead."[79]

Then it was the turn of Peter Pelkey, Spopee's jail mate, also convicted of murder. And after Judge Conger had ordered the French-Canadian laborer to stand, he intoned on behalf of the court "the county is content and judgment shall be followed by execution; your crime will be expiated, and the majesty of a broken and outraged law be restored. You will be taken from this room and kept in close confinement until the 4th of February next, and then taken to the place appointed by law, and between the hour of 11 o'clock a.m. and 3 o'clock p.m. hanged by the neck until you are dead."[80]

The *Benton Weekly Record* reported that both Spopee and Pelkey "listened to their sentences with characteristic Indian stolidity."[81] According to the *Helena Daily Herald*, Pelkey, who was not Indian, exhibited no emotion as the judge read his sentence, but "on its conclusion made a low bow and with the words 'Thank you,' resumed his seat."[82] With this the prisoners were removed from the room, and the court was adjourned. It was two o'clock in the afternoon. Execution was scheduled for February 4, 1881.

CHAPTER 4

COMMUTATION

Citizens in Montana Territory generally loved a hanging; they thought executions were entertaining as well as socially beneficial. Executions were public events, if not public spectacles, in spite of the laws of the territory that stipulated expressly that executions were to be held in a "private enclosure" and that only those few invited by the sheriff could be present. Those few included the judge of the court, the prosecuting attorney, and the clerk of court, together with two physicians, a minister, two relations or friends of the condemned, and twelve reputable citizens selected by the sheriff.[1] But denizens in the scattered territorial communities, aware of the role vigilante justice had played in their history, still awaited a good legal hanging, however infrequent in the 1880s, with considerable anticipation.

Spopee's scheduled hanging was no different. No one wanted to miss out, and location was critical. Arguing that it was, after all, Fort Benton's notorious lawman J. J. Healy who had arrested Spopee, the *Benton Weekly Record* reported, "An effort is being made to have Spopee the Indian murderer, hung in Benton."[2] The reasoning behind this assertion was two-fold. First, the capital city of Helena did not need to have two executions at the same time, and in early February 1881, both Peter Pelkey and Spopee were scheduled for execution. But if a hanging was "most powerful in the suppression of murder," then these legal deterrents needed to be spread around. Helena should not monopolize them. Second, this needed to be a show trial. If Spopee was to be hanged in Helena, it would "signally fail to inspire among the Indians the awful dread of the white man's laws—a dread so necessary for them to be imbued with to prevent further crime."[3] Fort Benton, on the other hand, was close to the Blackfeet Reservation and was frequented by large numbers of Blackfeet and other northern Indians. Hanging Spopee there would give Indians a welcome opportunity to "behold the execution" and the necessary lesson that "the law will be revenged . . . will be brought home to the Indians."[4]

Helena paid no attention to such objections and briskly moved ahead with preparations that were almost ghoulish as the February 4 executions of Pelkey and Spopee came closer. Workmen, reported the *Helena Daily Herald,* were busy erecting the necessary scaffold, and the paper thought "many have been attracted to the vicinity by the feelings of curiosity and to gratify, if possible, the desire to inspect the grim instrument of death."[5] Visitors to the jail were numerous.

The finished scaffold stood in the jail yard. It was a "small, dreary enclosure, surrounded by a high board fence which completely shuts out all view from the world beyond."[6] The apparatus was quite large, about fourteen feet square, large enough to hold not only the doomed individual but a variety of officials and guards, as well as the executioner. The platform rose some eight feet above the ground, with "two substantial upright timbers" placed on either side, surmounted by a crossbeam seven feet above the platform; from this beam hung the rope and noose.

When the *Daily Herald*'s reporter visited the Helena jail in order to write a story on the preparations for the two hangings, he noted that from the scaffold, reached by a short flight of steps, he could "catch a partial view of the city, the valley and the mountains beyond." This reassuring, peaceful winter landscape was disturbed, however, because "lying in a small drift of snow were two ropes, which have been used at previous executions. . . . The hangman's knot which served to terminate the lives of two human beings has not been untied and remains in the same condition as when last used."[7] If this were not enough detail for the general public, the *Herald* reporter went on to describe the three-foot-square trap door upon which the condemned men would be placed, as well as the character of the hinges on one side and the "two heavy lips, which project from an iron rod" on the other. "The rope is so arranged that the body of the prisoner will fall about four feet before the rope becomes taut."[8] With reporting such as this, the citizens of Helena were bound to turn out in large numbers.

The Helena sheriff, Charles M. Jefferis, had already issued invitations to several spectators, as allowed by law. This small audience would be present inside the confines of the jail yard and its fence. The larger public, although ignored by the legal restrictions, was by no means without a presence. There were a large number of houses, barns, and stables whose roofs, porches, and windows overlooked the jail yard and the scaffold, and these, observed the reporter, would "doubtless be crowded . . . by an eager throng, attracted thither by feelings of curiosity to witness the final act in a most horrible tragedy."[9]

At the same time, the newspaper ran an enlightened article on how public opinion regarding capital punishment had been fluctuating. People were repudiating the notion that public executions and public displays were a necessary deterrence, and hangings were becoming "more or less unpopular." "Facts," asserted the *Helena Daily Herald,* "did not substantiate theory," and it went on to note that "familiarity with the life, career and fate of criminals does not always or generally beget abhorrence." Worse still, people who assembled to witness a public execution were often "incited to crime" rather than warned against it, and "it frequently occurred that murders were committed in the very sight of gallows." The editorial concluded, "Those who have a morbid taste, that delights to read of crime, to see it pictured or punished have already . . . reached the half way station towards being criminals themselves."[10]

None of this pious editorializing as to the barbarous nature of public executions or the jockeying to obtain a position to witness the hanging helped Spopee as he awaited his end, however oblivious he might have been. Nor was it at all clear to Spopee's court-appointed lawyers, Wilbur Fisk Sanders and William Chumasero, how they should proceed in their efforts to defend the convicted Spopee, or if they should defend him at all. Judge Everton Conger had already overruled their motion for a new trial. An appeal to higher courts, first to the Montana Supreme Court and eventually to the U.S. Supreme Court, was a possibility, but one that they decided to forgo.[11]

One of the probable reasons for not appealing to the Montana Supreme Court for the 1881 January term was the fact that it was a three-person body made up of the same three judges, Decius S. Wade, Everton J. Conger, and William J. Galbraith, who presided over the three territorial district courts.[12] In effect, this meant that each territorial judge had both trial and appellant jurisdictions, depending upon the situation; individually they sat as trial judges, collectively they heard appeals. Judge Conger would be again hearing and trying an appeal from his own previous ruling and pleading his own previous judgment with the other two judges. This did not seem to be a promising avenue to redress the earlier verdict. As Andrew P. Morriss has observed, "some territorial courts justly earned the nickname given the Arizona court: the Supreme Court of Affirmance."[13] This situation of overlapping jurisdictions was viewed as a weakness and would be changed in 1884—too late, however, for Spopee and his lawyers.[14] They were stuck with Judge Conger. In any event, seeking redress from the Montana Supreme Court would not address the prevailing racial prejudice and bias already encountered in Helena, the legislature, and the territory. If the first trial had been unjust for these reasons, then in all likelihood so would the appeal.

The February 4 execution date was also a problem—there had been less than one month from the end of the trial, insufficient time for the defense team to develop an adequate appeal. Costs inevitably would have mounted, as well as time and effort. An appeal would have been expensive. Sanders and Chumasero's legal work had been pro bono—how much of their professional time could be devoted to this public endeavor? Sanders was by all accounts an intense, extremely independent man who went to heroic lengths defending what he deemed to be right. He liked championing the underdog, as he had proved in the Helena extradition hearing associated with the Cypress Hills massacre; he did not weigh costs, personal or otherwise. Once he got hold of an issue, political or legal, he did not let go, and the Spopee case had allowed him one more jab at the Fort Benton Democrats. He was also convinced that Spopee's conviction had been wrong, and he might well have had twinges of conscience about what he should have done. But the judicial obstacles in the Spopee case went beyond time and money, and the prospects for a successful appeal did not look good. Perhaps an alternative route to equity or some semblance of remedial justice could be found outside of the federal courts.

Either a petition for executive clemency from the governor of Montana Territory or a U.S. presidential pardon or commutation, changing one legal penalty for a lesser one, might be such a path. When this idea first surfaced as a possible route was never recorded, but the constellation of Republican political offices in Washington, D.C., had to have played a part in Sanders's thinking.[15] President Rutherford B. Hayes was in office, another Republican president in a phalanx of stalwart Republicans who followed Lincoln and the Civil War. Territorial problems in Montana had frequently led its Republican minority to appeal to Washington, D.C., for help. In fact, the path from Montana Territory to the Potomac had become almost a boulevard—wide, frequently used, and, to the consternation of the Democratic majority, often effective. As a "Republican warhorse" with Ohio ties and experience, Sanders was well known in national party conventions, in Congress, and to President Hayes. His relationship with Ohio Senator James Garfield, who had come to Montana in 1872 to settle Flathead claims in the Bitterroot Valley, was more than cordial. Garfield had visited with Sanders on numerous occasions while on that trip, referring to him later as "our old comrade Sanders."[16] Senator Garfield had been welcomed initially in Virginia City by Sanders and friends from Ohio—Montana Territorial Governor Benjamin F. Potts and Supreme Court Justice Decius Wade. Garfield's diary of the trip described any number of social occasions that included Sanders. It was not at all surprising that Sanders, finding himself a party to what he considered to be a case of racial injustice nine years later, turned east to Republican friends to find a possible remedy for Spopee and his legal problem.

He had to move carefully, however. Not only was Judge Conger a Republican appointed by President Hayes, but his brother was the Republican senator Omar Conger of Michigan.[17] The national political arena was complicated.

Sanders attempted to enlist the support of the Republican governor, Potts, a close personal friend of President Hayes. He did so by presenting a petition for executive clemency to Potts, as provided for by territorial law, hoping that Potts would either grant it in his capacity, as he was empowered to and often did, or forward the petition to Washington and the White House.[18] Potts, however, was unwilling to do either and returned the petition to Sanders. However, he did endorse it and seemingly was willing to allow his name and friendship with President Hayes to be used.[19] This was a surprising concession. Potts and Sanders, although both Republican, were bitter enemies and had a long history of feuding. In fact, Potts, in an 1878 letter to his friend President Hayes, had termed Sanders "the most unscrupulous man that ever disgraced the legal profession."[20] Uninterested in allowing the well-entrenched Sanders to retain control of the Republican Party machinery, Potts had challenged Sanders and his reputation, terming him "a disappointed office seeker" who had "abused and maligned every man who ever held office in the territory." On another occasion Potts declared that Sanders was "bankrupt in morals, purse, and reputation."[21] Even in the spring of 1881, Sanders was using all of his political connections to have Governor Potts replaced, and there was much talk that Sanders would be the new federal appointee.[22] So Potts's reluctance in helping Sanders with Spopee was hardly surprising. What was surprising was his willingness to endorse anything connected to his archrival.

In the end, Sanders and Chumasero turned directly to the U.S. attorney general, Charles Devens, writing to him on New Year's Day, 1881.[23] In making his appeal for executive clemency, Attorney Sanders raised many of the uncertainties of the case, including the specific questions that Spopee himself had pointed out while making his statement to the court prior to his sentencing. Most important, in Sanders's opinion, was that the prosecution had not proved that the crime had been committed in the United States. "It appeared," he wrote, "by a very large preponderance of the evidence, that the homicide of the white man was perpetrated in the British Northwest Territories and north of our International Boundary. Both the Indians so swore and that they brought the body down into the United States some thirty miles and left it where it was found."[24] Despite every effort to pressure Good Rider to locate the killing south of the boundary, despite what Sanders thought was a succession of "inquisitorial examinations, some of whom we fear do not always seek to deal justly by Indians and what the Indians or this defendant was alleged to have said was given in evidence before the jury," the prosecution introduced no evidence that the crime had taken place in the United States. In the words of the petition, "the verdict was contrary to the proof[,] for no witness swore that the defendant or Good Rider had at any time said that it [the crime] had been perpetrated this side of the line."[25]

Further, the statements of the two Indians had been taken by the grand jury, by a separate examining commission, and, while they were confined in prison, "by men who were eager to secure their conviction." The two defense attorneys, on the other hand, had not been allowed to "converse with our client, to prepare for the trial, to ascertain the circumstances of the homicide as under other circumstances we should have done."[26]

Such actions hardly fulfilled Spopee's constitutional right to "due process of law." If that were not enough to shed "reasonable doubt" on the facts connected with the murder and its subsequent proceedings, there was the issue of language. Spopee and Good Rider spoke only Blackfoot, and, as the lawyers pointed out, "in interpreting from Indian speech into the English language so much difficulty was experienced and interpreters so different that we as the defendant's counsel were greatly embarrassed to know what to believe in the conflicting interpretations which were made."[27]

Whatever the shortcomings, Spopee's defenders had a difficult task. They were essentially appealing the judgment of the Third District Court—while not directly impugning its fairness, impartiality, or legality. Sanders and Chumasero had to couch their objections and the flawed or uncertain nature of the trial as delicately as they could. In their petition for executive clemency they were courting the support of Judge Congers, U.S. District Attorney for Montana James L. Dryden, as well as his rival, Governor Potts.

Superficially, Spopee's case appeared to have been conducted following clear and orderly procedures and protocols—in other words, according to due process. On the other side, however, Sanders and Chumasero unequivocally charged procedural shortcomings and especially racial discrimination. They insisted, not once but twice, that race had skewed the outcome. Again, they wrote, had "this been a white man on trial, no jury here or elsewhere . . . would have found on the evidence that the homicide occurred on the reservation named or within the exterior limits of the United States and we doubt if a jury here under such circumstances would have found that the man killed was Charles Walmesley."[28] Secondly, while Sanders and Chumasero wrote that they regretted having to resort to a presidential appeal, recognizing it as "an unsatisfactory method," they felt compelled to because they could "not contemplate the taking of this life under these circumstances of doubt without a shudder." Yet they did not leave it there. Again, the more concrete reason was race: "We feel certain had it been some other race than this, the occasion for this appeal would not have arisen."[29] The verdict was seen as a travesty of justice. Spopee's conviction should not have happened in Montana Territory given its exceptional record of legally recognizing the right of Indians to provide testimony as witnesses and even its registered concern with language misunderstandings. But it did.[30] And the explanation had not changed since the Cypress Hills debacle—too many of the citizens of the territory felt that there was a double standard, that "whitemen could take the law into their own hands against the Indians," and that Indians were not worthy of due process.[31] The very atmosphere was prejudicial, and the reason for this, as identified by Sanders and Chumasero, was race.

There were in addition to race many uncertainties—including the identity of the murdered man, the location of the killing, whether or not it had been done in self-defense, and, of course, the inability of the court to provide for proper and certain translation and interpretation, to say nothing of the extralegal inquisitorial hearings and Spopee's lack of understanding. All were addressed. The plea for presidential clemency minced no words. "To him [Spopee] the trial has been a pantomime; he does not comprehend our laws, institutions, or language—and he seems profoundly impressed that the verdict is one of great injustice." Finally, Sanders and Chumasero spoke to the issue of deterrence, concluding that the execution of Spopee would "add nothing to the security of life on our frontier, will not impress the [Indian] survivors with the impartiality or justice of our laws, will not commend to his race our methods of dealing with them."

All in all, this was a most effective plea. To top it off, the attorneys for the defense not only sought but secured the written endorsement of Judge Conger. Curiously, he was now of the opinion that "the statement of Counsel is truthfully Presented, and while the trial was fair and impartial, and the jury had Evidence reasons to sustain the verdict, yet on the whole I cheerfully recommend commutation of the sentence." His choice of the adverb "cheerfully" seemed a bit odd; supposedly it was employed because a human life would be legally spared, but it could just as easily be understood as the judge's signal of complete agreement.

Governor Potts, who had originally offered the reward for the arrest and conviction of the murderer, was by no means neglected. Writing from Helena on January 8, 1881, in support, Governor Potts acknowledged that "the case was a peculiar one and a commutation of the sentence to imprisonment for life will probably meet the ends of justice."[32]

The process must have been nerve-wracking for Sanders and Chumasero. They had staked the appeal for clemency on President Rutherford Hayes, an old friend of Governor Potts. Potts had evinced a long-standing enmity toward Sanders, one that Sanders fully reciprocated. Nonetheless, whatever the personal and political calculations, Spopee's counsel had presented a skillful and persuasive case. Much of this case, as noted above, had been made previously by Spopee himself. The petition for executive clemency utilized this information, organized it, and gave it a legal veneer. This was what should have been presented at the Helena trial but was not. Sanders must have been sensitive to this charge, for in his careful treatment of the justness of the trial and the rulings of the judge, he quite defensively pointed out that he and Chumasero had not omitted "to do such things as seemed our duty on that occasion."

Yet the federal petition process allowed for new information and a different format. No longer bound by the restrictions of the territorial court, Sanders and Chumasero used the Spopee statement to demonstrate the shortcomings of the trial, including those of their own defense. They asserted that they had not been able to converse with their client, "to prepare for the trial, to ascertain the circumstances of the homicide as under other circumstances we should have done." In sum, they had been negligent. The vigorous arguments now presented appear almost as compensation for the flawed nature of their defense, of what had been neglected in the trial. They appear, as well, to be the motivation for the effort at clemency. This was about professional redemption. There were things Sanders and Chumasero should have done, and for that reason, they said, "we can not consent that the sentence which dooms this poor Indian to be hung on the 4th of next February shall be carried out if in our power to prevent it."

Sanders's strategy proved to be successful. Spopee was not hanged on the fourth of February. Seventeen days after writing the petition, on January 18, 1881, Attorney General Devens sent Alexander C. Botkin, U.S. Marshal, Montana Territory, a telegram: "The President [Hayes] has ordered a postponement of the execution of Spope, or Turtle, a Piegan Indian, till Friday, May 6th next."[33] A warrant of reprieve would follow. This, of course, was not clemency, only a reprieve, but it was welcome progress. Having partially prevailed, Spopee and his defense counsel had to wait to see if President Hayes was willing to do something more than simply stay the execution before his term in office expired on March 3, 1881. Time was running out. Ultimately, the outgoing president proved to be recalcitrant. He was not willing to act. Instead the whole issue of clemency for Spopee passed to the new incoming president, Republican James A. Garfield, who nine years earlier in Montana had referred to Spopee's attorney as "our old comrade Sanders." Perhaps President Hayes's decision not to act had been for the best.

President Garfield was sworn in on March 4, along with his new attorney general from Pennsylvania, Wayne MacVeagh. A month later, on April 9, the Helena defense team learned that Alexander T. Gray, clerk of pardons in the Department of Justice, had concluded his review of the petition for clemency and accompanying documents. Gray concluded that it appeared that "more than ordinary difficulty was encountered in the preparation for and conduct of the defense" and that Spopee had been "provoked by insulting and cruel treatment of the white man whom he killed, including personal assault." The clerk of pardons, while by no means offering a ringing endorsement of the plea for clemency, nonetheless concluded with the suggestion that "[p]erhaps such commutation would be more useful than the execution of the sentence" and that "the Detroit House of Correction—a humanely conducted institution—would be a suitable place of imprisonment."[34]

Evidently Gray, while waiting for the change of administrations in Washington, had also been in touch with both Judge Conger and District Attorney Dryden prior to submitting his conclusions. On March 29 Dryden grudgingly had informed Gray that "Spopee's was a plain case fairly submitted to a good Jury and the territory will be as well off with him in the spirit land as in the penitentiary."[35] Having offered this opinion, Dryden awaited his final days in office, resigning in June to make way for a new federal appointee.[36] If this was a brokered deal, it was not apparent. There was no haggling or bargaining for a full pardon. Sanders had to take it or leave it. A commutation was what was politically possible and that is what was being offered—a life had been spared.

Years later, long after the fact, a friend and biographer of Sanders remembered that "an Indian boy, accused of murder, who would doubtless have been railroaded to the gallows but for Sanders' investigation of the case," had been saved. Sanders had not reversed the conviction, but he had "presented such a case to the governor that pardon became a necessity."[37]

However correct this evaluation may be, it seems certain that with the support of the principal figures in the Helena court in hand and with the assessments of Governor Potts, there was sufficient political and legal cover for the new attorney general, MacVeagh, to advise the recently elected President Garfield, in writing: "Upon the within report and the recommendation of the Judge who passed sentence, I recommend commutation of sentence of death to imprisonment for life in the Detroit (Mich.) House of Correction."[38] Three days later, news came from the executive mansion: "Let sentence be commuted as recomd'd. By direction of the President."[39] Spopee would not die. He would, however, be incarcerated for the rest of his life. For an Indian convicted of the murder of a white man, this was as good an outcome as could have been expected. Had justice been served? That was another question.

Word of Spopee's commutation spread fast. The *Helena Daily Herald*—after reminding its readers of Spopee's case, his trial for murder, his conviction, sentencing, and execution date—relayed the news: "This morning the Marshal received a dispatch from the Chief of the Bureau of Pardons, saying: The sentence of Spo-pe has been commuted by the President to imprisonment for life in the Detroit House of Correction."[40]

Why the Detroit House of Correction was suggested, rather than the U.S. Penitentiary at Deer Lodge City, Montana Territory, was not clear. Spopee's case was a federal one, not a territorial one, suggesting federal responsibility. However, the decision to send Spopee to Detroit was certainly opaque to the editors of the *Helena Daily Herald*. They thought it was an oversight. So, according to their reports, did U.S. Marshal Botkin, for he had telegraphed the Justice Department "recommending a change," presumably to the U.S. Penitentiary at Deer Lodge.[41] Whatever the reason for the choice of the Detroit prison, the decision would be a critical one for Spopee, replete with any number of unimagined and unintended consequences.

The recommendation may have stemmed from the Detroit House of Correction's progressive reputation for rehabilitation. It had also long been eager to board federal prisoners from federal courts outside of Detroit and the state of Michigan. For many jurisdictions in the sparsely populated West, it was more economical to board their long-term prisoners elsewhere than to build their own institutions. That had been the case in Montana Territory before the construction of the federal prison in Deer Lodge.[42] In 1880, however, the reason was more likely the lack of cell space in the Deer Lodge prison, for overcrowding had been a problem from the beginning. This chronic issue became acute by 1881 and would remain so, coming to influence a great number of decisions.[43]

The Deer Lodge institution began as a "penitentiary on a shoestring," and throughout the territorial period in Montana it was never able to escape its impoverished federal beginnings. Built in an isolated high mountain valley amid a sprawling agricultural community, far from water or railroad transportation, it was in an awkward location. Above all, before and after 1881, the prison lacked space, was overcrowded, and, as historian Keith Edgerton has shown, officials were forced to compromise too often.[44] In January of 1881, Governor Potts in his message to the legislature reported that he had obtained a reduction in what the territory paid the federal government for "keeping the Territorial convicts" to seventy-five cents per day. Yet the number of convicts steadily increased, he said. His solution was to recommend that the legislature "authorize the confinement in county jails of such convicts as cannot be kept at the Deer Lodge prison."[45] At the time, the number of convicts at Deer Lodge was fifty-six.

Another compromise was to dramatically shorten sentence times by allowing for executive clemency to commute or pardons. So, for example, writes Edgerton, no matter how heinous the crime, sixty-three percent of Deer Lodge prison's convicted murders received pardons during the territorial years. The men serving life sentences served an average of 11.3 years in the period between 1871 and 1889. Spopee's chances of a shortened prison term, in other words, would have been significantly greater at the Deer Lodge penitentiary than at the Detroit House of Correction. On the other hand, Deer Lodge had far fewer reformatory and humane ambitions than did Detroit, and those would also come to play an important role in Spopee's continuing odyssey.

As for Spopee, he did not seem to care where he was to be sent. When the news reached him, "he was enjoying his postprandial smoke" and he laughed "joyfully," seeming to understand that he was not to be hanged. But the newspaper report was unwilling to leave his response at that, for it wryly noted that it was not clear why he laughed; his "amusement may have been occasioned by the efforts of the officer to make himself understood." Spopee's first question, however, revealed his essential understanding—"How many snows?" Then, when Spopee was told that he would be shut up for life, "his continence fell."[46] Distrustful of Marshal Botkin's statements (Spopee called the marshal Ma-koop-ah, or "Lame in the

Knees," because of his paralysis and confinement to a wheelchair), Spopee wanted an acquaintance, who spoke Blackfoot, "to read 'the paper' (dispatch) to him."[47]

Interpretation had again proved to be a stumbling block—and at Spopee's expense. As if to underline the problem, the *Helena Daily Independent*, under "Brief Items," reported a final incident of misunderstanding under the guise of humor. "The deputy U.S. Marshal left Helena via Dillon yesterday for Detroit, Michigan, having in charge Spo-pe, the Indian prisoner. . . . Spo-pee was under the impression yesterday morning that he was going on a visit to the U.S. President, and he left the jail in high glee."[48]

Although widely known and well regarded for its innovative methods of rehabilitation, the Detroit House of Correction was not physically imposing. Completed in 1861 and located in the downtown area of Detroit on about three square blocks, it was described as "a great grey fortress-like structure [that] stood grim and foreboding, brooding over a dismal section of the city which became one of Detroit's first and worst slums."[49] By 1880 the number of federal prisoners boarded there from other states and territories stood at about two hundred, but record keeping was not the prison's strong suit, and the total prison population or how many Indian prisoners it included remains unclear. There were periodic complaints about the treatment of prisoners, of course. Yet when a prison inspection agent from the Department of Justice visited in 1885, four years after the beginning of Spopee's tenure, he assured the attorney general that "the prisoners of the United States who are confined here receive good food and kind and humane treatment."[50]

Spopee was delivered to the Detroit House of Correction on May 15, 1881.[51] Following his delivery, U.S. Marshal Botkin reported to the Blackfeet agent, John Young, writing from Helena "Spo-pe was delivered safely to the Detroit House of Correction." At the same time he confided to Young his own bewilderment: "Why his sentence was commuted is a mystery that I have never solved."[52]

The Detroit House of Corrections proved to be but a brief way station on Spopee's adventure out of Montana. He was discharged from the prison and transferred to Washington, D.C., on August 8, 1882, just less than a year and a half after arriving. Unfortunately, the records of the Detroit House of Corrections offer precious little information on Spopee's time there. The Montana territorial newspapers were even less helpful. In Fort Benton and Helena the public was informed that late in December of 1881, "Spopee, the Piegan Indian who murdered Chas. Warmley in 1880, and whose death sentence was commuted to imprisonment for life, died in the Detroit house of correction."[53]

We have, however, one small piece of evidence about Spopee's time in Detroit. On November 16, 1881, an unknown correspondent and translator wrote a letter on behalf of Spopee's wife, Tharhibuski, or One-Who-Goes-Under-the-Water. She had been in contact with Spopee through the efforts of the Blackfeet agent, John Young, and the new U.S. attorney for Montana, James W. Andrews, Jr., through whom she sent small parcels, including moccasins and "Indian tobacco."[54] Her letter of October 16 was in response to a letter Spopee had sent to her just a month earlier, which had been interpreted and read out loud to her, although we do not know the circumstances. One-Who-Goes-Under-the-Water replied through the interpreter that she would like to see Spopee, "and that she lives now with 'Painted Wing' [Mick-a-nin-ye-ma] and her two girls are with her, and Painted Wing sees that they get enough to eat, but they are poor. She has only three horses." Then, in the next paragraph, Spopee's wife confessed that she "gave the boy to another Squaw, whose baby had died." Her sight, she said, was so bad that she could "scarcely see to walk." The letter, unsigned, appeared to break off as if there were a missing second page, after which it reiterated that she would like to hear from him again and that "any letter addressed to 'Painted Wing, Care of the Agent, Piegan PO, Montana' will reach her. The Agent is the same that Spopee knew. White Calf is still head chief, and the other head men Running Crane, Fast Buffalo Horse remain unchanged."[55]

It is difficult to imagine the fortitude it required for this young woman to deal with the agent in order to stay in touch with a distant Spopee. The difficulties began with being in a nomadic camp some distance away from the agency on Badger Creek, with no control over when and where the camp went. The difficulties continued with the need to cross the invisible but forbidding boundary that separated a young Piegan woman and her children from the intimidating, authoritative white agent, sitting in his chair behind the imposing door at the agency and surrounded by subservient assistants. But she did it.

It was One-Who-Goes-Under-the-Water's only letter—or at least, it was the only one of this period to survive. Then, there was silence.

CHAPTER 5

THE PARALLEL CONFINEMENT

Sheriff John J. Healy and his deputy, Jeff Talbert, had hauled Spopee in handcuffs out of the snowy hunting camp in the Judith Basin just as the New Year arrived in 1880. The sprawling winter camp had numbered about three hundred Indians and included Bloods, Piegan, and Blackfeet, with other tribes nearby.[1] The Niitzitapi bitterly resented Healy's unexpected intrusion. According to James Willard Schultz, an eyewitness or close to it but writing long after the fact, the Bloods in particular "swore they would not allow him [Spopee] to be taken from them" and the Piegan under White Calf were "noncommital but inclined to side with the Bloods."[2] In such a dangerous and volatile situation, the Fort Benton lawmen were lucky to have gotten away with their daring episode.[3]

A month later, in early February, the disruptive reach of territorial authority arrived once again in the scattered winter hunting camps of the Blackfeet in the Judith Basin—this time in the shape of the U.S. Army. Lieutenant William Krause, Third Infantry, and fourteen mounted enlisted men, with a supply train in tow, had left their military post at Fort Benton early on Saturday morning, February 6. Making their way over the ice-covered Missouri, they climbed up out of the protected river bottom to the bluffs above, hit the wind, and made their way some distance to Shonkin Creek (Pahksi

Piskwo). Only then did they set out south and east across the heavily drifted, frozen terrain in the direction of the Arrow River. It was
slow going. There were gusting winds and little shelter. Having
threaded their way through the Mauvais Terres on the blown-in
road, the bulkily dressed company of soldiers eventually arrived
in the Judith Basin. The same severe wintery conditions that Healy
and Talbert had experienced again prevailed. The military operation, however, was different in that it did not involve apprehending
a single individual Indian wanted for murder.[4] This time Colonel
Thomas H. Ruger, Eighteenth Infantry, the commanding officer of
the District of Montana, headquartered in Helena, had ordered Captain Edward Moale, commanding the Third Infantry at Fort Benton,
to move all the Piegan Indians under White Calf and Running Crane
from their established hunting camps in the Judith Basin, however
dispersed, back to their reservation on the north side of the Missouri
River. It did not matter that it was in the middle of one of the worst
winters on record, or that eight hundred to a thousand people were
involved, along with horse herds numbering in the thousands. Orders were orders.

This U.S. military action against the Blackfeet took place under
the color of the legal authority of the president of the United States
to create or modify Indian reservations by executive order. This
came about in 1871, when Congress decided that it would no longer
make treaties with Indian tribes as if they were sovereign, independent nations.[5] Instead, the federal government would conduct its
business by means of what came to be called "treaty substitutes."
These replacements for treaties included bilateral agreements that
were confirmed by Congress and, important in this case, executive
orders that involved no negotiation, involvement, or consent on the
part of Indian tribes.[6] In short order, executive orders became "the
dominant means of establishing and modifying" Indian reservations and their boundaries.[7]

Not only had the United States established by executive order
in 1873 a new reservation for the Blackfoot tribes, the Gros Ventre,
the Assiniboine, and the River Crows, but the following year President Grant issued another executive order moving the reservation's
southern boundary and reducing significantly its size. The United

States also relied upon more than a decade of administrative decisions on the part of the Office of Indian Affairs in the Department of the Interior and the War Department in its efforts to regulate tribal behavior. So, for example, hoping to protect the growing number of white property interests and settlements, the two federal agencies formulated a regulatory dictum that limited the tribes' continued exercise of off-reservation hunting rights in their former territories, as provided for in the Blackfeet Treaty of 1855, without written permission from the reservation agent.[8] As early as 1872 the commissioner of Indian Affairs, Francis A. Walker, had written of the government's need for a "legalized reformatory control" by which federal authorities would have the right to keep Indians on reservations. Essential to this control was the authority to "arrest and return them whenever they wander away."[9] Such "paternal control," however desirable from the perception of the federal government, had not proved workable in Montana Territory, given the amount of land and the size of the federal army.

Indian depredations remained an ongoing problem, made more difficult by 1879 with the rapid expansion of the open-range cattle industry. Although stockmen lived in isolated circumstances outside of established settlements, they were every bit as adamant that their sprawling properties needed the same protections and that cattle killing was a property crime. Consequently, in the case of the Blackfeet collectively and of Spopee individually, government officials alleged that in addition to being off-reservation without permission and without escort, both had committed serious crimes. This added still another legal charge to help validate the interference of the army.

The decision to restrict the American Blackfeet, or Southern Piegan, to their reduced reservation began when Captain Moale, commanding the military post in Fort Benton, complied with instructions from above and issued Special Orders No. 1. The date was February 5, 1880. Not only was Lieutenant Krause "to order the Piegan Indians . . . to move to their reservation," but he was to "endeavor to impress upon the Headmen . . . the necessity of obeying the orders without unnecessary delay."[10] This meant immediately, and there was the clear understanding that if necessary, Lieutenant Krause was to use force to compel compliance.

Unbeknownst to the multiple Piegan bands in the Judith Basin, this decision stemmed from an action that began during the first week in January. A Judith Basin pioneer and stockman, Henry P. Brooks, had alerted his business partner in the Judith Cattle Company, Thomas C. Power, one of the trading magnates of Fort Benton, via a telegram sent from Fort Assiniboine on the Milk River, that "Chief White Calf with seventy five lodges of Pigans Indians camped amongst my cattle. Have killed some cattle already, scattering Cattle all over the range. What shall I do?"[11]

Whether or not this report was true or only suspected by Brooks is now hard to discern. The previous October, the *Benton Weekly Record* noted that "[b]uffalo are so numerous in the vicinity of the Judith that stock men are obliged to guard their herds."[12] The ranchers were "to guard their herds" because otherwise the cattle were likely to run off with the bison. That was before the first snow fell. Later in the season, when the wind kicked up blinding ground blizzards and the encrusted cattle drifted in small clusters, heads down, into the surrounding buffalo herds, the mingling became even more pronounced. On January 2, for example, the same newspaper observed that "Brooks is having quite a time with his cattle, as the Indians and stormy weather have scattered them badly."[13] However, there were no reports of cattle-killing by Indians or anyone else.

Upon receiving the alarming news of cattle depredations from Brooks, on January 6, Thomas Power, ever anxious about his investments and politically powerful, did not dither. He went straight to the top of the governmental pyramid, sending an alarmed telegram on the following day to E. A. Hayt, commissioner of Indian Affairs in Washington, D.C. Hayt, in turn, reported the news of the cattle killing to the secretary of Interior. From there the alarm went to Alexander Ramsey at the War Department: "Piegan Indians are running and killing stock in the Judith country."[14]

Something needed to be done. Power's telegram had included two additional items—first, a suggested remedy: "[I]f authority is given, Genl [*sic*] Ruger will have them [the Piegan] removed on Reserve 50 miles north side of Mo River. If authorized please act at once valuable property in danger."[15] Powers also suggested that Hayt should refer to "this telegram, only say you are reliably informed. I showed this to him [Colonel Ruger]. He thinks Brooks is

Caught in the Act, by Charles M. Russell, oil on canvas, 1888. (Montana Historical Society, Mackay Collection, X1952.03.03.)

more scared than hurt. But I know Brooks is right and is a truthful honest man."[16]

A month later, on February 6, 1880, the secretary of War responded to Interior that he concurred with the decision that "Colonel Ruger be directed to return these Indians to their reservation." The War Department enclosed a copy of its telegraphic instructions, dated January 28, to Colonel Ruger as proof that E. A. Hayt's recommendation had been complied with.[17] The mission to confine the Blackfeet to their reservation was launched.

In 1880, the boundaries of the Blackfeet Reservation already had a complex history. The current boundaries were established, as noted, with an executive order by President Grant in the summer of 1873. This federal action sought to end uncertainty regarding earlier agreements. This confusion had arisen because Congress had not ratified two treaties between the United States and the Blackfeet, negotiated in 1865 and 1868. This failure had left in place the boundaries of the long-antiquated 1855 treaty with the Blackfeet, also called Lame Bull's Treaty after the then head chief. In that treaty the southern boundary had been a line, drawn eastward from Hell Gate or Medicine Rock passes on the Continental Divide, across the Missouri River, to the nearest source of the Musselshell River, down that river to its mouth on the Missouri, and then down the Missouri to the mouth of the Milk River (see map 2). Designated as the "exclusive territory" of the Blackfeet, this area adjoined a delineated and defined "Common Hunting Ground," which the Blackfeet were to share with Indian buffalo hunters from west of the Rocky Mountains. These rich hunting grounds, however, experienced the discovery of gold in 1862 at Grasshopper Creek, in 1863 at Alder Gulch, and in 1864 at Last Chance Gulch, soon to become Helena. The result was wave after wave of irrepressible miners, disorderly mining camps straddling streams and gullies, town plats, freight roads, and increased steamboat traffic on the Missouri. White settlement, including cattle ranches on range land, became frequent. The landscape experienced dramatic change, and Lame Bull's Treaty of 1855, with its provisions and assurances to the Indians, became obsolete.

No one paid any attention to the articles of the 1855 treaty—not the newcomers, to be sure, but not the buffalo-hunting Indians either. The Common Hunting Ground had disappeared for them. The buffalo were no longer there, and therefore there was no reason for the Blackfeet to go there. Determined to end this legal artifact as well as to provide title and to promote territorial growth, President Grant, via his 1873 executive order, had created a new reservation that included all of Montana Territory east of the Rockies and north of the Missouri and Sun Rivers.

Almost immediately there was determined political pressure to reduce the western portion of this new reservation by moving the southern boundary. Instead of following the Sun River from the Continental Divide east to the Missouri River, the proposed new reservation boundary line would be shoved north over sixty miles to follow the Marias from its mouth on the Missouri to Birch Creek, and from Birch Creek to the summit of the Rockies. The severed

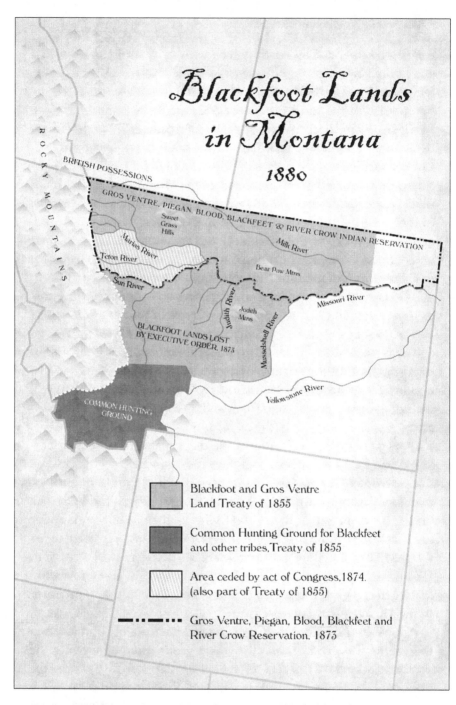

Blackfoot Lands in Montana, 1880. (Map by Neal Wiegert.)

territory included the very heart of the country belonging to the American Blackfeet. Its threatened loss occasioned immediate and spirited opposition from both the Blackfeet and their agent. Nonetheless, the territorial delegate to Congress, Martin Maginnis, introduced this boundary change in a bill to Congress and it was enacted into law on April 15, 1874. The reduced size of the reservation meant not only the abandonment of the existing Blackfeet Agency on the upper reaches of the Teton River, known as the Four Persons agency, but also the loss to the Blackfeet of the rich buffalo hunting grounds along both sides of that river, as well as the hunting grounds along the Sun River. It did so, moreover, without addressing any of the off-reservation hunting and gathering rights of the Blackfeet guaranteed by the 1855 treaty, without any consultation with the Piegan, and without any compensation on the part of the United States. Instead, the Blackfoot tribes were squeezed and confined to a smaller and smaller space, with less and less access to buffalo. As for the buffalo, they were being pressured and hunted by both whites and Indians as never before.[18] To make matters worse, the Blackfeet were further restricted even on the reservation they shared with their competitors and enemies—the Gros Ventre, the Assiniboine, and the River Crows—because although designated as a single reserve, known as "the Blackfeet Reservation," there were internal tribal hunting boundaries that could be crossed only with peril.

As for the new southern boundary, John S. Wood, who had been appointed Blackfeet agent in April of 1875, noted in his annual report that the new "lines" or boundaries were "a source of continual complaint." White Calf was one of the three head chiefs elected by the band leaders in 1875. He too "kicked" about the how the "lines" had been moved, the encroachments of the whites, and the loss of the fairest portion of their reservation.[19] The southern boundary line, however, was not restored. Consequently, in 1879 the Blackfeet Reservation was north of the Missouri River and its tributaries, the Marias River and Birch Creek. If the Southern Piegan were anywhere else, they were "off the reservation" and subject to all manner of surveillance, limitations, and constraint.

As early as the beginning of November 1879, local officers of the U.S. Army had been aware that 150 lodges of Piegan were across the

Missouri and scattered along its southern tributary, the Musselshell River. They had been there for some time. Colonel Nelson A. Miles, commanding Fort Keogh on the Yellowstone River, for example, wanted to know from the secretary of the Interior and the Office of Indian Affairs "whether they [the Piegan] had permission to hunt off their reservation?" His question had been sparked by Crow Indians, whom he reported were "displeased with their [Piegans'] killing game there."[20] At the same time, the Blackfeet agent on Badger Creek, John Young, already apprehensive about white concerns regarding the Piegan, weighed in on both this issue and the matter of their permission to be off the reservation. In his monthly report for November to the Office of Indian Affairs, he observed: "Nearly all the Indians camped near leaving for the hunting grounds. . . . I talked earnestly to the Chiefs impressing them with the necessity for the utmost vigilance in preserving order and preventing the purchase of whisky as they were going off the Reservation and beyond my jurisdiction, all which they promised to observe."[21]

Earnest talk, however, did not include any official action on Young's part, even though some of the Piegan headmen specifically asked the agent for written support.[22] Notwithstanding their appeals, Agent Young declined to write letters of introduction granting them permission to leave the reservation, "at the same time admitting the necessity for their going to get meat and robes, especially now that their farm work is over for the season."[23] That was where the matter stood in the fall of 1879. The Piegan were off their reservation without their agent's specific permission, but there was nothing he could—or wanted—to do about it.

For the first two months, there were no reports of trouble on the part of the off-reservation Piegan, although the opportunities to get into trouble were many. Agent Young's monthly report for November included only the brief mention that there was "no unpleasant news from the great Camp on the winter hunt—south of the Missouri near the Muscleshell—the buffalo reported plenty there." December's report was much the same—to the clear relief of the agent. Hearing once in a while from the Judith camps, Young was of the opinion that it was "all quiet there and meat plenty."[24] Agent Young, relieved, had informed the *Helena Weekly Herald* of the same circumstances based on "reliable advises from them [the Indians]" that they "are in the midst of buffalo, are securing an abundance of meat, have fat ponies, and are making plenty of robes."[25]

On December 27, prior to T. C. Power's urgent telegram, Commissioner Hayt, already aware of the off-reservation Piegan reported earlier by Young, questioned the situation. Agent Young responded on January 14, writing that yes, the greater part of the Piegan were in the Judith Basin for a very important reason—they had no alternative. They were hungry and had been drawn there by the presence of significant numbers of buffalo. "They have *no permission*," he assured the commissioner, "but with their large force, it would have been utterly impossible for me to have prevented their going, as there is no game on this side of the Missouri."[26]

Having defended his decision—and denied any culpability— Young repeated his earlier warning from the previous November, writing that he had admonished the leaders to be on their best behavior and that they would be beyond his jurisdiction. Still, in his bureaucratic manner, he wanted to assure Commissioner Hayt that not only were the best men of the tribe in charge, but the recently established Indian Police Force was also there to compel obedience to the chiefs, and all reports available to him indicated that their behavior off the reservation had been excellent. Then Young specifically addressed the solution proposed by the Office of Indian Affairs: "If these Indians are to be ordered back to the Agency, it will be necessary for the Government to furnish them their entire subsistence, and the supplies allowed under the present appropriations will not feed the entire camp two months. There is now no game in this vicinity, so that they would have no choice but to live upon the government." The clearly troubled agent closed his remarks with the observation that the Musselshell River was, in good weather, a week's journey from his new agency on Badger Creek, a tributary of the Marias. The current winter weather, with its deep snow and cold temperatures, made it "impossible for me to communicate with the Indians, nor could they move camp, just at this time." Unwilling to close his letter on this negative note, the agent added a final sentence. "At the earliest possible moment, I will endeavor to bring them upon this side of the Missouri."[27]

On January 27, Young informed Colonel Ruger in Helena that the commissioner of Indian Affairs had advised him "of having recommended that the Military Authorities be requested to remove the Piegan Indians belonging to this Agency and now in the Judith Basin Country, on their winter hunt, back to their reservation" and that the commissioner had directed Agent Young's full cooperation.

Young did his best to convince Ruger that this was a bad idea. He began by again relating how some 150 lodges had left the reservation in October to hunt buffalo, and that they were then reported to be south of the Missouri. He noted as before that he had refused to grant permission for them to leave, although he was aware that this was "their most congenial way of making the necessary addition to what Congress allots for their support." He reiterated his earlier cautions—telling the headmen that this was a risky business, and that they should keep together and hold their young men under complete control so "that no destruction might occur, or any damage be done to property and no cause be given for complaint by white men."[28]

Given this situation, and particularly given the fact that the Blackfeet Indian Police Force under The General, or Double Runner, were along, Young expressed his confidence in the good behavior of the Piegan. He closed his letter with a reference to the Thomas Power telegram, stating that he "hoped to find that the complaint made on investigation will prove to have been wrong."[29] Young was also of the opinion that as soon as White Calf and Running Crane learned of the wishes of the "Great Father," they would immediately do as they were asked and return to the reservation. But, as with his letter to Commissioner Hayt, Young wanted Colonel Ruger to know that there was not much that he could do; after all, the distance was great and travel currently so difficult that he could not send a messenger to what he called "the great Camp" on the Judith, even if he wanted to. He concluded, however, by reporting that there was recent news that some of the bands were trying to make their way back to the agency, and that they would do so "if this weather allows of their traveling."[30] A short time later, penning his monthly report for January, Young related to the Office of Indian Affairs further news regarding his charges: "They have taken a good many Robes, and there is no scarcity of meat." The monthly report also mentioned that the Piegan were moving as the weather permitted, to the Missouri River, which "they can cross on the ice and so be on their own reservation again."[31]

Colonel Ruger's reply on February 1 from Helena must have come as a surprise to Young. Ruger informed the Blackfeet agent that he had sent orders to the commanding officer at Fort Benton to dispatch a detachment of troops to the Judith with instructions to return the Piegan to their reservation, and he suggested that Agent Young send a messenger under his own authority as well, with orders to interrupt their winter buffalo hunt and to return to the agency.[32] There should be no doubt as to the cooperation between the military and the civilian Indian service in this important matter. Acting together and in concert would leave the impression that there was nothing to be done but to obey.

Young's initial response was to attempt to head off the operation. He pointed out in a number of letters that his information demonstrated that the Piegan were "endeavoring to cross the Missouri to their own Reservation, in which case it will be unnecessary for any steps to be taken by the military." Defending his charges, Young also indicated that he did not think any depredations had been committed by the Piegan. "I feel satisfied that the Piegans would not kill cattle, as too much of their well being depends upon their continued good terms with the whites." This last was a not-so-veiled reference to the fact that just ten years earlier, the Piegan had suffered terrible carnage from the U.S. Army on the banks of the Marias River, when Colonel E. M. Baker, led by Indian trader turned scout Joe Kipp, erroneously attacked an innocent camp of Piegan under Heavy Runner, striking them when the camps were vulnerable, again in the deep snows and bitter cold of winter. (As we have seen, Spopee and his mother were there, and this is where Spopee received the gunshot wound in the hips that left him with his crabbed gait.) In other words, the Indians were already pacified; this was not a collective outbreak or a rebellion, and there was little or no chance of their resorting to armed resistance or significant violence. The Piegan were convinced that they would be the losers in such a contest; of that they had no doubt.[33]

In addition to the reports that the Piegan camp had reported plenty of buffalo robes and meat, Agent Young indicated another extenuating circumstance: "The Judith country has for some time past," he wrote, "been occupied by many different tribes of Indians, drawn there by the abundance of Buffalo, and from all that I can learn, what cattle killing has been done has been the work of Indians from the North."[34]

These objections came too late. Captain Moale issued Special Orders No. 1 on February 5, instructing Lieutenant Krause and his company to proceed to the camp of White Calf, then located on the Judith above the mouth of Warm Springs Creek.[35] The detachment left Fort Benton on the morning of the sixth with three heavily laden wagons containing rations and ammunition for the men and forage for the animals, and despite the difficult weather and snow conditions, they arrived at White Calf's camp four days later, on the tenth. However trying, the wintry journey was evidently uneventful or at any rate went unrecorded in Krause's later report.

Unfortunately, the Indian trader Joe Kipp, whom Lieutenant Krause had counted on to do the interpreting, was not at his recently erected post at the confluence of Sage Creek and the Judith River. He was away on a hunting trip. There were others, both Americans and members of the tribe, who could speak both English and Piegan. But Krause recognized that his mission was a delicate one and was afraid that he might be misunderstood. It would be better to wait. Four long, uncomfortable days in the snow and intense cold passed in his camp before Kipp returned. The wait, however, proved particularly productive. Kipp brought with him, in addition to his acknowledged personal expertise, a letter for Lieutenant Krause. It was dated "Headquarters, Fort Benton, February 10," and signed by Captain Moale. Containing good news, it advised that "the Indians could delay, if necessary to await the return the hunting party then out after buffalo." This released some of the explosive pressure felt by both soldiers and the Piegan. Both now had some room and time to maneuver. On the morning of the fifteenth Lieutenant Krause finally "had a talk with the principal chiefs." Once more he failed to report in any detail either the conversation or their immediate reaction to his orders.

Of the leading chiefs, White Calf found himself in a difficult situation. Although elected head chief of the Piegan following the death of Little Plume, much of his authority and influence, according to

White Calf, chief of
the Southern Piegans.
(Courtesy Richard
Lancaster to Hugh
Dempsey [1965] to author
[2005]. Author's collection,
unnumbered.)

Army Captain J. M. J. Sanno, rested on his acknowledged diplomatic abilities, which owed a good deal to his "supposed popularity with the whites, by reason of which they [the Piegan] expect to profit." Sanno knew White Calf well and doubted, for example, his influence over the band chiefs. "It is questionable if he has sufficient force to compel obedience in case of dissensions. . . . Fast Buffalo Horse, Running Crane, Running Rabbit and Big Nose Bear Chief are chiefs of considerable influence and when aroused would be dangerous enemies. Big Nose is a hereditary chief and expected to be head chief."[36] White Calf's authority, in other words, was not without criticism, political enemies, and competitors. Some charged him with drinking too much whiskey. Others doubted his leadership skills.[37]

Whatever his shortcomings among the Piegan, White Calf in addition had already had a number of run-ins with Agent John Young.

The prickly federal Indian service employee, to his dismay, had learned how willing White Calf was to criticize and seek out countervailing authorities—the military, for example—when dissatisfied with his agent, or how wily and politically conniving he could be, including giving an interview in 1877 to the *Fort Benton Record*, which published his complaints at his request.[38] According to White Calf, since the arrival of John Young, no coffee or sugar had been issued. And as for rations, "Seven days rations for 20 persons consists of 10 pounds of fresh meat, 20 pounds of flour and 5 pounds of bacon, but no bacon is issued. . . . The buffalo are two hundred miles away, and the Indians are without ammunition and provisions to hunt them." Remaining at the agency, he concluded, was impossible. His family was suffering. In singing out his litany of broken white promises, including the lack of agricultural equipment with which to learn to farm on the inhospitable prairies of the reservation, the newspaper reported in 1877 that "the Chief asks the great father at Washington to take pity on his people and give them more food, for they cannot live upon the rocks, and now that the buffalo are gone, they have no means of support except what they receive from the Government."[39]

Always lynx-eyed when it came to his rivals, even within the prestigious and newly created tribal police, it was White Calf who now stepped forward in the Judith camp to lead the effort to move the Piegan back to their agency. We know of this, and in considerable detail, because unlike the official army reports of Captain Moale and Lieutenant Krause, which remained disappointingly silent regarding the Indian responses, there was an observer on the spot who spoke Blackfoot tolerably well, who knew something of the Indian leadership involved, and who was eager, in later years, to report what had transpired. His name was James Willard Schultz, subsequently a popular storyteller and author, first with the George Bird Grinnell's national magazine, *Forest and Stream*, and then with the established publisher Houghton Mifflin.

Schultz, at age eighteen, had come up the Missouri River to the middle of Blackfeet country on the steamboat *Benton*, already known as "the Old Reliable," from St. Louis.[40] He arrived at Fort Benton's crowded levee abutting the notorious Front Street probably in July of 1877, carrying a letter of introduction to the management of the firm I. G. Baker & Company, under the local direction of the Conrad brothers, William, Charles, and John. Once in Fort Benton the impressionable young man met Indian trader Joe Kipp, called Raven Quiver, or Mas-tun-opachis, the son of the famous James Kipp, who had opened up trade with the Blackfeet on the upper Missouri with the building of Fort Piegan. Joe Kipp's mother was Earth Woman, or Sah-kwi-ahki, a daughter of the great Mandan chief, Four Bears, or Manto-to-pah.[41] Schultz and Kipp immediately hit it off, with Kipp taking the tenderfoot under his wing. Working as a clerk for Kipp at his various trading posts, Schultz learned Blackfoot, married a young Piegan woman named Natahki, and eagerly learned as much as he could about tribal ways and tribal history.

Schultz happened to be there in the Judith during the winter of 1880. He was an employee at Kipp's post, purchasing bison robes and other peltries from the Piegan, when Lieutenant Krause arrived with his mounted detachment. In other words, Schultz's account of Lieutenant Krause's parley with White Calf and Running Crane in 1880 is a contemporary, autobiographical account, and while much of Schultz's remembrance was subject to the demands of a good story, it is also as close to factual as we are going to get.

Schultz knew the story well, as he did the events surrounding Spopee and his capture, and he told it often and with the indignation of an insider and member of the tribe.[42] In his telling Schultz determined that this encounter with Lieutenant Krause was White Calf's finest hour and one in which he performed his greatest service as the Father of his people.[43] In his multiple versions, Schultz had Lieutenant Krause arriving, to the surprise of all, one winter's afternoon from Fort Benton. With his detachment of soldiers behind him, Krause announced he had come to escort the Piegan camp immediately back to their own country, to their agency on Badger Creek. Schultz skipped over the four long days of waiting for Joe Kipp. He did not mention the ameliorating news from Fort Benton that the Piegan obedience need not be immediate, but could be delayed, to await the return of the scattered hunting parties.

Instead, Schultz had officer Krause informing the chiefs and warriors that Thomas Power's manager, "Colonel" Henry Brooks, had complained that the Piegan were killing his cattle. The response was immediate and outraged. "Why, why," asked White Calf, his face tense and hard with suppressed anger, "is this to be done? By what right? We are on our own ground. It was always ours. Who shall say that we must leave it?"[44] In another account Running Crane roared, "That white man is a liar. We have killed none of his [Brooks'] white horns [cattle]. We would be foolish to kill them when we have constantly all the real meat [buffalo] that we want." For his part, White Calf, according to Schultz, added: "Why should [my] people kill bad tasting meat when they had their choice of fat good meat—antelopes, buffaloes, elk, and deer?"[45] White Calf, moreover, countered, "Our hunters have seen this white man's white horns grazing with our buffalo even as far down as Bear River [Musselshell]. That is where his white horns have gone."[46] This conclusion was corroborated by the agency reports, both before the arrival of the soldiers in November and December and in late February, when a visitor from White Calf's camp had indignantly denied any agency Indians had engaged in killing cattle, saying, "Why should we[?] . . . [W]e had plenty of meat."[47]

In response to White Calf's insistent questioning as to why they must leave their own ground to return to an agency with no food and no game, Lieutenant Krause could only say that they were south of the Missouri River and therefore "off the reservation," an assertion immediately corrected by White Calf, who reminded the "soldier chief" of the Blackfeet Treaty that had been conducted in 1855 at the mouth of the Judith River. White Calf had been twenty years old at the time and had signed the treaty under an earlier name, "Feather."[48] Three Suns, or Big Nose, had been there as well and still had in his possession a medal that he had received from Governor Isaac I. Stevens at the conclusion of the treaty.[49] White Calf knew full well what the treaty had contained: "It was written," he said, emphasizing the documentary character of the agreement, "that we own all of this country, from the country of the Red Coats [Canada] south to the Yellowstone River, and from the Backbone-of-the-World [Continental Divide] east to the mouth of the Yellowstone. The Great Father's men signed that paper; we signed it."[50] What White Calf chose to ignore was that, using the convenient legal instrument of the executive order, new reservation boundaries had been established and that the provisions of Lame Bull's Treaty south of the Missouri River were no longer valid.

No wonder the Piegan were now surprised. Schultz shared their confusion. In his description of their encounter with Lieutenant Krause, Schultz has Krause saying, in essence, "Does White Calf not know that the U.S. government, by means of an executive order or a congressional act, has twice moved the reservation boundary north?" The answer came when White Calf, dumbfounded, turned to Joe Kipp to ask for confirmation: "Have the Great Fathers . . . really stolen from us the greater part of our country?" In one of Schultz's accounts Kipp's answer was unequivocal. "They have stolen it, as he says."[51] In another, Kipp answered Lieutenant Krause's question: "No, they know nothing about it and I won't tell them of it for God knows what might then happen."[52] Whatever the case, tempers flared. A hubbub ensued, replete with threatening cries, and only after being reminded of the horrible carnage of the Baker massacre on the Marias were the Piegan, and especially the young warriors, dissuaded from immediate bloodshed.

White Calf should have known of the government's changes in the reservation's southern boundary. After all, the changes had generated any number of meetings and protests on the part of the Piegan, especially as they impacted buffalo hunting on both sides of the critical Teton River, flowing west to east, from the Rocky Mountains to its confluence with the Missouri. Both the Blackfeet and the Assiniboine and Gros Ventre of the Fort Belknap Special Agency, as a result of Grant's executive order and under the initiative of their two agents, had become involved in a case of "bison diplomacy," in which they established relations of peace and friendship in the Fort Benton Treaty of 1874.[53] Under this intertribal peace, they promised to "engage in no warlike or hostile acts against each other" and to forbid killing and horse stealing, and they "extended to each other cordial consent to hunt and camp upon the territory as assigned to us respectively and all meetings that may by chance occur upon the prairie shall be friendly." Although Cut Hand was then the head chief for the Piegan, White Calf, the future head chief, signed the peace treaty and must have been apprised of the new reservation's external and internal boundaries. Even more to the point, White Calf must have remembered his earlier objections to the loss of the Teton River valley and how bitterly he had complained.

Cattlemen had not only initiated the critical reductions of the reservation reflected in the presidential executive order, but they had also aggressively moved into much of the grasslands north of the Sun River and south of the Missouri and on the Musselshell and Judith Rivers. Colonel Thomas Ruger, for example, noted that an increased feeling of hostility on the part of cattle owners and settlers had surfaced prior to 1880 and that they were extremely concerned about the presence of roving, hungry Indians who were converging on them from every side. Stock owners had organized to be politically effective and were determined to keep the Indians away from what they now considered to be their ranges, either by having the government confine the Indians to their designated reservations or by doing it themselves. Solving the problem of roaming Indians had become a pressing priority, and increasingly the answer the stockmen found most acceptable was the confinement of Indians to their reservations.[54] However, whether White Calf adequately understood the political import of their actions with the military is doubtful. Then, as now, people hear what they want to hear.

Captain Moale's decision to allow the Piegan time to call in the various winter hunting parties prior to their forced departure from the Judith and to prepare themselves and their horses for the difficult February journey proved to be a godsend. It allowed Lieutenant Krause to give the totally unprepared Indians a reasonable amount of time to ready themselves for what promised to be a most difficult winter ordeal. "I told them," Krause later reported, "that they must be ready to start in eight days or sooner." This timetable, although arbitrary, was predicated on the ability of White Calf and others to get word to the scattered distant hunters, who were as far as seventy-five miles away, in the vicinity of Black Butte. Given the wintry circumstances, eight days was not much time to call them back. They would have to move fast and willingly.

Reports in the *Benton Weekly Record* on February 17 mentioned that "[a]dvices from Lieutenant Krause state that the Piegan are moving this way [toward Benton] slowly. Many of the camps were after buffalo and had not returned. The removal of the Indians to their reservation will be slow." Delays were to be expected, "as their horses are poor and many are without transportation." The weather was not helping either, as it was "impossible to move on the prairies between Judith and Arrow Creek and the Missouri, while the cold weather lasts, these points being destitute of fuel, and distance from 30 to 40 miles."[55] Three days later the newspaper told its audience that the Piegan whom Lieutenant Krause was "to arrest and compel to remove to their reservation, are badly scattered and it will take some time before they can be collected."[56] In addition, the Piegan "piteously" pleaded for understanding. "They say they would willingly return to, and remain on, the reservation, if the military officers could guarantee them a full supply of rations according to treaty stipulations." The newspaper article concluded that the government should demonstrate some regard for White Calf's and Running Crane's bands of Piegan, for they had been "staunch friends to the white people and crowding them into a corner looks unjust."[57]

No one made the eight-day deadline, which fell on February 23. The leadership was reluctant to force the issue, and the collected camp remained hunkered down and in place. Miraculously, however, most of the lodges came down early on February 24, and a slow start was made toward Fort Benton. Lieutenant Krause stayed behind with the last stragglers of the camp, making sure that "all the lodges were down and in motion" before leaving to catch up with the wagons carrying his camp equipage, which he had ordered to Arrow Creek. He did not directly accompany the ponderous Piegan cavalcade, with its ungainly collection of women and children, horses and hordes of dogs. The ponies were piled high with what dry meat the Blackfeet had been able to preserve and their cache of green and already tanned buffalo robes. Although heavily encumbered, the Indians were moving. It was a beginning.

A third party would take part in the arduous trek, one never identified by the military commanders in their reports—Joe Kipp and his trading outfit, including James Willard Schultz. And once again Schultz, or Apikunni, provided intriguing details passed over in the abbreviated official reports. "We went with them," he wrote, "for during the winter our four-horse teams and wagons had hauled our buffalo robes and furs to Fort Benton about as fast as we traded for them."[58] It had been a very profitable trade. They had taken in more than 1,800 buffalo robes and 3,000 elk, deer, and antelope hides, plus a few other pelts. Now, given the lateness of the season and the departure of the Piegan, winter trading in the Judith was essentially over. Kipp's outfit might as well stay with the Piegan and go back to the reservation and to Fort Conrad on the Marias, which Kipp had purchased in 1878.[59]

Although it meant leaving the ragged line of struggling Piegan long behind, Lieutenant Krause had decided to head directly to Arrow Creek for a number of reasons; there was no fuel wood any closer, he sensed the weather was worsening, and he feared encountering a storm on what amounted to a high and barren plateau already covered in snow. Moreover, his horses were already stressed, as they had been unable to graze at the great camp on the Judith. Grasses there had long since been cropped off by the large numbers of Indian horses or buried under a thick coat of ice and snow. Given this situation and fearing that his horses might either drift away in the blowing snow or disappear as they sought shelter, Krause had ordered them tied to the wagons. They had remained there, sometimes plastered with snow, for six days while the Lieutenant waited for the Piegan. Their only feed was the dry forage the wagons had brought with them. Now they "were sadly in need of grazing and there being no grass between these two points," Krause hoped to find some feed among the cottonwoods along the river bottoms or enough cured grass blown free in the broken country to tide them over.[60]

Lieutenant Krause's intuition about the weather proved to be correct. By the time the soldiers set up camp on Arrow Creek the next day, it had become very stormy. On their second day in camp, fine, sand-like flakes were falling so hard, wrote Krause, "that no one could live without shelter." The soldiers were forced to spend three days at the Arrow Creek camp before they could move. No mention was made in the later reports of the plight of the Blackfeet, far to the rear. Krause's men struck camp on February 28, when the weather let up a little, although there was still severe drifting, with snow swirling and dancing to intermediate gusts. In any case, the detachment had to get to Fort Benton. They had "but two days rations and forage." Striking camp and marching as quickly as they could, they began a critical race that they almost lost. It took the men and wagons a full two days, until February 29, to finally drop down to the frozen ice of the Missouri, in sight of their barracks.

The ordeal was by no means over. Replenishing their supplies and displaying considerable fortitude, the detachment turned around and started back across the Missouri, retracing their trail from Arrow Creek. On the second of March they found the majority of the Piegan camp as they had expected. The Indians were in bad shape. After waiting two more days for knots of stragglers to string in, basically those without horses or those whose horses were in the worst shape, the soldiers and Indians pushed on relentlessly to Fort Benton and to provisions. They reached safety after noon on Saturday, March 13. The Piegan under White Calf and Running Crane, numbering about eight hundred, set up camp across the Missouri River among the bleak and bare cottonwoods that sharply etched the bottom half of the barren horizon down river, east and opposite the town.[61] The forced march had taken them twenty days from the Judith Basin to Fort Benton, a distance, estimated Colonel Ruger, of less than eighty miles. During this trial they had lost more than two hundred of their worn-out and over-loaded ponies.[62]

On Sunday the Piegan and "several families of Northern Indians" were allowed a day of rest, and on Monday they received permission to go into the town of Fort Benton "to trade to provide for the trip to the reservation." Among the "noted personages of the camp" were The General, or Double Runner, and Black Weasel, who now went by the name of Mountain Chief. "It may be remembered," intoned the *Helena Daily Herald*, "that Black Weasel was the scoundrel who led the party of murderers against Malcolm Clark in 1869, and why he should be allowed to run at large until this time is one of the mysteries of Indian Affairs."[63]

Captain Moale took all the proper precautions to prevent the whiskey traders from taking advantage of the miserable situation. He stationed numerous guards at the large camp and tried, said the *Benton Record*, to inhibit "too free intercourse between the Indians and their old time acquaintances." This was difficult to do, for the buffalo hunting that season had been surprisingly good. The Blackfeet were "well supplied with robes, peltries and dry meat" that they

Fort Benton, Montana Territory, 1878. (Glenbow Archives, Calgary, Alberta, NA-2446-11.)

had hauled with them, hoping their robes would bring higher prices than Kipp had been willing to pay. Short of supplies and wanting to lighten their burdensome loads, they were now eager to trade in Fort Benton, where the demand was lively.[64]

The Blackfeet removal under military escort had by no means relieved the concerns of either the stockmen of Chouteau County or the citizens of Fort Benton. Reporting another large camp of Blood Indians, "of about 150, or 200 lodges, in the Judith, fifteen miles below the Moccasin Mountains," the *Benton Record* was of the opinion that there would be trouble, and that "settlers in that section justly demand that these interlopers shall be removed, as they have no more rights in that section than the peaceable Piegan, who are now being removed back to their reservation by Lieutenant Krause."[65] At least the newspaper recommended consistency.

The *Benton Weekly Record* also wanted to know "Why the Indian Department should insist upon moving the Piegans from an isolated game country to a reservation, without having provided means for their support, and leave the turbulent and dangerous Indians from across the line, at large?" Attempting to answer its own question, it could only come up with a reflection on the federal government, calling the situation "one of the unaccountable tangles of red tape."[66]

The Blackfeet agent on Badger Creek, John Young, was also well informed of the progress of the military escort action and, as might be expected, was apprehensive about his ability to feed them. What would he do when the battered bands arrived and became once again his responsibility? A month earlier, Colonel Ruger, commanding from Helena, had raised the obvious question, requesting from Agent Young "information as to whether the means at your disposal for feeding the Indians attached to your agency are adequate on the supposition that they should not be permitted to go for purposes of hunting across the Missouri." Young had long since answered that question in the negative. He could not supply the Piegan with full rations. He had known that back in the fall of 1879, and so did White Calf and the other Piegan chiefs. Nothing had changed since.[67]

Anticipating the problem—although not by much, for the Piegan were already in Fort Benton—on March 16 Young requested permission from the Office of Indian Affairs to call for and receive the twenty-five per cent additional beef and flour supplies provided for in his initial contract. "These additional supplies are necessary for the reason that the Indians belonging to this Agency have been ordered back to their Reservation by the military authorities, (they having gone beyond its limits in the pursuit of Buffalo), and will thus be deprived for the coming season of their principal source of subsistence." Young went on to say that they were presently "traveling toward the Agency as rapidly as the weather and the weakened condition of their ponies will permit, and as there is now an almost total lack of game on this side of the Missouri River, they will have to depend entirely upon the Government for support, and with the main camp here, the present supplies will be exhausted *before* July 1st,"[68] which was the beginning of the new fiscal year when additional supplies would be available.

In Fort Benton, following a two-day respite, Captain Moale gave orders that the march to the agency was to be continued, again under

Lieutenant Krause's direction. But Krause was unable to continue. Although he had been "well clad and well mounted," as his report pointed out, he had suffered so severely from the cold and exposure during the relentless ground blizzards that he could not report for duty on the fifteenth and was confined to his quarters for ten days.[69]

With little latitude and even less in the way of government supplies, Captain Moale took over the escorting detachment. "[B]y slow marches" they, together with the Blackfeet, travelled up the valley of the Teton to a point some twenty miles from Fort Benton, near what was called the Leavings of the Teton, on the Whoop-Up Trail. The Indians could go no further. Their horses, just skin and bones, were totally played out. They had to rest their animals. There could be no thought of continuing up out of the sheltered valley and across the treeless plains in the direction of the Marias and Kipp's trading post, Fort Conrad.[70] The camp rested there in sight of "the Knees," or as the Blackfeet called it, "Mutoksisiko," a critical landform marking the direction north, for three days.

During the march's interruption, Captain Moale organized a talk with the leading men of the camp—White Calf, Running Crane, Fast Buffalo Horse, Four Bears, and others, including Running Wolf, a Northern Piegan, and one or two Bloods. Running Wolf had been with the Piegan all winter. By this time the Indians had passed any outlying settlements, and Moale decided that given the fact that they had promised "not to go up the Teton towards the old Agency [called Four Persons or Nissue Tupi], although a great many of the old squaws and those who are accustomed to loaf around the settlements wanted particularly to go that way," it would be safe to let them travel the rest of the way on their own. As a result, when it came time to resume, Moale remained in camp until the last lodge had come down, excepting the eleven lodges belonging to Iron Breast, whose wife was then dying, and the attendant medicine men and women. Moale sent the rest on their way. The others would follow them when they could, also "via the Knees" to the Marias and Fort Conrad, and from there on to their agency on Badger Creek. To be certain this happened, the military escort, absent Captain Moale, followed behind for another five miles and again reminded the Indians that no one should head toward the Teton River and its trail to their former agency. It was not that Captain Moale did not trust White Calf and Running Crane, he said, but that "some few might get away from them as they have a great fondness for a Mr. Hamilton, who lives at the old agency about 29 miles from Fort Shaw."[71]

Having sent the Indians on their way, the escort returned to rejoin Captain Moale, and together they retraced their way down the Teton, returning to Fort Benton and their comfortable permanent quarters. It must have been a relief.

When it came time to write up his report the following day, March 26, the commanding officer expressed his discomfort at what had happened to the Piegan, disagreeing with both military and civilian authorities—first with the allegations regarding the killing of cattle, and second with Agent Young's repeated denial that he had given any of the Indians written passes to leave the reservation. Captain Moale was not shy. "To my own knowledge," he wrote, "I have seen the passes in the hands of some of the Indians and have read them myself." Moreover, he tried to impress upon Headquarters how ashamed the Indians felt at their "being ordered to return to their reservation as they assert there was no reason for their removal." At this point, however, there was little that he could do other than to set the record straight and to relay to his superiors the wishes of the Piegan now that they had been compelled to return to their agency: that the military authorities "try and obtain for them greater assistance to sustain life than what they receive from their agent."[72]

Clearly the Blackfeet were unhappy with their agent and were seeking help from the army. They had complained bitterly about Young to Moale. "I did not hear a favorable word said in regard to him," confessed Captain Moale, "by one of them."[73] Once again, the military had to do the dirty work of enforcing regulations with which it was uncomfortable, and of remedying the mistakes and political incompetence of civilian agents and the Office of Indian Affairs.

By now it was early spring. Most of the Indians continued on to the vicinity of Fort Conrad on the Marias River, resting there for as long as several months. Men and women spent their time recovering from their losses; the men hunted antelope and deer in the area with some success while the women tanned whatever green hides they had brought with them in their haste, hoping to trade them with Kipp, who had returned with them and was now again in charge of the post he had bought two years earlier. The Blackfeet were in no hurry to reach their agency. There was little or no food there, and it was still some fifty long miles distant to the west, with the grass only beginning to green up. Schultz estimated that another two hundred Piegan horses had expired from exhaustion moving from Fort Benton to the Marias.[74] Now even greater numbers of Blackfeet would be returning to the agency on foot, and doing so with little more than they or their surviving dogs could carry. For the moment, then, they were happy to be at Fort Conrad.

Before long, in spite of multiple warnings, some of the Piegan decided to strike out on their own. Instead of heading in the direction of the agency, they made their way into the Teton country. Almost immediately there were reports of camps as well as bands being off the reservation, south of Birch Creek, and in the vicinity of their old agency. There were allegations of cattle killing, too.[75] When inquiries were made to Agent Young, his response was that "the few Indians on the Teton are some stragglers from the main camp who halted on the homeward journey in order to rest their horses." Then, attempting to present their side of the story regarding the previous winter, he wrote, "My Indians complain bitterly that they, who were doing no harm, were compelled to leave the hunting grounds, while other tribes, having no right on this side of the Canadian line, were allowed to remain where game was abundant." Moreover, he asserted, whatever wrongdoing had occurred had been the "work of foreign Indians," and the Piegan indignantly denied that any of their people were involved in killing cattle. He also reported the complaint that "the speed with which they were compelled to move was productive of great loss to them as they had to leave behind a large number of horses as well as mares in foal that were too weak to make the journey."[76] Agent Young also explained that the Indians felt their wealth to be in the number of horses they possessed, and that as a result of their horse losses "these people all feel that they have been badly treated without having given cause for it."[77] Finally, addressing the issue of their subsistence and need to hunt off the reservation, Young once again equivocated, stating that in his opinion, "the supplies at my disposal will *with what game they can find along the mountains,* [emphasis added] support them for some time to come, comfortably."[78] These words would soon come to haunt Agent Young.

The two winter events of 1879–80—the arrest of Spopee late in December, followed by the military arrest of the Blackfeet and their forced removal to the reservation—did not sit well with the Piegan. Some connected the two incidents, as can be seen from the account of Charlemagne, a young Nez Perce Indian, who had been hunting buffalo with the Blackfeet on Flat Willow Creek in the Judith Basin. While there, one of the Blackfeet warriors told Charlemagne that the Blackfeet were going to make war with the whites and had therefore made a treaty with Sitting Bull, their encroaching Sioux enemy. They were going to fight, he said, "on account of a Blackfoot having been hung by the white men some months ago. White men had got two Blackfeet; one they hung, and the other they put in jail." While incorrect, the reference, of course, was to Spopee and Good Rider. And while this information regarding a prospective Sioux alliance proved to be erroneous, it nonetheless registered the growing undercurrent of Blackfeet hostility toward the white population, as well as providing a rationale for such unprecedented action.[79]

Nor was this hostility limited to a single expression that somehow managed to survive in print. Later in 1880, after White Calf and the Blackfeet had undergone their winter exodus out of the Judith Basin, the *Benton Record* gave another Blackfeet response to Spopee's arrest. Jeff Talbert, deputy sheriff for Chouteau County, who along with Sheriff Healy had arrested Spopee, had returned from the Musselshell Country, where he had attempted to arrest "an Indian horse thief." Talbert had found his man, but he was "among one hundred and fifty lodges of Bloods and Piegans," and Talbert was unable to extricate him from the camp. The Indians surrounded Talbert with cocked guns and "told him that he could not take his prisoner; that they were friends of the whites and did not want to fight them, but now their hearts were getting bad." Again, the reason for their "bad hearts" was that Spopee had been wrenched out of their camp last winter and was now in prison waiting to be hanged. The Indians swore that was not going to happen again without a fight. With cocked guns pointing at him from all sides, Talbert "had found it impossible to bring his man away."[80]

The Blackfeet did not forget the example of Spopee, but it was the humiliation of White Calf and their forced return to the Blackfeet Reservation while other parties continued to hunt that galled most. This was a tribal event involving the whole of their leadership and their 1855 treaty rights; many people were involved, and the action resulted in irreversible changes that would remain impossible to forget. More directly, in returning to the reservation the Blackfeet lost the ability to provide for themselves and in their confinement became depressingly dependent upon the federal government. Taking away their "liberty of motion," their ability to follow the buffalo, and restricting them to a single place that had been hunted out had consequences for both the Blackfeet leadership and representatives of the federal government. Either the government would have to provide full rations for them, or the Blackfeet would starve. The huge joint reservation, particularly west of the Bear's Paw Mountains, was devoid of game. East of that landmark, the territory either belonged to those Indians associated with Fort Belknap—the Gros Ventre and the Assiniboine, augmented by all manner of Canadian Indians, both Blackfoot-speakers and otherwise, including Cree and Métis—or had been overrun by the Sioux expansion west. As a result, Blackfeet confinement to the reservation essentially meant confinement only to the most western parts. That was the reality.

The situation was dire. And it did not end with the Blackfeet return to the agency, or rather, their portion of the reservation. During April and May, unable to secure adequate food in the mountains as Agent Young had suggested, either those involved in the forced retreat or other Blackfeet bands subsequently drifted over the newly defined southern reservation boundary in their continued quest for food. Breaking up into small camps, families and bands surreptitiously went west and south, returning to their old haunts near the Four Persons agency on the Teton River. Once again the army was called upon to haul them back.

This time a mounted military patrol from Fort Shaw under Lieutenant John W. Hannay, Third Infantry, searched in mid-April for the small, scattered camps of the Blackfeet. Once discovered, hungry clusters of men, women, and children were fed by the patrol and again slowly prodded and escorted back to the north side of the new reservation boundary, Birch Creek. Once more, the precipitating cause of the action was a complaint by a prominent white stockman, alleging the killing of a single cow. The lack of game in the foothills made such depredations predictable if not inevitable, and when combined with the apprehensiveness of other stockmen for the safety of their cattle, the two fused together to make a flammable situation.

Lieutenant Hannay dutifully investigated the incident and in his subsequent report confirmed the killing. He also observed that the Piegan were "in a state of destitution," and that the main source of their food was "the putrid meat of cattle which had died from disease or exposure on the prairie, during the past winter." The Indians were in such bad shape that they had traded their ponies and their buffalo bed-robes for food; their lodges "were very poor, full of holes, and rent and they have no means of renewing them unless by buffalo hunting." In such straits, Lieutenant Hannay sent for additional rations from Fort Shaw to the south, on the Sun River, and issued food to the Indians along the way as his detachment marched them toward Birch Creek. By April 25, the patrol had collected thirty-two lodges, warned others, and moved those on the wrong side of Birch Creek over to the reservation side of the boundary. Once back on the reservation, Lieutenant Hannay also met with White Calf and told him of his orders. White Calf gave him assurances that he would "send out runners and move all his tribe to their reservation." The rounding up of the off-reservation Indians, however, was by no means over.

Upon leaving the Badger Creek agency, Lieutenant Hannay made his way south again to the Four Persons agency and from there proceeded once more to scour the countryside for smaller bands. His successes included finding a small encampment of Kootenai Indians under Big Head (Pascal), Medicine Pipe, and Left Arm, "which had been lurking about the mountains in this neighborhood for over a year." The Blackfeet refugees he found were in a "pitiable state." They had moved away from the reservation because, as one man expressed it, "Our children on Birch Creek are cryin' for food."

The reason for this, wrote Lieutenant Hannay, stemmed from their having been driven "from the Judith Basin before they had laid in their usual supply of buffalo meat and robes." The crisis had been exacerbated because moving at that time of year had caused them "to leave many of their ponies—two hundred is one estimate—behind, and since their return, many more have died or have been abandoned."[81]

As desperate as they were, the Blackfeet were still anxious to get along with the white authorities. As Lieutenant Hannay expressed it: "[T]heir action in quietly submitting to being taken from their hunting ground and hemmed in on their reservation, where, they say, they must starve, is powerful proof of their sincerity in this matter."[82]

Efforts to confine Indians to their reservations as a method of controlling them and teaching them "civilized occupations and pursuits" had been around for decades.[83] Indian fears in this regard were long-standing as well. Following the 1855 Stevens Treaty at Walla Walla, where signature tribes were assigned territories, the influential chief Yellow Bird, or PeoPeoMoxMox, had presciently remarked that "he was not a hog to be put in a pen and to be fed by the whites."[84] Over time territorial newspapers, stockmen, and citizens in Montana had developed a long rolling drumbeat of criticism regarding off-reservation Indian "roaming" that culminated with the advent of the 1880s. Then, when everyone was expecting to see or hear about the "last tail of the last buffalo," when there was no longer much game anywhere, even in the Judith Basin, the cries to confine Indians to their reservations in Montana and Idaho reached a pitched crescendo. In the minds of white Americans, whatever rationale there may have been for Indians to leave their reservations, including the solemn and legally binding promises contained in the articles of congressional treaties, was now gone. As far as most citizens were concerned, "that was then and this is now," and to facilitate territorial progress there had to be a separation of the races until such time as tribal authority had been pulverized and set aside and Indians individually had been rendered similar to the national culture, if not the same.[85]

As recently as 1879, the starvation year for the Canadian tribes on the other side of the Medicine Line, Niitzitapi such as Spopee had been free to go where ever they wanted without interference; they could seek to relieve their gnawing hunger pangs by crossing the abstract international borderline, as they had done from time immemorial. There, south of the Missouri, they could again find buffalo and make meat, and do so without fear of U.S. government intervention. The same was true for a surprising number of Indians from west of the Rocky Mountains. Nez Perce, Cayuse, Spokane, Coeur d'Alene, and many other tribes annually exercised their off-reservation hunting rights as set down in the Blackfeet Treaty. Inexplicably, arbitrarily, these same rights, from the same treaty, were now denied the Blackfeet, causing their arrest, removal, humiliation, and forced confinement in 1880. It was a signal event. Confinement heralded a new dispensation. The Piegan were unjustly or illegally confined to a portion of their homeland void of game, when others were not. Their freedom was gone. Without the "liberty of motion" and without any means of providing for themselves, the Blackfeet lost their political independence and became depressingly and totally dependent on the government for food; there would be either government rations or actual starvation. As the slogan of the day went, it was "feed them or fight them."[86]

Hank Brooks, the Judith Basin stockman who in desperation had set in motion the forced removal of the Southern Piegan at the beginning of 1880, came to reflect on this "feed or fight" attitude in a Christmas interview with the Helena newspaper, the *Daily Independent*. Even ten months after the forced Blackfeet removal, he was still complaining about roving bands of Indians, most of whom he now described as "British Indians." They were, in his opinion, preying upon the stockmen's herds with "comparative impunity." Feeling inadequate to resolve the situation himself and unprotected by the government, Brooks humorously reported that he had opted to "establish an Indian restaurant on his ranch and entertain those dusky warriors by the score," preferring to give them "cooked beef to having the Indians help themselves to the raw article on the plains." In this way he proposed to save "the wastage which would result from the indiscriminate slaughter of his herd."[87]

Many whites decided the same thing—to feed the Indians rather than fight them. But feeding them required confinement—not only was it a legal administrative tool, but many thought that under the right conditions it was a good thing—in fact, therapeutic—for it would compel the Blackfeet bands to address the imminent demise of the buffalo and would wean them away from their reliance upon the chase and upon gathering. Bounded, unhorsed, and dependent, these deprivations would jolt them into a much needed recognition; it would push them in the right direction, toward agriculture and stock-raising as alternative and necessary livelihoods. Even hunger had its proponents. As early as 1875 the commissioner of Indian Affairs, Edward P. Smith, had praised the "moral suasion of hunger" to compel the Indians "to do what they dislike"; in other words, if it took hunger and confinement to enforce civilization, so be it.[88]

There were two flaws in this thinking. The first, of course, was that the legality of imposed reservation confinement was questionable, to say the least. The second was that the federal authorities, especially the Office of Indian Affairs, was talking about mere hunger, but the reservation reality for the Blackfeet was not hunger but actual and miserable starvation, with high mortality rates among the young and the elderly. Federal authorities had not adequately prepared for the transition to agriculture by any stretch of the imagination. They knew of the likelihood of crop failure on the northern plains due to weather; they knew that Congress declined to increase emergency appropriations; they had already experienced the calloused delays of territorial merchants in delivering contracted food rations, however difficult the road and weather conditions or how high the costs. Blackfeet confinement was predicated upon adequate food provision and storage—yet food was not there, and everyone knew it—the Blackfeet, their agent, and the Great Father in the form of the Office of Indian Affairs. Inevitably this chain of events led to the subsequent infamous "Starvation Winter of 1883–84," when as many as one-fourth of the Piegans in Montana perished.[89]

These government failures, however well documented, undermined the more basic, "therapeutic" argument—that the confinement of the Blackfeet was an opportunity, for it would lead to their incorporation into American society. The Blackfeet were now governmental wards, and their future well-being was the rationale for control and confinement. Their guardians were doing this for their benefit, and although the Blackfeet might not understand, in the long run it was best for them. The same was argued for Spopee. By 1884 both his trial and the Detroit House of Correction were behind him. Now he was at a new institution, the Government Hospital for the Insane in Washington, D.C., where he too, like the Blackfeet, would be a government ward, confined for a very long time, in the hopes that he would "come to his senses" and experience a therapeutic recovery.

Analogies, however, can only be pushed so far. The ironic reality was that Spopee would be well fed to the point of concern in his institutional confinement at St. Elizabeths, with its dining halls of starched linen table cloths, tableware, and elegant Palladian windows. The Southern Piegan would, on the other hand, amid a winter landscape alternating between snow drifts over their heads and patches of prairie swept clean by brutal winds, ignominiously starve on their reservation, without explanation, widespread concern, or relief. Huddled in rags in lodges around the forlorn agency on Badger Creek, they waited, and they died. For both the Blackfeet and Spopee, however, the result was the same—their way of life as independent buffalo people was extinguished. They were no longer free.

CHAPTER 6

THE GOVERNMENT HOSPITAL
FOR THE INSANE
A Case of "Undifferentiated Psychosis"

It has never been clear why in 1882 Detroit prison officials trans-ferred Spopee to the only federal mental asylum in the nation, the Government Hospital for the Insane in Washington, D.C. Ostensi-bly, they reported that Spopee suffered from melancholia and that this condition presumably had become more pronounced after his admission.[1] With this diagnosis and a lifetime sentence, he left the Detroit House of Correction, a penitentiary, for the sanctuary of the Government Hospital for the Insane, there to be removed from the stress, tensions, external influences, and mental excitements that had brought about the problem in the first place. Officials hoped Spopee would be cured. At least that was the theory. The reality may have been as simple as one institution ridding itself of an expensive liability that did not belong there. He was an Indian who exhibited strange behaviors and attempted to communicate by hand signals and gestures. He did not speak English, in fact did not speak at all, and he was both a convicted felon and a government ward. Foisting him off onto another federal institution, one more capable of han-dling such eccentricities, was an attractive solution.

An interview with Spopee himself, long after the fact, indicates why he decided to stop talking and suggests a reason for his trans-fer. Catherine M. MacLennan, who championed his eventual release in 1914, wrote that "feeling he could not understand the white man's language and that the white man could not understand his language, he [Spopee] resolved to keep silence, thereby hoping to receive better treatment from those in whose care he was." MacLennan went on to relate how Spopee's resolve was misunderstood and the favorable treatment he had hoped for failed to materialize. Instead, "his silence was interpreted as a species of melancholia and he was sent as a criminal insane patient to the Government Hospital for the Insane."[2]

When Spopee arrived in 1882 at the Government Hospital for the Insane, or St. Elizabeths, the name that Union soldiers in the Civil War preferred to use, it already had a long institutional history. Established in 1855, its original mission was to provide "the most humane care and enlightened curative treatment of the insane of the Army, Navy, and District of Columbia." Congress had shouldered this burdensome responsibility, which was unusual. Normally public insane asylums were viewed as the responsibility of states and cities. Largely because of the indefatigable efforts of Dorothea Lynde Dix, then a leading prison and mental health reformer, Congress provided the resources to purchase a 185-acre farm at the southeast edge of Washington, D.C., commanding a spectacular view of the Anacostia and Potomac Rivers and with a clear view of the capitol. It became the first and only federal mental institution with a national scope, providing a place for "persons under the immediate supervision of the federal government."[3] This mandate came to include American Indians.

Congress acted in part because of the current optimistic view that madness or insanity was eminently curable, particularly if treated outside of the family and home in distant, state-supported, public institutions by experienced and qualified professionals.[4] Critical to this assumption was the notion that "a person's immediate surroundings influenced his or her conduct," and that surroundings with the proper design and setting would engender critical therapeutic values, which in turn could be further enhanced through a structured, organized supervision. The reigning nineteenth-century authority on the matter was Dr. Thomas S. Kirkbride, who directed the Pennsylvania Hospital for the Insane and was the author of the influential text *On the Construction, Organization, and General Arrangements of Hospitals for the Insane,* published in 1854.

When it came time to commission the architect for the Government Hospital for the Insane, authorities selected Thomas U. Walter, who had gained distinction designing the dome of the Capitol. Working in tandem with the medical superintendent of the yet-to-be constructed hospital, Dr. Charles H. Nichols, Walter settled upon the then popular "Kirkbride Plan," in which the design and the building itself were thought of as possessing curative powers. Only within the embrace of such structures, through institutionalization, could effective treatment of the insane transpire.

Kirkbride's asylum design featured a blunt, fortress-like exterior of red brick with an imposing central main entrance. The building was flanked by a distinctive set of "wings" on either side, which contained wards—large rooms where patients were accommodated. The original plan was linear, but Superintendent Nichols modified the Kirkbride plan, arranging the "wings" in a novel way.[5] They were "in echelon," meaning they were stepped or staggered, designed to break up the long, straight corridors that conventionally marked such institutions. In the process the broken segments allowed for more windows, letting in more light and ventilation. These smaller wards housed fewer inhabitants per room and thus provided greater privacy. The reduction in size of the wards also made them more manageable. Each hosted a day room with tall imposing windows and dining halls at the end of each pavilion, and the design promoted a more residential atmosphere than other conceptions. The plan also was unusual in that the wards farthest from the grandiose central entrance were often stepped down, lower in height, reflecting the fact that the untidy and noisy units for more deranged patients were fewer in number, farther away from the public central spaces, and that the sickest patients did not need, nor could they benefit from, the companionship and therefore the social parlors of the other wards.[6] Palatial institutions built on this plan, referred to by Kirkbride as "a special apparatus for the care of lunacy," were set amid extensive surrounding grounds, "highly improved and tastefully ornamented"—sanctuaries where the insane could find peace of mind as they awaited recovery.

St. Elizabeths Hospital, Center Building, Old Administration Building complex. (National Archives and Records Administration, Still Pictures Unit, Image 418-G-9. Reproduced from the Blackburn Laboratory Archives at St. Elizabeths Hospital. Copies of this image exist in other repositories. The Hospital wishes to acknowledge the holdings related to the Government Hospital for the Insane in the National Archives and Records Administration.)

Congress set out the purposes of the Government Hospital for the Insane in positive terms. As noted, it was to offer "the most humane care and enlightened curative treatment of the insane" available at that time. In context, this made perfect sense. In the days before of a wide array of specific medications and antipsychotic drugs, curative treatments were in short supply. Most asylums attempted to address mental diseases by relying upon what then was termed "the moral treatment," a therapy that used emotional or spiritual approaches as opposed to material intervention in the way of medicines or physical devises. The moral treatment was also an approach that took into consideration the whole of the individual: mind, body, and spirit. Fundamental to this holistic avenue were

St. Elizabeths Hospital, detached dining hall, 1897, seating 500. (Reproduced from the Blackburn Laboratory Archives at St. Elizabeths Hospital and the National Archives and Records Administration. The Hospital wishes to acknowledge the holdings related to the Government Hospital for the Insane in the National Archives and Records Administration.)

"pleasant surroundings, kindness, personal attention, entertainment—in short, the basic humanities."[7] Simply put, environments were important to well-being. Hospitals were required to have a park or garden-like setting if they were to offer an alternative to the unhealthy stresses of urban and family life. Few doubted nature's therapeutic effects, and these should be brought to bear, diverting "the melancholic from their distressing fantasies, furnishing inexhaustible occupation and delight to the convalescent."[8] Freed from the cares of the world, the "strolling invalid" could "woo nature for their health that spurned nature had denied."[9]

In addition to redemptive natural surroundings, the asylum should also assemble a structured daily schedule with periods of fresh air and exercise, as well as modest amounts of physical labor in what amounted to an early form of occupational therapy. These features would exert a positive, curative influence, especially when done under the direction of caring ward attendants and interested, personally involved medical doctors. Inmates in the process would find themselves protected and sheltered, not only from the distresses of the outside world but also from the ridicule and abuse of the mentally sane. Patients could be themselves, free to concentrate on their shortcomings, even their madness, as they made their remedial return to restored sanity.

This nonmedical, disciplined, and humane approach to mental and physical health was, of course, expensive, and it worked best when designed for small patient numbers. After the Civil War, the patient population of mentally ill veterans and government officials exploded, and the "moral treatment" had to be adjusted. By the 1890s St. Elizabeths embraced, or at least tried to embrace, 1,073 patients.[10] Mental asylums elsewhere experienced similar growth, and everywhere institutions first became overcrowded and then ballooned into increasingly immense, overcrowded complexes. Large numbers of patients, including the criminally insane, inadequate funding, and a paucity of curative successes slowly undermined public confidence in the viability of the public enterprises, their cost, and the feasibility of "the moral treatment" itself. Protean reform initiatives accompanied increased accounting efforts.

At St. Elizabeths, multiple alterations aimed at remediation were introduced, particularly after 1878 and the arrival of Dr. William Whitney Godding, the new medical superintendent, who would remain in charge of the hospital for the next twenty-one years, until 1899. Doctor Godding pioneered the first "cottage plan," an effort that resulted in the construction of eighteen new patient buildings that provided dormitory accommodations independent of the main institution. He also was instrumental in acquiring significant tracts of land to increase the size and physical layout of the institution.

Dr. William Whitney Godding,
medical superintendent, St.
Elizabeths Hospital, Washington,
D.C., 1878–99. (Reproduced from
the Blackburn Laboratory Archives
at St. Elizabeths Hospital and the
National Archives and Records
Administration. The Hospital
wishes to acknowledge the
holdings related to the Government
Hospital for the Insane in the
National Archives and Records
Administration.)

Thus not only did the capacity of the hospital grow to 1,603 beds, but the introduction of cottages reflected a new approach to patient rehabilitation. These cottages were designed to leave the "cathedral" or palatial lunatic asylums behind and to establish a more home-like environment. The buildings were smaller, housed fewer people, emphasized porches and separate grounds, and promoted a more casual, even family atmosphere. It was a new direction. In line with this, Godding also emphasized recreational opportunities, including walks, sunbaths, the frequent use of twelve- and six-seated horse-driven carriages for entertaining drives, a large number of John Philip Sousa concerts, as well as the possession of pet animals. He thought of these innovations as "prominent modes of treatment at the hospital."[11] And while there were still patients who had to be restrained by means of straitjackets, cuffs, sleeves, bed straps, and cribs, an outside evaluation in 1880 reported that these devises at St. Elizabeths were used on only about 1 percent of the asylum population.

Spopee arrived at St. Elizabeths on August 9, 1882, after many of these reforms were under way, but it was clear to most observers that asylum care had deteriorated dramatically since the Civil War and that the early promises for the effective cure of mental illnesses were illusionary. There was no cure for most madness. Mental patients piled up in the immense institutional asylums for decades, at government expense, and remained there without significant improvement and without rehabilitation. The "moral treatment," however, was not abandoned—far from it. And for good reason. Dr. Godding, for example, hung on to the basic notion that good care was itself therapeutic. "If it be said that the primary object of a hospital is to bring a cure, not to make a home, I admit it; but I deny that the two are incompatible with each other; indeed, the content which the home feeling gives is most favorable to recovery; the moral treatment, so called, is in a majority of cases more efficacious than medicine."[12] Along these same lines, Godding observed that "the best road to quiet content if not to cure lies through the regular occupation of the mind and body with some work not too hard of comprehension, nor too taxing in the strength in its performance."[13] He did not rule out "rides, walks and sunbaths," which he pronounced "are prominent modes of treatment at the hospital."[14]

From his arrival, Spopee enjoyed the benefits of this humane approach as well as the enviable freedom to be as different or as "mad" as he liked. He was not being punished. The doors of the hospital were open, and the windows were without bars. There existed a remarkable freedom of movement, or what was called "ground parole," within the restraining walls of the hospital complex. There was also periodic entertainment, welcome social privileges, and, above all, a sense of caring, community, and companionship. One of the new facilities was Atkins Hall, a fifty-bed cottage, which a visiting charity official in the 1880s described as "light, cheerful, and clean."[15] This stood in marked contrast to what Spopee had experienced in the Detroit House of Corrections or to what he would have encountered in the territorial penitentiary in Deer Lodge, Montana. Incarceration could have been worse, much worse. Spopee was not being punished; he was being "treated" in the hopes of being made whole.

Such liberalities were, of course, accompanied by the prejudices of the time. African Americans after the Civil War were treated within St. Elizabeths in segregated buildings for the "colored Insane." Men

and women were also kept separate, with even the distances between their buildings and the main edifice to be specified—"not
less than two hundred feet nor more than four hundred feet."[16]
Any distance closer than that would constitute an "objectionable
proximity."[17]

There were no guidelines for the segregation of Indian patients
simply because there were so few. While Spopee was at St. Elizabeths, there were never more than five Indians present as patients.
Spopee was housed for the first six years of his hospitalization in
the West Lodge, a "lodge for colored males." Given the trifling numbers of Indians and reflecting the social biases of the day, in which
Indians were ranked higher on the evolutionary ladder than black
Americans, later Spopee was transferred to Howard Hall, which
had both "white and colored male criminal wards."[18]

Astonishingly, for the first twenty years of Spopee's commitment
in Washington, D.C., his official record is blank. There are no extant
ward logs or much else beyond his initial admission papers. These
too were minimal in the extreme. What did Spopee do during his
waking hours in this distant confinement, we might ask him? The
answer, however sincere, would probably have been much like that
of another Montana Indian, the last great chief of the Crow Nation,
Plenty Coups, when answering the question, "What did you do
after the buffalo were gone?" Plenty Coups replied, "When the buffalo went away the hearts of my people fell to the ground, and they
could not lift them up again. After this nothing happened."[19] Another prominent Crow warrior, Two Leggings, after leading what
was considered the last Crow war party in 1888, confided "Nothing
happened after that. We just lived. There were no more war parties,
no capturing of horses from the Piegans and the Sioux, no buffalo to
hunt. There is nothing more to tell."[20] Memorable events and people
were no more. The Piegan leader Elk Horn, who had kept a winter
count of the earlier days, had much the same feeling; when asked
why in later years his winter count featured primarily the deaths of
prominent warriors, he replied that since confinement to the reservation, "nothing else happened worth remembering."[21]

And so it was with Spopee. His situation had so dramatically
changed from what it had been that nothing significant could

happen anymore, and nothing made sense. There were no bench marks. It was difficult to measure the slowing tempo, the loss of freedom and decision, the difficult adjustment to language loss, the choking off, the steady retreat. Spopee, the buffalo hunter, so used to a bustling, nomadic life of moving camps, horses, seasonal vagaries of wind and weather, became disoriented, alienated, and listless in the humidity of Washington, D.C. Other mental patients sometimes described this process as "sinking," or "gradually falling into a torpor, like that of a living corpses"[22] For Spopee it was more like the disembodiment experienced by ghosts on their spiritual way to the Sand Hills, their special afterlife location at the eastern edge of the Blackfeet territory.

Even for American Indians who stayed home and in place on their reservations, life following the unbelievable extinction of the buffalo and confinement to the reservation became a bewildering struggle in which spiritual rejection, want, and actual starvation figured prominently. Two Leggings, again, said it best: "Nothing happened after that. We just lived."[23] Spopee's story too breaks off. What was there to say? He chose silence, for there was nothing to say, nothing to tell and no one to tell it to. There were no listeners, animate or inanimate, real or spiritual—no one who understood. Spopee was still there, but his story had come to an end. And although he tried to touch his former life, momentarily, by writing to his wife, he also revealed his view that things had stopped happening when pitifully he dictated to an unknown scribe, "I have nothing important at present."

It is no wonder that after the commotion of the Helena trial he had become mute, depressed, and dejected—in a sense, he ceased to be. No wonder that prison officials in Detroit had described his state as one of melancholia. Nothing could continue in the same way after he left the Helena jail for the Detroit House of Correction, and the break was made even sharper in Washington, D.C. The distance was greater. Nothing made sense or mattered. Nothing significant could happen.

Mental asylums, of course, were supposed to slow the bewildering tempo of life. The speed, stress, tension, struggle, and complexity associated with "civilization" were deemed to be the major causes of insanity in the first place; individuals had to "get away," to "find asylum," to experience a "retreat." Once away, patients were to be isolated, protected from "the dangers loose in the community," from the distorting reach and stress of friends, family, and others.[24] What solace the asylum could be with its structured order and predictability is revealed by Anna Agnew, an inmate at the Indiana Hospital for the Insane. In 1878 she observed, "This place reminds me of a great clock, so perfectly regular and smooth in its workings. The system is perfect, our bill of fare is excellent, and varied, as in any well-regulated family. . . . We retire at the ringing of the telephone at eight o'clock, and an hour later, there's darkness and silence . . . all over this vast building."[25]

How the pendulum's tempo slowed in Spopee's case remains a mystery. His earliest patient record at St. Elizabeths is a letter dated August 1, 1882, from the Department of the Interior, Office of Indian Affairs, to Dr. Godding, St. Elizabeths' medical superintendent. The federal authorities informed Dr. Godding that the department had received "satisfactory evidence" that "Spopee alias Turtle, a convict, who was placed in the House of Correction at Detroit Michigan, under the laws of the United States is insane." Dr. Godding was then authorized by the secretary of the department to admit Spopee under the provisions of Section 4852, of the Revised Statutes of the United States.[26] The statute in question had to do with persons convicted of a crime who had become insane while imprisoned and provided that "upon the application of the Attorney-General the Secretary of the Interior . . . be authorized and directed to transfer to the Government Hospital for the Insane in the District of Columbia all persons who during the term of their imprisonment have or shall become and be insane." Other than asserting "satisfactory evidence," there is no indication as to how or why the determination was made; there was no accompanying diagnosis, no disciplinary record that would account for the determination so soon after Spopee's arrival in Detroit. Had he been difficult to handle or manage, was he threatening or despondent and depressed? There is no record.

Upon Spopee's admission at the Government Hospital for the Insane, his age was listed as thirty-three years, and his diagnosis,

under the category of "Mental Disease," printed on the admission
form, read, "Chronic Mania." The response to the heading "Supposed Cause" featured one word: "Exposure." What was meant by
this cryptic note is unclear. Did it refer to the natural world of wind
and weather, storm and below-zero temperatures common on the
northern plains and especially in the worn and tattered hide lodges
of nomadic camps? Or was it an exposure of a different kind, the
exposure that came from a dark, overcrowded, and violent prison
situation? And if the former, was this diagnosis an opinion as to the
cause of Spopee's affliction, or speculation based on romantic delu-
sion? We do not know. Other headings on the form included "Du-
ration on Admission," after which had been entered the response,
"1 Year."[27]

At the very end of Spopee's incarceration, in a conference report
dated May 11, 1914, hospital officials noted that upon his admission,
August 9, 1882, there was no family or personal history other than
that Spopee was age thirty-three and an "Indian, Indigent Convict"
who was admitted from the House of Corrections in Detroit, Michigan, "where he was serving a life sentence for homicide." As for
marital status, Spopee was listed as single, although at the bottom of
the page under "Addresses of friends" it was incongruously noted:
"Wife: Tharhibuski, or One-Who-Swims-Under-the-Water, c/o H. S.
Young, Piegan, Choteau Co., Mont."[28]

As late as May 11, 1914, hospital officials were still of the opinion that no personal information or medical record could be obtained from the patient "owing to his limited knowledge of the
English language and the extreme difficulty which is experienced
in making the patient understand what is said to him."[29] This excuse had been a perennial one, repeated again and again, to account for the absence of any information of a clinical nature on his
charts. The only significant information from the earliest years is
contained in a letter from Dr. Godding in 1883, where he stated,
"the patient is as a rule quiet and well behaved, but when his delusional ideas become marked he seems somewhat depressed."
Other than that, Spopee's file at the hospital before 1901 is empty.
The only exception is the surprising existence of a few touching
personal letters he had either exchanged or attempted to exchange

with his wife, One-Who-Goes-Under-the-Water, after admission in Washington, D.C.

The first, dated October 24, 1882, was from "One-Who-Goes-Under-the-Water" and was postmarked "Piegan, Montana," sent from the Blackfeet agency on Badger Creek. She had dictated the letter to one of the Blackfeet agent's grown children, H. S. Young, who had in turn translated and written her words out on paper. The small letter began, "My Dear Husband. Some friends from the north told me that you had written two letters saying that you would be out in a year or two and wanted me to be in Canada with your mother when you came. I want you to write to me very soon and tell me if this true. If you are not coming back I will send the children to your mother as we are very poor. Your brother was killed about a year ago and we miss his support. Big Lake is taking care of the baby. One of his wives is a relation of mine." In other words, One-Who-Goes-Under-the-Water had not given the baby to just "another Squaw," as stated in her earlier letter to Spopee (see chapter 4), but had given him to a relative. She had done so because of her striated conditions as well as because the relative had just lost her own baby. One-Who-Goes-Under-the-Water then informed her husband that "Painted Wing (with whom we live) is the only relation who takes any care of us. Write to me soon."[30]

Late the following spring, in June 1883, a second letter arrived for Spopee, this time addressed to Dr. Godding. "Will you be so kind as to inform the Indian 'Spo-pee' that his wife, One-Who-Swims-Under-the-Water, previous to the receipt of your letter, had supposed him to be dead. It was a comfort to her to hear otherwise. She is lonesome without him and the four years he has been away seems a long time to her. His little girl 6 years old died about a month ago, after a long illness. His wife and his mother Owa-cus-ah-kee (Antelope Woman) are living together.[31] She is very grateful for your kindness in writing to her of her husband's condition." Again, the letter was written for Spopee's wife by H. S. Young, and the envelope was stamped "Washington, January 2, 1884, dead letter."[32]

Little wonder that One-Who-Goes-Under-the-Water thought Spopee to be dead. Two of Montana Territory's most prominent papers, the *Helena Daily Herald* and the *Fort Benton River Press*, reported that "Spopee, the Piegan Indian who murdered Chas. Warmley in 1880 and whose death sentence was commuted to imprisonment for life, died in the Detroit House of Correction about a month ago. Our citizens will remember this case. Spopee was to have been hung at the same time with Pelkey, the murderer of Chas. Tacke, but his sentence was commuted by President Hayes. Good Rider, arrested as an accomplice, was acquitted."[33] This information, relayed among the Piegan by word of mouth from camp to camp, via the so-called "moccasin telegraph," probably reached Spopee's wife in one of the bands, whether on the Blackfeet Reservation or in Canada with the Bloods, apparently confirming her worst fears.

Finally, the file contains Spopee's own soulful last letter to his wife. It is dated June of 1884, dictated, of course, to an unknown person who then attempted to turn Spopee's crude and broken English, often helped by sign language, into a comprehensible letter. His words, revealing his growing sense of despair and isolation, began: "Compliments to you my dear wife," before reminding her that already he had written to her three times, "but received know answer." He wanted to know why this was so and asked about his little boy and how the two of them were doing. "I have much to relate to you if ever we meet again in this life," he explained. "You must write me an immediate Answer if possible. I have nothing important at present, so think of me far away. Give my respect to friends. The Doctor don't understand my language. When you write sind [sic] your letter in care of Doctor Stocks, medical physcianer. I have some hard custermers having unable to speak plain English. Remember me. Yours, Spopee, Snake."[34]

So far as is known, with this letter the sporadic, pitiful efforts of Spopee and his wife to stay in touch with each other come to an end. Both had to cope with their own deteriorating, if not desperate, situations alone. One-Who-Goes-Under-the-Water and her children lived in a bewildering world of inchoate reservation life, sedentary and confined. Hunkered down along multiple water courses, in scattered clusters of hastily constructed log cabins, everyone waited. Everywhere there was hunger, if not actual starvation, and the grinding poverty of confined and total dependence. Spopee too was confined and alone in a foreign place, not only buried in the institutional environment of the asylum but also without speech or comprehension, cut off from whatever had been meaningful, unable to make decisions, bereft of hope or intention.

The experience of other deranged and delusional patients such as Anna Agnew offers some insight into how Spopee might have reacted in these undocumented years. In a sense the institution of St. Elizabeths took over, wrapping Spopee in the embrace of its meticulous routines, its protective patterns of sleep, supervision, restraint, and, increasingly, occupational therapy. Seasons changed, new physicians came on board, ward assignments shifted, but the great efficient clock, so regular and reliable, so mechanical and remorseless, prevailed. If the moral treatment represented therapy or initiated an improvement in the patient's well-being, it was often through their exposure to this discipline. Spopee, the independent Blood warrior who had counted his Kootenai coup and killed Charles Walmesley, slowly ceased to exist, and with that gradual erasure, a quieter Spopee could let go of his former identity, the good humored joking and familiar noises of the camps, and move into a reduced, but still insistent present.

With the years, the voices of the past slipped away. Living must have gotten easier. Generally the daily life in the asylum and on the hospital's farm was an orderly, if not monotonous, affair. Spopee worked in the tailor shop, he gardened and did farm work, helping to support the complicated functioning of the hospital. These activities were thought to be therapeutic. Spopee did not object. On weekends Washingtonians visited the asylum, interrupting the daily routines and strolling through the manicured gardens with their narrow gravel paths as if they were inside a most magnificent park; or they visited the cramped wards with their numerous patients. Sometimes the visitations took the shape of an exercise in moral rectitude or responsibility as they walked past patients slumped over in their chairs, oblivious to the passing parade. It other cases, visitors looked forward to the titillating possibility of viewing the antics of the mad or anticipating the threat of an emotional outburst. Both were condoned. These visits were seen as a form of public involvement in a public institution, or as a citizens' safeguard, a way of making sure that the patients were clean and cared for, and that they

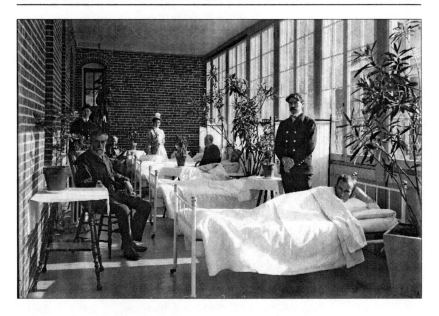

St. Elizabeths Hospital, Allison Sun Parlor, 1910. (Reproduced from the
Blackburn Laboratory Archives at St. Elizabeths Hospital and the National
Archives and Records Administration, 418-G-15.)

were not being abused. Politicians and citizens alike availed themselves of this welcome diversion, hiding their morbid curiosity and
self-congratulatory smugness under a screen of concern. Sundays
were busy with such events and other entertainments. Spopee, as
a "wild Indian" from the Wild West, had to have been an object of
considerable interest.

While Spopee's medical records, periodic evaluations, behavioral
observations, notes, ward records, and work assignments are absent,
or, more likely, were never recorded, his list of housing assignments
and the appropriate dates over the years are remarkably complete.
At the top of the list there is his name, "Spopee alias Turtle," then
under "Organization:" his affiliation, "Indian Convict," and the
date he was admitted, August 9, 1882. His first housing assignment
was to West Lodge No. 2, where he stayed for six years before being
transferred to Grey Ash on June 3, 1888, and four months after that to
the well-known Howard Hall, No. 1, on October 30. The subsequent

listing of his housing transfers, and there were many, fills a very detailed page.[35] There were periods when Spopee would be transferred up to five times in a single year—the year 1900, for example. No reasons, institutional or personal, are given for these shifts, but Spopee must have found them disruptive, and it is hard to imagine them contributing to his sense of security and self-determination.

Still, by all accounts Spopee's life at the hospital was quiet and uneventful. In 1903, after he had been incarcerated for years, a new medical superintendent, Dr. William Alanson White, was appointed to St. Elizabeths. He injected a new spirit of scientific inquiry into the causes of mental illness and insisted upon more research. Not surprisingly, there was a rise in the quality of medical attention. He tried to move away from mechanical restraints and compulsion, brought greater organization into the hospital, and created a humane blend of old and new. In spite of the changes and St. Elizabeths' growing size and complexity, the hospital remained much as it had been. Routines remained entrenched, and more often, as can be seen in the extant records, Spopee's lengthy confinement amounted to little more than a benign custodial care.

Dr. White, for example, wrote retrospectively about Spopee in the following terms: "During his entire sojourn here the patient has been of exemplary habits, quiet in behavior, and has at no time exhibited any vicious or harmful tendencies. For a great number of years he enjoyed the privilege of parole of the grounds and did some light work in our vineyard and on the lawns."[36] At the bottom of the page appears the comment that there were no recorded visitors or correspondence.

After June of 1901, official documents known as "ward notes" came into use. These observations were jotted down routinely by what appear to have been ward attendants, who were responsible for measuring vital signs, administering already prescribed medicines, recording information on individual patient charts, and generally helping patients to cope with the routines of the institution.

Spopee's file for that year harbors three short, but interesting, mentions. June 30 bears the notation that Spopee "went to work in the garden, paroled." The second declared he had been transferred to Akins Hall, and the third, the December entry, noted that Spopee had quit work for some time past and "was found selling clothing to colored people." He did so while working in the sewing room, and the file states that "he was in the habit of repairing old clothing given him by various employees, which he then sold to the colored people around the grounds."[37]

By the spring of 1904, at least for a short time, Spopee was no longer free to go where he wanted inside the protective walls of the asylum. On April 9 the superintendent had issued a general order that discontinued the "parole of all criminal patients," and Spopee was "transferred from Relief-5 to Howard Hall-8." This prohibition did not, however, keep him from being employed out in the grounds; it just ended his parolee status. The ward attendant, this time in full sentences, also helpfully observed, "At that time he was noticed to be in the same condition in which he had been for years, didn't understand or speak English very well, and it was difficult, therefore, to detect any delusions if present."[38] Later that year there appeared a note stating that Spopee was "somewhat discontented at times," and by November he was often talking, obviously in English, of going home, although he "shows no violence, if not interfered with."[39]

One of the most telling observations among the ward notes came in 1905. The ward attendant revealed that the "physician's note states there has been no change in his condition for years" and then offered his own evaluation. "Being an Indian and not being able to speak much English it is somewhat difficult to understand him, although he gives no trouble and works in the work room." Clinically "he seems to be well oriented for person, but not for time or place."

Another personal peculiarity of Spopee's emerges in this report. It has to do with money. Money compelled Spopee's attention, fascinated him, and endlessly provoked him. This idiosyncratic interest in money took two forms. First, as would be noted multiple times, he had a "fondness for collecting five cent pieces and putting them in the shanks of soldiers buttons and then sewing them on his clothes." What at first glance may have been strange to uninformed members of the hospital staff might have been to the Blood Indian from Montana quite natural. Everyone at home decorated their clothing, be it with feathers and animal skins, a perforated stone with seven holes for a star constellation, American coins with portrait busts, colorful beads, peace medals, brass wire, elk's teeth, or dyed porcupine quills. All this was quite common, and it need not have been a sign of Spopee's eccentric behavior. On the other hand, Spopee's other habit of "making money"—that is, of morbidly drawing and replicating paper money and personal checks in pen and ink, and writing or having letters written about his interest in money matters—was truly delusional. According to the ward notes, Spopee made "imitation money and checks and puts the names of some of the hospital officials upon them and gives them to some of-ficials of the institution." Often the checks or bills were for amounts that were equal to the pay of the ward attendants, and Spopee ex-pected to be paid that exact amount. This hobby of making money rendered his interest in collecting and decorating his clothing with coins equally suspect. Still, as one of the attendants noted, "Yet he doesn't give any trouble if he doesn't get it."[40]

Just as bizarre was an extant, albeit undated, letter, ostensibly written in Spopee's own handwriting, in which he addressed one Dr. John E. Toner, asking for money. "Please give me your money said twenty five ($25.00). Me a poor Indian in chief with no money needing all your money or give me six dollars ($6.00) will do. I am a crooked Indian in chief goes. . . . You are a good man however you are a counter feiting money maker. . . . You must give me money. Please give it to me on the holy Sabbath day before your Shadow passes me." Another of these shake-down notes Spopee signed, "yours affectionately, Washington D.C. D2." It began: "oh my heart I would forsake you if you don't grant me as to the money I ask. My head troubles me for no money in the Indian fashion for a long time to wait. Many many & hundreds of thousands days. Million ching bugs [chinch-bugs, Blissus sp.] can creep in the head to wisdom on money matters. You are a nice fellow liberal with your money I suppose. I cling you as the bed tick does for money. Indeed money money & money indeed. Don't forget me."[41] These behaviors per-sisted. The July 1, 1911, comment in the ward notes was typical: Spopee "continues to manufacture paper money which he gives the physician on his daily rounds to give it to Dr. White," the head of the hospital.

Spopee's official file also includes periodic evaluations by a num-ber of physicians. These began in March of 1908, and although these reports generally were better written and a bit more helpful than

U.S. paper money featuring a portrait of Washington, drawn by Spopee. (National Archives and Records Administration, RG 418, St. Elizabeths Hospital, Case File 54465.)

those of the ward attendants, they remained exasperatingly repetitive. "The physical condition of this patient is very good," wrote a doctor with the initials "CRB"—one C. R. Bell, a medical intern. Dr. Bell went on to describe Spopee as "well nourished, strong and active." That part was easy. A mental diagnosis, however, proved beyond him. "The mental examination of this patient is very unsatisfactory. It is very difficult to get an intelligent answer to a question, from lack of knowledge and from the indifference due to his mental disorder. Imagines he has plenty of money—makes it out of pieces of paper. The condition has remained unchanged for some time."[42] Another physician, Dr. Frank H. Dixon, wrote in 1913, "Patient speaks no English. Spends most of his time by himself, drawing pictures, which he calls making money."[43]

During the last decade of Spopee's confinement there were a few revelations that, however skimpy, serve to punctuate the monotonous record. In 1906 and 1907, for example, Spopee "suffered from malarial attacks from which we are told he made good recoveries. He continued in the same habits and exhibited the same traits as previously noted." In the winter of 1908 Spopee experienced an attack of influenza from which he recovered. In 1910, as always, the report has Spopee well behaved and notes that he "willingly assists the attendant with the ward work, and whenever the occasion arises helps them to look after the other patients on the ward. Although it is very difficult to conduct a conversation with him, he gives evidence of being accurately oriented concerning his immediate environment, distinguishes correctly between employes and patients and knows most of the latter by name."

During the summer months Spopee had developed the habit of frequently asking to go home, although he did not describe or locate where that might be or what made it so desirable. In 1911 this desire became more insistent, becoming a complaint: "Says this place no good; wants to go home." Yet Spopee, it was also noted, did not "exhibit any dangerous tendencies" and continued "throughout quite good natured." Doctors complained again and again how hard it was to get an intelligent answer from him regarding his thoughts and concerns. "He is quiet, obedient and orderly. Works, it was reported in the sewing room. Imagines he has plenty of money— makes it out of pieces of paper. The condition has remained unchanged for some time."[44]

Spopee, as noted, also worked outside on the grounds of St. Elizabeths in the informal gardens and the vineyard, and he seemed to enjoy the landscaped nature, thought by contemporaries to be beneficial and calming—a counter, for whites, to the devastating effects of civilization and the chaos of the city that so affected their advanced society.[45] Whether it would do the same for American Indians, so-called primitives or noble savages, was never covered or dealt with because the institutional asylum was not designed with them in mind.

In 1912, standardized and printed ward forms for each month became a part of the record for the first time. They generated comments that were as obscure, repetitive, and habitual as before. "Patient remains in his usual condition, quiet and orderly. Helps with the Light-Ward work daily. . . . Neat and tidy in his habits. Eats and sleeps well." There was, however, as with all subsequent reports, the additional observation that Spopee spent "most of his time in his room making pictures on pieces of paper. Says he is making money to run away with when he gets out and says this place is no good and he wants to go home."[46]

The next month's report is but one short sentence: "No change in this patient's condition since last report." The March 1 report is no different—"Patient remains as usual"—and concludes, "Can see no change in this patient since last report." The August notes are again the same: "Patient quiet and orderly. At this time gives no trouble, helps with the Light-Ward work daily. Tidy in habits and appearance. Appetite good. Bowels regular."[47]

Each month is much the same as the previous—sometimes it is verbatim or the doctor writes, "Can see no change in this patient since last report." Only in the month of October did the ward notes indicate anything different: that Spopee received Quinine, sulfate, Bellodonme.[48] The next year, 1913, is no different, with one notable exception. In February "the patient refused to let the doctor vaccinate him." There is also the note: "Patient has nothing to say to other patients but spends most of his time in making as he calls [it] money[:] taking articles from the newspaper painting them and calling them money."[49] Here and there are other references to medicines, or reports that Spopee would not talk to the other patients but would talk to the attendants, with whom he was very friendly. Finally, during the last days of his confinement, on May 17, 1914, the ward notes reveal the presence of the Blackfeet delegation from Browning, noted earlier, with the cryptic notation "Patient visited by friends from the city."

Dr. John E. Lind, the physician in charge of Howard Hall, may have conducted a number of physical examinations of Spopee in 1913 and 1914; the report of only one, however, is extant. His general comment read: "A well nourished, rather obese Indian male. Height 68-1/4 inches; weight 207-1/2." Dr. Lind's examination revealed that Spopee had a crucifix tattooed on his left forearm, that his teeth were in poor condition with a number missing, his pulse rate was "88 small and firm," and that his sight in both eyes was somewhat impaired. Other notes had to do with tongue color, regularity of bowel movements, condition of stool, and the like. As for Dr. Lind's other comments, they were restricted to Spopee's appetite—"[P]atient is an enormous eater and is very negligent in regard to his bowels, allowing himself to become quite constipated . . . and about once in two weeks he asks for a dose of castor oil." Then in the next line, without pause, there are further comments regarding Spopee's money-making activities, as well as the observation that Spopee also copied sentences found in newspapers, such as the following: "In addition to the admitted assets as given above the company had on October 31, 1912 non admitted assets consisting of subscriptions to the increased capital stock and sur twelve dollars $12.00." According to Dr. Lind, Spopee also traced silver dollars on checks, filled whole check books with checks for five dollars, and wrote out on slips of paper the day's date and the phrase "Wanto. Gohome." This was as close as he came to examining Spopee's mental condition. As for a neurological examination that should have followed the physical examination—one word sufficed: "Negative." Such an examination was not done.

After thirty-two years there was not a lot more to be said about Spopee the person, or about the causes of his insanity or its possible cure. He had grown old and peculiar at St. Elizabeths and would die there. The cemetery there was full of veterans and others who had done the same thing. The accumulation of physical examinations, ward notes, and treatment had been unimaginative, belated, and sporadic. The little information gathered did not bring analysis or insightful recognition of patterns, only a matter-of-fact repetition of previous observations. Spopee had no reason to expect any change, with money or without. There were no more stepping stones ahead of him—in fact, the stones had ended a long time ago. After that nothing had happened.

Miraculously the situation changed in May of 1914. Suddenly Spopee became "an object of interest." So wrote Dr. Bernard Glueck on a conference report, dated May 11, 1914. On the synopsis of record for Spopee, "Diagnosis of Mental disease on admission" was listed as "Chronic Mania," and the "supposed cause" was once again identified as "exposure." At the time of his discharge, an examining panel of five doctors was of the following opinion: "It is difficult to state just what is the matter with the man. He is suffering at present from a certain degree of deterioration, but it is impossible to state whether or not this is original or acquired. I would call it an undifferentiated psychosis." The other doctors, Glascock, O'Malley, Schwinn, and White, agreed.[50]

CHAPTER 7

"The Ends of Justice Have Been Met"

Miraculously, Spopee's confinement to the Government Hospital for the Insane came to an abrupt end in the summer of 1914. Spopee, the once forgotten nonentity, became momentarily an object of intense outside interest. It began, as already noted, with a chance visit to Spopee by two competing Blackfeet delegations from Browning, Montana, who were on business in Washington, D.C. Each represented conflicting political and economic positions as they sought to influence the belated implementation of the General Allotment Act of 1887, which was not completed on the Blackfeet Reservation until 1912. The Blackfeet visit to St. Elizabeths, totally independent of their political agendas, set in motion a cascading sequence of events that would eventually lead to Spopee's release.

The unlikely event began with Mrs. Ella Hamilton Clark, the Blackfoot speaker who first enticed Spopee out of his self-imposed silence in March of 1914, and ended on July 6, 1914, with President Woodrow Wilson issuing Spopee a presidential pardon for his conviction, with an immediate release from the asylum. The story is one of heart-warming redemption, but sad and tragic as well. Ella Clark told it in writing from her personal perspective on her way back home to Montana from Washington. She and her delegate husband, Malcolm, were in central Pennsylvania visiting the Carlisle Indian

School, her husband's alma mater, and her story about Spopee was published that September in the school's publication, *The Red Man*, a monthly magazine.[1] In this article, Clark reported that upon learning the details of Spopee's story, including his territorial trial and incarceration, during her visits to St. Elizabeths, she went directly to Capitol Hill and the office of Cato Sells, who had only recently been appointed commissioner of the Indian Office of the Interior Department. A Texas Democrat and Southern Baptist, Sells later recounted that the facts of this strange case "aroused my immediate interest," and he promised to investigate.[2] True to his word, Sells quickly followed up her unexpected initial visit by ordering a search of the surviving court records in Montana. Then the commissioner, in an accelerated process, "laid this data before the Department of Justice."[3]

Later, in the afterglow of President Wilson's presidential pardon, Commissioner Sells acknowledged Clark's initiative with a personal letter dated July 28, 1914, thanking her for her decisive intervention. "When first advised of the circumstances surrounding his [Spopee's] imprisonment," he wrote, "I became fully convinced that it was so unjust and un-American as to demand the prompt and aggressive action of all who were able to lend him assistance in securing release from his almost worse than death surroundings. But for the discovery of him by your party it is not likely that my attention would have been called to him, and that he would have remained at St. Elizabeth the rest of his life."[4] Subsequently, while submitting his annual report to the secretary of the Interior, Sells again addressed his motivation. "It seemed wholly out of harmony with the genius of American institutions that anyone could be permitted to pay such a terrible penalty for the commission of an offense against our laws, particularly that the punishment should be imposed under the very shadow of the Capitol of this great Democracy."[5]

There is no doubt that Commissioner Sells, following the visit of Ella Clark, became a sympathetic and influential official who decided very early on to champion Spopee. In fact, a presidential pardon of Spopee became a personal priority of the commissioner and his office. Sells took enough interest to interview Spopee himself at the Government Hospital for the Insane and to do so with the help of the Blackfoot interpreter Robert J. Hamilton, a contentious, self-appointed tribal delegate who had remained in Washington to counter the political ambitions of the other delegation, made up of James Perrine, Charles W. Buck, and Mrs. Clark's husband, Malcolm. And while seeking Hamilton's help may have been awkward, given that the initial contact was made with Mrs. Clark, it was necessary because Sells needed to better understand reservation politics as well as Spopee's opaque past. Having done so, he determined a critical central rationale for executive clemency—that the ends of justice had been met—which was eventually successful, liberating Spopee from his sentence of life imprisonment and from St. Elizabeths Hospital.

Commissioner Sells's argument attempted to avoid the technical legal questions of jurisdiction or Spopee's plea of self-defense, focusing instead on his unusual and severe punishment. It seemed to Sells that "without regard to the nature of his crime or the justice of the punishment to which he was sentenced, this Indian had long since paid the penalty for his offense."[6] Sells was incensed at the "unjust and un-American" punishment that had occurred under the American justice system; something had gone wrong that had resulted in a terrible injustice. He thought of it as a blight or blemish and worthy of his direct attention and his best efforts as head of the Office of Indian Affairs. He said he couldn't stop thinking about it. Spopee became a preoccupation.[7]

This was not that surprising, given the new place of Indians in the perceptions of Americans. No longer were they thought of as threatening enemies or reviled as "savages," incapable of cultural progress, caught in a collective, tribal embrace from which there was no escape. As historian Sherry Smith has demonstrated by examining popular writers on Indian themes at the turn of the century, Indians and their cultures, as well as the injustices that had befallen them, had become more interesting to an anxious and nostalgic American public than ever before.[8] Gradually this aroused public interest in and reevaluation of Indians seeped into policy concerns as determined by government officials such as Cato Sells.

In Spopee's case, these important shifts and the proximity of Spopee in his asylum just across the Potomac helped move the application process along. Several days after Spopee's initial encounter with the local attorneys of the Blackfeet delegates, A. R. Serven and A. C. J. Farrel, the *Evening Star* in Washington, D.C., reported that Sells "had already taken active steps to procure a pardon and freedom."[9] The decision to pursue a presidential pardon also appeared in the New York papers. The *Sun*, for example, noted Commissioner Sells's argument that "the crime for which Spo-pe was condemned has been expiated by a penal service of far greater length than the average term of a 'lifer.'"[10] A further justification for his release, according to the commissioner, had to do with the "[t]he extenuating circumstances of his mother having been killed by the troopers in a battle for which the commanding cavalry officer was severely reprimanded."[11] Again and again in the emerging newspaper coverage, reporters linked Spopee's crime to his determination to avenge his mother. "Pious atonement" as the noble or at least the extenuating impetus for the killing of Charles Walmesley only fed the public's interest in the case and enhanced the melodramatic image of the by now old Indian warrior.

Commissioner Sells was the probable author of the idea of a presidential pardon, but there was no doubt that the attempt would be officially made through the pardon attorney and the offices of the attorney general in the Justice Department. Sells was confident that a pardon for Spopee could be obtained, particularly since the secretary of the Interior, Franklin Lane, had received Spopee's documentation and indicated his early support. Blackfeet attorneys Serven and Farrell, knowledgeable Washington political insiders, were also on board and were "pushing with vigor."[12]

Armed with a persuasive rationale and enjoying the support and advice of key officials, Sells set out to mobilize additional help. Much of this came via the expanding newspaper coverage that played upon a renewed and transformed popular interest in Native Americans at the turn of the century, an interest that emphasized their fundamental humanity, their worthy and threatened, if romantic, "otherness," and the injustices of their conquest.[13] But in addition to exploiting this public interest and general sympathy with American Indians, Sells needed solid evidence of what had happened to Spopee. The case would be strengthened with the backing of the Blackfeet on their reservation in northern Montana. Although he had been in office only briefly, Sells recognized that both Spopee in particular and Indian people in general had experienced terrible hardships and alienation in the late nineteenth century and that their decisive incorporation into the dominant society now was both necessary and desirable. Spopee's suffering was not an isolated case, however peculiar. Like Spopee, Indian tribes had been geographically confined and, if not always intentionally, abused and exploited, impeded and ignored. Sells's goal was to use the contemporary, more positive changes in the public perception of Indians to elicit a more sympathetic and just consideration for an individual Indian, Spopee, thought to be demented by white authorities simply because he could not, or did not, communicate.

The progressive commissioner from Texas learned it had not been easy for the Blackfeet after the early 1880s, after the buffalo and the great hunts were gone. Not only had they been confined to their reservation, but their agricultural efforts had also been subject to serial crop failures due to late spring and early fall frosts, their lack of experience, and inept local agents and agency farmers. In addition there was significant miscalculation and corruption among merchant suppliers of government rations and a cumbersome, if not bungling, distant congressional oversight, slow to recognize how desperate and hungry the Blackfeet had become absent the buffalo. These experiences with malnutrition and growing hunger culminated in the "nightmarish years of 1883–1884," when some four to five hundred Southern Piegan, men, women, and children, died miserably from lack of food. Described as the "Starvation Winter," the catastrophic results generated national outrage and investigation.[14]

Given this situation and in an effort to avoid future seasons of horrible want, the Southern Piegan, now numbering around two thousand, agreed to sell to the United States the eastern part of their portion of the reservation they shared with the Gros Ventre, Assiniboine, and Sioux. This sale, which included negotiations with all of the tribes, was conducted by the congressionally appointed Northwest Commission in January and February of 1887 and was meant to "enable them [the Indians] to be self-supporting, as a pastoral and agricultural people, and to educate their children in the path of civilization."[15] The Blackfeet, for their part, referred to the sale as "when we sold the Sweet Grass Hills." Bringing them $150,000 per year for ten years, it allowed them to address their immediate needs and nourished the hope that they could develop a fledgling cattle industry.

Yet hope for the cattle industry was in short supply in 1886–87. This was the "Hard Winter" that broke the speculative back of the open-range approach to raising beef on the northern Plains. Cattle had been pouring into the short-grass Montana ranges following the near extinction of the buffalo and the ranges had become over-grazed, leaving the animals in poor condition even before onset of one of the hardest winters on record. Cattle would have to be raised more carefully and under different conditions in the future, with fences, irrigation, and winter feed.[16] It would not be easy for the Blackfeet stockmen to overcome many of these obstacles.

Ten years after the sale of the Sweet Grass Hills, the tribe's money, administered by the Office of Indian Affairs, was gone. With little to show for their effort and with no other solution at hand, the Black-feet had to repeat the process once more. Once again the Blackfeet had to give way to white demands to reduce the size of their reser-vation and to unwillingly negotiate another land sale. This time, in 1895, they surrendered the so-called ceded strip, the mountainous area from the Continental Divide eastward, which in 1910 became the eastern portion of Glacier National Park. The rationale for the sale was much the same as with the Sweet Grass Hills.[17]

The monies from the sale of these lands were again administered by the Office of Indian Affairs. Bureaucrats in this office were the tribe's government guardians and had sought to secure an economic base for their needy wards. First it had been cattle, then irrigation and agriculture, and then cattle again. None of these economic de-velopment efforts had brought the proverbial flood tide of com-merce that would raise all tribal boats. The coming of the railroads held great promise for cattle—after all, this had been and remained unparalleled grazing land. Dams and irrigation canals brought water and the promise of flourishing hay crops, but short growing seasons, early frosts, and battering winds also brought repeated ag-ricultural failures, discouraging Indian engagement. Just as disqui-eting was the fact that on the reduced reservation, Blackfeet land ownership—legal title—wandered, inexplicably but increasingly, into white hands.

The provisions of the General Allotment Act, often referred to as the Dawes Severalty Act, enacted in February 1887, made this transfer of ownership more pronounced and more threatening. The act contained provisions intended to break up Indian reservations where the tribal land base was held in common ownership, and to allot to individual Indians the equivalent of 320-acre homesteads and no more. Reservation lands left over following the allotment process were deemed surplus, and these, according to the law, reverted to the public domain to be sold to the highest bidder for cash.

If these alarming novelties were not enough, the Blackfeet tribe itself had changed. Intermarriages between Blackfeet and whites resulted in a tribal population that was becoming more mixed-blood than full-blood in lineage, language, and culture. The Blackfeet Reservation already provided multiple opportunities to benefit whites both on and off the reservation. The policy of government wardship had been difficult to effect—too often government officials squandered tribal monies, allowed illegal cattle trespass, leased land to neighboring whites for less than market prices, permitted tribal lands to pass via marriage to whites, and offered preferential treatment for white economic interests, whether local or regional.

The Allotment Act arrived late on the Blackfeet Reservation. Congress did not authorize its implementation there until March 1, 1907, and it was years before officials developed an allotment census and surveyed and plotted the reservation into 320-acre tracts prior to actual assignment to individual Indians, to be held in trust by the federal government. The work was done at a snail's pace, and it was not until 1912 that the process had determined how much land remained in the "surplus" category, where these 156,000 acres were located, and whether or not the surplus lands were watered by the reservation's multiple irrigation projects.

Blackfeet allotment exacerbated previous divisions within the tribe and pitted those supporting the mandated sale of the leftover surplus lands against those opposed. As historian Paul Rosier has convincingly argued, the prospect of this mandated sale split the tribe in two, fathering ongoing and acidic factionalism that corroded any effort at a united political policy. The less adventuresome and more impoverished full-bloods, comfortable with tribal ownership and control, struggled against the mixed-blood population and allied whites, who wished to be freed from the controls and limitations imposed by the federal government in the form of the Office of Indian Affairs. The full-bloods, hoping to block the sale of the surplus lands and to protect their tribal base, organized to oust their new agent, Blackfeet Superintendent Arthur E. McFatridge. The mixed-bloods, led by wealthy cattlemen, defended his administration and pushed hard to commence the sale, thereby opening the eastern half of the reservation to settlement and economic development. The resulting factionalism on the reservation left no one out. There was no neutral ground. The projected sale of the "surplus" reservation lands colored every decision. It was a tangled mess in which both sides took their legal cases to Congress in the form of delegations, signed petitions, official inquiries, and scandalous charges.[18]

News of Spopee's discovery and tragic plight broke into this turbulent and clashing world of determined Blackfeet rivalries. The contending delegates, the battling reservation coalitions representing numerous concerns and families, and the supervising government officials of the Blackfeet agency were at first reluctant to say or act negatively in the Spopee affair for fear of public reaction. All would cooperate to try and bring this case of obvious injustice to a successful resolution. If anyone suspected that they might be able to use the unexpected national interest in Spopee to their own advantage, as they had used other issues and other events, they kept it to themselves. This included McFatridge, who aggressively promoted the allotment process and the selling of surplus lands favored by the prosperous mixed-bloods and allied business interests.[19]

Commissioner Cato Sells's position regarding these contentious allotment issues has been described as "conventional."[20] In his first annual report to the secretary of the Interior, for example, Sells confessed, "[I]t is my fixed purpose to bring about the speedy individualization of the Indian"—coded language for getting rid of wardship and dependency in favor of private property, individual homesteads, freedom from federal restrictions, and full assimilation into the dominant culture.[21]

Arthur E. McFatridge, superintendent, Blackfeet Agency, 1910–15. (Courtesy Helen Chase and Keith Partell, author's collection, no. 1477.)

Living up to his early promise to Ella Clark, Sells wrote to Superintendent McFatridge as early as April 22, asking him to investigate the Spopee case. Tipping his hand, Sells indicated to McFatridge that he and the Washington office were interested in applying for a presidential pardon. Sells wanted information from certain reservation elders who may have had some contact with Spopee, or from those who knew about the events in question, including the Baker massacre in 1870, and whether or not Spopee's mother had been among those killed on the Marias. He also inquired about the availability of whatever court records might be extant.

There was due diligence. McFatridge, uncharacteristically, replied to Commissioner Sells less than a week later. He admitted that of the names Sells had suggested, prompted by either the delegation or by Spopee himself, he had been able to speak only with Mountain Chief, who happened to be in the agency office in Browning when McFatridge received the request.[22] The rest of the individuals Sells had proposed resided in the scattered full-blood communities and were too far away from the agency headquarters to be reached on short notice. He promised, however, that he would attend to the matter in the near future.

But McFatridge already had learned many of the details of the 1879 murder of Charles Walmesley by poking about in the agent records on file in the agency office in Browning. These included copies of Agent Young's outgoing correspondence. Most of the particulars therein were reasonably accurate. These included how the two Indians, Spopee and Good Rider, had "concealed his [Walmesley's] body under a wagon, after having taken the wheels off the wagon near a bluff, and made an effort to cover the wagon over by the caving of the bluff." In addition, McFatridge assured Commissioner Sells that he had written "to the Clerk of the Court at Helena requesting that he furnish me information relative to the trial" and would forward that material on to Washington as soon as he received it. McFatridge also indicated that although Spopee was a Blood Indian from southern Alberta, he did have a daughter living on the Blackfeet Reservation. Her name was Mary Takes Gun, but she went by Minnie. McFatridge had not yet spoken to her about her father because at the time of the murder she was a very small girl and he did not think she knew anything. He doubted as well that "she knew that her father is still living."[23]

McFatridge's speedy compliance was uncommon. He had been notoriously unresponsive to Washington, D.C., inquiries in the past, and more significantly, he was under investigation by the Office of Indian Affairs, as well as having been the object of an official inquiry in February before a Joint Commission of Congress regarding agency corruption and rampant reports of malnutrition and starvation among the full-bloods in the southern portions of the reservation.[24] In the "Digest of Charges Against Arthur McFatridge," Chief Inspector E. B. Linnen of the Office of Indian Affairs pointed out that the records of McFatridge's administration "contained many instances of his failure to answer Office letters" in spite of repeated requests, and that in other instances he answered them only after considerable delay.[25] On April 13, 1914, in a "Memoranda for Commissioner Sells," the inspector was of the opinion that "it appears beyond any question of doubt that Superintendent McFatridge is not an office man and is not a man of good administrative capacity. He has repeatedly neglected to answer important correspondence with this Office and has neglected important matters."[26] There were many other charges as well. The local criticism reflected to some degree the political struggle on the reservation over the mandated sale of the surplus reservation lands. As noted above, this issue, as well as conditions on the reservation, had festered as factions jockeyed for political advantage or control, both on the reservation and through maneuverings in Washington. Already on the defensive in both places and not wanting to compound his current troubles, McFatridge kept his head down and quickly complied with Commissioner Sells's request.

In spite of this mounting pressure, McFatridge was stubbornly independent where he could be. He was by no means convinced of Spopee's innocence, nor was he overly eager to support Sells in securing a pardon for Spopee. While he agreed with the commissioner that Spopee had "certainly been severely punished for the crime committed by him," confined as he had "been for 32 years in the hospital for insane without having an opportunity to converse with any person speaking his own language," he believed that had little to do with his guilt or innocence. In fact, he wrote, "those whom I have talked to relative to the matter, who knew both Walmesley and Spo-pe, state that Walmesley was an exceptionally good man, and that Spo-pe was a man whose reputation was bad."[27] Moreover, he put no stock in the view, then current, that Spopee had murdered in order to revenge his mother's killing by a white man at the Baker massacre in 1870. The superintendent was aware of the "old Indian belief, that the soul of the mother who met death through violence could not repose in peace until her death had been avenged by one of her relatives," but he was convinced that in this case, Spopee murdered in order to "secure the money that Walmesley had on his person at the time."[28] Given this situation and in spite of the commissioner's obvious interest, McFatridge did not want to make a recommendation to the president. Calling it a "pathetic case," he did, however, agree that because "the ends of justice have been fully met," he would offer no objection "should an application be made to the President for his pardon."[29] That was as far as he was willing to go.

In the meantime, McFatridge had informed Minnie Takes Gun, Spopee's daughter, that her father was not dead but very much alive in Washington and had told her something of his circumstances. We know this because two days after McFatridge's letter to the commissioner's office, writing through a translator, she too sent a letter, via McFatridge, addressed to Commissioner Sells. She told him that she had just learned that her father, Spopee, who she thought had died years ago, was in fact living as a patient in St. Elizabeths Hospital for the Insane and that he had been there for over thirty years. Her purpose in communicating was to "plead" with Commissioner Sells to use his best efforts to secure Spopee's release. Giving a bit of background, Takes Gun pointed out that at the time he was sent away she was an infant and did not remember anything about him. Now she was thirty-five, married, and "aside from a sister of his who lives in Canada, I think I am the only relative he has living." She remarked that Spopee must be a very old man, and further stated, as if she had been coached as to the situation and the necessary rationale, that "as he has been confined in that institution for so many years away from his people, being unable to speak the English language, it seems to me that he has been justly punished for any crime he may have committed."[30] Mrs. Takes Gun concluded by saying, "I am very anxious that my father be released in order that he might spend his old days with me, his only child, in order that I may care for him and be of some comfort to him during the last few years of his life."[31]

The next week, on May 4, McFatridge reported that George Sproule, clerk of the U.S. Court in Helena, had furnished him with all the information in the case that he could find. These data were among the old territorial records that had been sent over to Sproule's office when the court was organized in 1890.[32] McFatridge then sent the documents in question to Washington and the Office of Indian Affairs. McFatridge went on to deal with the death of Spopee's mother, informing Sells that "there is a difference of opinion of the people who are acquainted with these people, some saying that Spo-pe's mother was not killed at the Baker Massacre, but died near

Fort Benton, Montana. Others have advised me that the mother of these Indians is still living in Canada. I have as yet to verify the statements, and am only giving you what I have learned upon investigation."[33] It was clearly difficult to discern the situation in 1914. However, in 1882 One-Who-Goes-Under-the-Water, Spopee's wife, had written to Spopee at the Government Hospital for the Insane, indicating that his mother was still alive in Canada and that she, his wife, would be sending the children to her if Spopee was not coming back. In any case, according to most of the evidence, Spopee's mother had not been killed on the Marias River during the Baker massacre.[34]

Then McFatridge, who earlier had declined to make a recommendation, informed the commissioner that he had changed his mind. "After making a more careful investigation, I am of the opinion that this man has been justly punished and that the ends of justice have been met."[35] This change of heart, probably prompted by the momentum in the Office of Indian Affairs and McFatridge's investigations, elicited a telegram on May 7 from the commissioner's office. In it, Sells informed McFatridge: "Am about to ask for his [Spopee] pardon and if you favor same will thank you to at once send me your formal recommendation addressed to the President. Also want court record of indictment and conviction."[36] McFatridge responded the next day with a detailed letter, acknowledging receipt of the telegram and enclosing his recommendation to the president. Three days earlier McFatridge already had forwarded the court records, such as he was able to find, and he alerted the commissioner that they would probably arrive before the receipt of his letter dated the seventh.

McFatridge's closing paragraph spoke to a new issue. "In the event that Spo-pe is granted a pardon, it will no doubt be necessary to send him home with an escort as, I am of the opinion, he would be unable to travel the distance from Washington to this place alone. If the Office decides to return him at government expense with an escort, I have the honor to request authority to visit Washington on matters pertaining to this reservation, and if permitted to come to Washington, I could bring Spo-pe back to the reservation with me upon my return."[37]

The superintendent was not the only one offering to accompany Spopee home to Browning. His political nemesis on and off the reservation, Robert J. Hamilton, was already in Washington and had been, as a fluent Blackfoot speaker, able to communicate with Spopee, very involved in his discovery and promotion—more so really than the Blackfeet delegation, represented by James Perrine, Charles Buck, and the Clarks, who, with the exception of Ella Clark, took no pronounced position with respect to Spopee. Hamilton too offered his services to escort Spopee to Browning—as early as May 1. Representing the full-blood faction against the sale of the surplus lands, Hamilton had come to the Capitol to be a pivotal witness against McFatridge, his reservation administration, and his allies, represented by the Blackfeet delegation. The occasion had been the hearings of the Joint Commission of Congress called to investigate conditions on the Blackfeet Reservation.[38]

Interestingly enough, Hamilton, also known as Bobtail, had been either fathered by or adopted and raised by the trader A. B. Hamilton (Ella Clark's father), who had been the official interpreter at Spopee's trial in Helena. Hamilton later attended and graduated from Carlisle Indian School in Pennsylvania. Although of mixed ancestry, he was a fluent Blackfoot speaker who had married into a traditional family and who sought repeatedly to help and represent the majority of the full-bloods on the reservation, who remained committed to collective tribal authority and ownership of reservation lands.[39]

Hoping to prevent the sale of the reservation's surplus lands and improve the tribe's dismal living conditions, Hamilton had forcefully led the full-blood opposition against the mixed-bloods, who had the support of McFatridge. The long-standing struggle and finger-pointing, combined with deplorable reservation conditions and McFatridge's alleged malfeasance, had resulted in the congressional hearings in Washington during February of 1914. As the hearings began, Hamilton faced accusations tendered by the Blackfeet Tribal Council that he was "acting without proper authority from the tribe."[40] For his part, Hamilton had waved a tribal resolution and a letter from the acting commissioner of Indian Affairs authorizing him to act as a Blackfeet delegate.[41] With these bona fides in place, Hamilton argued that he was the legitimate representative of the reservation community. Following his critical testimony at the congressional hearings, he had remained in Washington to counter the influence of the opposing delegation of mixed-blood stockmen, Perrine, Buck, and Clark. Something of a political gadfly who had learned early on the power of the pen, he was frequently looking for tribal and federal monies to support his extensive political activities on behalf of his constituents.

In this case, Hamilton wrote Commissioner Sells about accounts he had submitted for his travel expenses as an unofficial, alternate tribal delegate. His requests for funding had been previously denied. Interrupting his presentation, and well aware of Sells's interest, Hamilton said of Spopee: "If it is possible," he wrote, "I would like to take Spopee home with me. I feel that his return to his people will be one of the historic events of the Blackfeet tribe, as well as of your administration. I would like to assist you in this event. I promised the daughter that [I] would learn about him this trip, and I should like to take him to her."[42]

Sells wasted no time in responding. He invited Hamilton's attention to earlier correspondence and telegrams, stating that his office would not "receive or pay expenses of [any] delegation unauthorized by the Office." Tribal funds were not to be expended. As late as February 11, Sells had written that it was not "deemed necessary for a delegation of the Blackfeet Tribe to visit Washington, either at their personal expense or at tribal expense." No authority had been granted to Hamilton, and the claim was summarily denied.[43] Then, seeing in Hamilton's desire to take Spopee home to Browning another ruse for staying longer in Washington at official expense, Sells informed Hamilton: "[Y]ou are advised that it will take some time before Spopee's case can be properly looked into and it is, therefore, not advisable for you to remain in Washington for this purpose."[44]

This rebuff did not faze Hamilton. Doggedly, he continued to write letters as he had before. Seemingly unsolicited, he also wrote directly to the president of the United States petitioning Spopee's pardon. Continuing to designate himself as a "Delegate Blackfeet Tribe of Indians," which was highly questionable, Hamilton asked that President Wilson "give the matter attention to the end that this Indian, now sixty-five years of age, may return to the Blackfeet

Reservation, Montana, to meet his daughter who survives him, and that he may not longer suffer unjustly."[45]

The White House staff referred this petition to the Department of Interior, rather than its subordinate, the Office of Indian Affairs. Responding, the Department of the Interior asked the Government Hospital for the Insane for information as to the date of Spopee's commitment, as well as for a statement regarding his present mental condition. The hospital administration took this request from across town seriously. On May 10, Dr. Bernard Glueck, a psychiatrist "on the Howard Hall Service for the Criminally Insane," who knew Spopee, examined him and reviewed the case (number 5445). Spopee was deemed "to be quite well oriented in all respects, except for time" and to be "clean and tidy in habits and willingly performs the work assigned him on the ward." However, according to Dr. Glueck it was "quite impossible to get any information regarding delusions and hallucinations." When he asked Spopee how he felt, for example, Spopee said, "Crazy, all crazy."[46]

The following day Dr. Glueck presented an abbreviated history of Spopee's case to an assembled four-person medical board that included the hospital's medical superintendent, Dr. William White. Glueck wrote, "No family or personal history obtainable from the patient, owing to the marked lack of knowledge of the English language and the extreme difficulty which is experienced in making the patient understand what is said to him." The summary of May 14 included the results of a physical examination, which showed Spopee to be in very good physical health. As to a diagnosis, Dr. Glueck suggested and the board agreed, as did the medical superintendent, that his problem should be called an "undifferentiated psychosis," evidently meaning "an unidentifiable psychosis," and that "there is no reason from our stand point why he should not go back to his home."[47]

Since psychiatric diagnosis then, as now, relied on patients to self-report their symptoms, it was difficult to proceed. Talk therapy was not an option with Spopee; there was little to do but to describe outward manifestations. Dr. White, in his own evaluation, informed the secretary of the Interior that "there is no question at all but that the man is suffering from a psychosis, but owing to his very limited

Dr. William A. White. (Photograph by Harris & Ewing. Reproduced from the Blackburn Laboratory Archives at St. Elizabeths Hospital and the National Archives and Records Administration.)

knowledge of English it is impossible to definitely classify the same."[48] He also admitted that because of the language barrier, "we were at no time able to make a thorough mental examination of the patient, but from observing his conduct and actions it is quite certain that the patient is suffering from a defective mental state which is either original with him since birth or has developed secondary to a mental disorder from which he has suffered during the early days at this institution."[49] Translation: They did not know what was wrong with Spopee—it was indeed an "undifferentiated psychosis."

This information was then forwarded to the Department of Interior. Previously, Commissioner Sells had written to the secretary of the Interior, Franklin Lane, that he was considering "the advisability of suggesting executive clemency in the case of Spo-pe." At that time Sells also registered a good many questions that he hoped to pose to the Government Hospital for the Insane regarding Spopee's physical and mental condition. These included "the treatment followed in his case, the method by which communication was had with him . . . and his knowledge, if any, of the English language, the effect of his mental condition on his ability to communicate, and how often and at what times he had been visited by persons who understood his language and could communicate with him." These sound suspiciously similar to the questions later posed by the Department of Interior.

All of this came together on May 16, when Secretary Lane summarized the panoply of documentation and investigations regarding Spopee in a lengthy letter for the attorney general, James C. McReynolds. By this time the assembled statements included the plea of Minnie Takes Gun, the favorable recommendation of Blackfeet Superintendent McFatridge, Robert Hamilton's letter to President Wilson, Dr. White's psychiatric evaluation, and most importantly, the thorough investigations of Commissioner of Indian Affairs Cato Sells.[50] Secretary Lane stated that Sells had made a personal two-hour visit to the hospital in addition to his other investigations of the case, and that although Sells did not "care to question the justice or legality of this Indian's punishment he asks a careful examination of the files of your office as to the facts upon which the commutation of this Indian's sentence by the President on April 12, 1881, was based." What Sells concentrated on was how Spopee had been taken away from any contact with "members of his race and people capable of communication with him"; how no one at the Detroit House of Correction or at St. Elizabeths had any knowledge of his language or customs; how he had never once been visited by any member of his tribe or, again, anyone else capable of communicating with him.[51]

As a result of these circumstances, Sells thought that Spopee had been subjected to a "practically continuous solitary confinement, a punishment not contemplated by the laws of the United States or of any State for crime." Sells was of the opinion that Spopee had "paid to society the penalty due for the crime he committed," and that the case was one that should be brought to the attention of the president for the exercise of "his mercy and executive clemency."[52]

Commissioner Sells, however, expressed a critical caveat. While he certainly recommended the presidential pardon, he did not "deem it advisable to recommend that this Indian be granted his freedom at this time." Sells was concerned about the reports from the Government Hospital for the Insane regarding Spopee's mental condition. Instead of granting Spopee his immediate freedom, he wanted to transfer Spopee to the recently established Indian Insane Asylum at Canton, South Dakota. There, Spopee could be "placed under the observation of men particularly skilled in the study of Indian psychology and with special knowledge of the aberrations peculiar to the Indians and their environment."[53] Convinced that a more comprehensive mental examination was in order, and also politically cautious, Sells offered his final thoughts. If after appropriate observation, he wrote, "and if it is determined that the Indian is harmless and can be safely returned to his people, such action can be taken." This presentation of the commissioner's case by his administrative superior, Secretary Lane, concluded with Lane "heartily" agreeing with Sells's recommendation and a request that the attorney general join them with the understanding that Spopee would be transferred to the Indian Insane Asylum in South Dakota.[54]

Spopee's mental condition was indeed a problem. It had been a concern for some time. He was not angry, nor had he hurt anyone. He was mild mannered and tractable, and in Dr. White's considered opinion, "[Spopee] has been of exemplary habits, quiet in his behavior and has at no time exhibited any vicious or harmful tendencies." Dr. White concluded that Spopee "would not be a menace to the community outside of the institution." Nonetheless, Spopee did exhibit what many had thought of as bizarre behaviors and had done so for a long time. These had included what Dr. White called "quite childish behavior," and White pointed out that Spopee had "always shown a tendency to decorate himself." In addition, the psychiatrist continued, Spopee had for a number of years been "in the habit of printing imitation checks and paper money which he every once in a while turns over to the physician in charge and in the value of which he fully believes."[55]

In a June letter to President Wilson, Catherine MacLennan, a former clerk in the Department of Interior, explained that in April she had become acquainted with Spopee and interested in his case.[56] Under her previous surname of Gallagher, MacLennan had been recognized by President Taft and was well known for her initiative in "having a law passed making discrimination against men in uniforms in public places of entertainment a misdemeanor." Recently remarried to Russell M. MacLennan, Washington correspondent of the *New York Evening Telegram,* she continued her altruistic interests with Spopee's case, although exactly how that happened is undocumented.[57]

Catherine MacLennan's interest was such that she made five visits to the Government Hospital for the Insane in the company of Hamilton, who interpreted for her, and would continue her support for Spopee until he left for Browning. MacLennan's letter attempted to explain to the president why Spopee had chosen silence and to relate how compelling she had found his testimony in Blackfoot. She was also of the opinion that many of the statements of the medical board at the hospital had been flawed because they had failed, like those of so many former officials, to make any effort to seek the aid of an interpreter. One of the issues she hoped to explain had to do with how Spopee came to print imitation checks and how innocent that activity was. In fact, Spopee had presented her with some of his artwork. He began this enterprise, according to her, when he saw some of the hospital employees preparing checks for the disbursing officer and wanted to do the same. One of the employees kindly furnished him "with a set of rubber type and pad and [he] was told to pick the numbers and letters out, using newspapers and magazines for copy." Spopee also copied freehand script without knowing what the words meant. Mrs. MacLennan wanted the president to realize that—contrary to the assertions of the medical board that Spopee fully believed in the worth of this "money"—"he has no idea of the use of checks. He simply knows that the receipt of these pieces of paper by the employees makes them feel happy."[58]

There were other voices with questions. James A. Finch, the pardon attorney in the Department of Justice, who had reluctantly visited the hospital at the behest of Spopee's supporters, reported to the attorney general on June 25 that he too was surprised that Spopee's recent examination to test his sanity had been done without the assistance of an interpreter. This was particularly noteworthy, he wrote, because Robert Hamilton, who had been interpreting for others at the hospital, including Sells, MacLennan, and himself, was "repeatedly at the institution to see Spo-pe." Finch thought it "unfair to claim that this man is insane and in need of further need

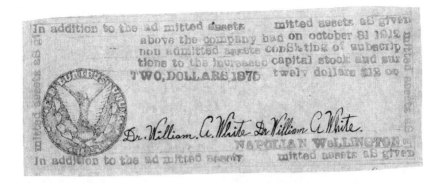

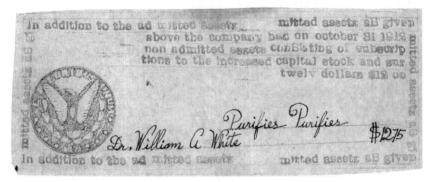

Checks or drafts made by Spopee for Dr. William A. White, medical superintendent, St. Elizabeths Hospital, signed by "Napolian Wellington" or "Purifies," a surname for Spopee. (National Archives and Records Administration, RG 418, St. Elizabeths Hospital, Case File 54465.)

of observation, when it is admitted that the authorities can not tell the nature of his insanity and that his conduct has been orderly and he has never shown, during the long years of his incarceration, any vicious or harmful tendencies, and that it is quite probable he would not be a menace to society if released."[59] Finch went on to report that Commissioner Sells, after speaking to Spopee through an interpreter, and Secretary of Interior Lane were both "persuaded that the Indian is possessed of his faculties" and that executive clemency was in order. Although they had reached this conclusion, the two officials had nonetheless recommended that Spopee should be sent to the South Dakota Indian Insane Asylum.

Finch could not have disagreed with this recommendation more. Calling such an action "unthinkable," he pointed out that he too had seen Spopee and had talked with him at length. "In my opinion," he wrote, "he shows no indication whatever of unsound mind but is a person of prepossessing appearance, intelligent and particularly responsive, so far as possible with his limited means of expression, to every inquiry made." The pardon attorney went on to adamantly reject Sells's suggestion that Spopee be transferred to the Indian Insane Asylum for observation. Instead, Finch was inclined to believe that "his whole incarceration has been a miscarriage of justice; that while he did kill the man in question, the chances are largely that he did it in self-defense, and but for the fact that he was an Indian . . . he would not have been convicted in the first place."[60] Agreeing with Sells that essentially Spopee had been in solitary confinement for thirty-two years, Finch reasoned that was enough. And to contemplate pulling him away from the people who had become his friends and to remove him from beloved and familiar surroundings to send him to another insane asylum, "to strangers without minds," would be cruel indeed. This decision "would not be understood by him but would be a further additional punishment which he would not understand." Finch's conclusion was that if Spopee was to be kept confined in an insane asylum, it should be where he already was. He should not be transferred.[61]

Having said this, Finch then returned to the issue of Spopee's trial in Helena in 1881 and the documentation for President Garfield's commutation of his sentence from death by hanging to life imprisonment. Finch had the original files in the Office of the Pardon Attorney. These included a newspaper account of Spopee's final statement to Judge Conger that had been delivered after the trial. Finch quoted these files in detail, going on to relate how he had interrogated Spopee regarding his final statement.

Neither Spopee nor Hamilton, who was interpreting, knew the source of his information, according to Finch, "and my inquiries were addressed to developing from the Indian, without stating them, therein recited. It was surprising, startling and almost uncanny the manner in which, after such a lapse of years, these statements, one by one, were drawn from him and developed in the interview." Convinced of the truthfulness of Spopee's statement, Finch concluded that "there is much doubt, in my mind, that he was ever guilty of the murder." Spopee also stated during the discussion that the killing had taken place "about two miles over the line in British America," but that he had decided to place the body in the wagon to transport it to the Blackfeet Agency. Good Rider had objected to his decision and upon arrival on Cut Bank Creek had persuaded Spopee to leave the body there in the brush. To prevent Spopee from changing his mind, "Good Rider had killed the ponies, not because they were worn out by hard driving, but in order to prevent Spo-pe from taking the body to the Agency."[62]

As for his recommendation to the attorney general, Finch was confident that Spopee "had abundantly satisfied every requirement of justice and should be released. In my opinion the sentence should be commuted to expire at once, without any condition regarding his future detention in an insane asylum."[63]

Evidently Attorney General McReynolds was completely swayed by this powerful brief, because in his own letter to President Wilson, on July 6, he fully endorsed the pardon attorney's views. Using the same arguments, he agreed that Spopee's sentence should be commuted, and again stated, following Finch's wording almost verbatim, that "it would be a refinement of cruelty to follow the suggestion of the Commissioner [Sells]."[64]

The morning of the following day, Tuesday, July 7, President Wilson exercised his executive clemency, unconditionally pardoning Spopee. He would not be sent to the Indian Insane Asylum. Commissioner Sells and the attorney general were informed of the decision, with the latter writing immediately to Dr. White at the Government Hospital for the Insane, "The president has commuted the sentence of Spo-pe to expire at once. You may release him immediately. Warrant of commutation will be prepared and mailed you in a few days."[65]

Commissioner Sells appears to have been delighted that his recommendation for further detention had not been followed. But instead of going personally that morning to St. Elizabeths to inform Spopee himself, he decided to send in his place an official from his office. Sells meanwhile would inform the press and put together a celebration for the evening. Spopee, for his part, had been totally ignorant of the specific efforts on his behalf. As a result he was taken unawares; he did not know that he was to be returned to his daughter in Browning. Moreover, reported the *Washington Times*, Spopee believed that his wife, One-Who-Goes-Under-the-Water, was still living.[66] It was left to Hamilton and Catherine MacLennan to explain the situation, and when they "broke the news gently to the old Indian and when he realized that he was finally free . . . he permitted himself a broad smile." During the afternoon, the MacLennans and Hamilton took Spopee for his first automobile ride—to the Capitol "for a spin around Potomac Park"—before having dinner at the New Capitol Hotel.[67] At nine o'clock that evening, Spopee was taken to Commissioner Sells's office in the Pension Building. There Sells, a group of twenty newspaper men, officials of the Indian office, and a photographer gathered to celebrate his freedom and to document the occasion for the media. The occasion also allowed them to "bid him Godspeed." Spopee had been told to pack his belongings, for he would be spending only one more night at the hospital before leaving the following day on his way back to his daughter and to the land of his fathers.[68] It had been a glorious day.

Spopee was dressed in a distinctive pinstriped suit, which he had worn that day while being chauffeured by automobile and would wear the next day when he had his photograph taken with Evelyn Finch, the pardon attorney's teenage daughter—she with her parasol and he holding in his right hand an American flag, standing outside a Washington office building. He had possessed this suit for some time, for his advocate, Mrs. MacLennan, had described him in it in her letter to President Wilson. In her opinion Spopee in his pinstriped suit and closely cropped hair, with his "courteous manner, gentile demeanor and evidence of superior intelligence," reminded her of the Japanese hero, Admiral Togo, whom she had met in Washington.[69]

Standing in front of what amounted to a press conference arranged by Sells, Spopee had his picture taken with Commissioner Sells, both with and without his certificate of pardon, and fielded a bewildering array of questions through the interpreter, Hamilton. Unrattled by the public attention, Spopee remained composed as he

Spopee standing before the Pension Building, Washington, D.C., following his executive pardon by President Woodrow Wilson, July 7, 1914. (Photograph by Harris & Ewing, Washington, D.C. Library of Congress, DIG-hec-04516.)

Commissioner of Indian Affairs Cato Sells, handing Spopee his presidential pardon, at the Commissioner's Office, Pension Building, Washington, D.C. (Photograph by Harris & Ewing, Washington, D.C., Library of Congress, DIG-hec-04515.)

Miss Evelyn Finch,
teenage daughter
of U.S. Pardon
Attorney James A.
Finch, with Spopee,
holding an American
flag. (Photograph
by Harris & Ewing,
Washington, D.C.
Library of Congress,
DIG-hec-04517.)

answered them carefully, without resentment, and even with a bit of humor. The queries ranged from the dopey and mundane to the serious and thoughtful—from what had his occupation been before his incarceration, to which he answered, "Chasing buffaloes with a bow and arrow," to why he had not talked, to which he answered, "I wanted to but could not speak your tongue and there was no one at the hospital that could speak mine."[70] When asked if he was surprised by the executive pardon, he related, through Hamilton, that "soon after I was sentenced, I made a petition to the White Father to pardon me. I was told the pardon would come. So I waited and waited. But now I guess it has come."

Yet although Spopee was without rancor, he did observe to those plying him with questions that he had doubts about the justice he had received in Montana: "I don't think your white men treated me white. It was not fair. I think white men are very peculiar[,] and why are they so curious about me now?"[71] He might have basked in the unusual attention, but he was also clearly puzzled by it. Nonetheless, Spopee signed his name to pieces of paper that were stuck in from of him by several admirers, something akin to an autograph. He wrote his name, "Spopee," with a legible and steady hand and took the occasion to add as a first name or prefix the word "Purify," which Hamilton said he took to mean to "make one good" or "keeping his heart clean." He was "Purify Spopee," and handing his signature back he added with a knowing smile "that his address no longer was Washington, D.C.," and glanced about to see if his joke had registered—laughter followed.[72]

These were remarkable responses. Ironically, once again, as he had during his multiple confessions, in the letters to his wife, and in his post-sentencing statement to Judge Congers, Spopee voiced his own thoughts and reactions. After a long silence, he recovered his voice and spoke directly and for himself, however mediated by white reporters, by translations and on-the-spot oral interpretation. His words disclosed what was on and in his mind, even if it was presented in caricature. For example, when Spopee was asked whether he would return to the garb of a blanket Indian, he replied: "Oh, no. White collar nice. Shoes nice. I like white man's clothes. Never go back to Indian clothes." The gist was there. He had registered his opinion. This was demonstrated as well when Spopee described his time in the asylum: "All about me I heard mutterings of the crazy men and women. How I stood it God only knows. It was a test."[73] While Spopee's words may seem trivial, they represent, then and now, a welcome departure from the norm. It is important to appreciate Spopee's relative fluency for the phenomenon that it was: Here is a voice that has been silent, or close to it, for many years, a voice far from home and family—and then this voice finally speaks, and speaks well! Amazing!

Spopee enjoyed the first day of his newfound freedom, July 8, by sight-seeing in the city. He visited the Washington Zoo, ushered there by the MacLennans and Hamilton, the interpreter. A knot of newspaper men trailed along. Spopee, dressed again in his pinstriped suit, was most impressed with the imprisoned bears.[74]

Commissioner Sells had already ordered an investigation to address the possibility of providing for Spopee's maintenance in the future, a problem for the Office of Indian Affairs because of his Canadian roots as a Blood Indian. This issue had already been alluded to in the attorney general's report. Now, Sells wanted to explore having Spopee adopted by the Blackfeet Tribe, given that Spopee's daughter was there and that he had been closely related to the Southern Piegan prior to his capture and trial in 1879–80. Once a member of the Blackfeet, Spopee would then be eligible for an allotment of land and farming tools. Whatever the outcome, however, Commissioner Sells promised that provisions would be made for his care.[75] On another occasion, Sells promised publically that his office would "see that SpoPee gets a square deal."[76]

Then it was time to leave for Montana. After visiting the Washington Zoo the morning of July 8, Spopee, accompanied by Hamilton and Dr. John Daugherty of the Office of Indian Affairs, went to the Union Station with its multiple arches, Ionic columns, and white marble. Amid the mahogany booths, counters, and seats and amid throngs of urban travelers, they waited to walk through the gates in the train concourse. Spopee had little baggage.[77] It is hard to imagine what was on his mind as he left behind the humid, lush Anacostia Hills of the hospital and its grounds or the smooth, white stone of Washington. The tracks west led him back over what had become a modern war trail to Congress, traversed by a new class of political warriors seeking federal booty, justice, or help. It was not a good time to return to the Blackfeet Reservation. Browning was turbulent. Spopee, however, did not know that. What he knew was that he was going home, returning to what was left of his family from his own long war trail. He was coming back alive and well, coming back, as the elder Blackfeet veterans would have said, "with berries in his mouth."[78] Life was sweet.

CHAPTER 8

HOMECOMING

News of President Wilson's unconditional pardon, the second major story of the year about Spopee following his April discovery, flew across the land via the major newswires such as the Associate Press and the United Press. Spopee became once again, if only for the moment, a small fragment of the national news that bubbled daily to the surface. His was a human interest story, much like those encountered today when, somewhere in the United States, DNA tests from evidence gathered long ago reveal an innocent victim, erroneously convicted and sentenced for so many years. In addition, Spopee's story was a romantic subject, for it involved an American Indian, a legendary warrior and buffalo hunter from the northern Plains, who had in fact "disappeared" just as Indians in the popular imagination were expected to do, only to reappear after thirty-four years in the havoc of the modern world. In the first week of July 1914, newspapers such as the *Washington Post*, the *New York Times*, and the *Los Angeles Times* ran versions of the Washington-released stories about Spopee under their own headlines—but so too did the *Minneapolis Journal*, the *Bellingham Herald*, the *Santa Fe New Mexican*, and the *Reno Evening Gazette*.

Local newspapers relying on small, overworked staffs fed off the wire services for a steady stream of national and international stories to augment their own offerings. These were often printed without byline and exhibited no attribution or dateline. Often the stories were edited down to meet space needs and allow room for breaking local news. Sometimes the resulting stories were so cut and pasted together that they made little sense. Nonetheless, in Spopee's case the country's readers were informed of his unlikely discovery in a "lunatic asylum" and enchanted with the merciful concern of government officials or sometimes appalled at what they perceived as the obvious injustice of it all. Herbert Quick, the well-known Ohio novelist and journalist who contributed a stream of editorials to the daily press, responded to the transmitted wire stories, so factual and objective, by asking, "What shall we do about Spo Pee's lost life?" He suggested remuneration but was of the opinion that "in our unfair land, we 'pardon' an innocent man for the wrongs we have done him, and make him no amends." Something should be done about this. "We should reinstate the case in court, and allow the tribunal which condemned him to record the fact of its shame, in lieu his. We should then pay him for his lost time. . . . In short we should try to do him justice."[1]

Such expressions of concern for those forgotten "in the spiritual cold and darkness of the living death of a prison" were quite rare, and even Quick's pointed editorial saw little print. For the most part, local paper after local paper, of all sizes and circulations, simply ran the story they received. People's reactions to this national coverage, their sympathy or their concern, moreover, went largely undocumented and unmeasured. Once in a while, when there was a specific connection to Spopee such as with the *Free Press* in Detroit, where Spopee had been first incarcerated after sentencing, a "Special" would be written emphasizing the local involvement.[2]

Newspapers in Montana and Alberta, Canada, geographically close to the 1879 murder of Charles Walmesley and Spopee's subsequent trial in Helena, followed the national press releases with much the same fidelity as other newspapers. Seldom did they provide additional context or comment. For the most part they registered no local opinion or "slant." Editing, for the most part, was limited to trimming the story. So, for example, shortened versions of the story about the Blood Indian from Fort Macleod, emphasizing the Canadian border, appeared in the local Canadian newspapers including the *Calgary Daily Herald,* the *Medicine Hat News,* and the *Lethbridge Daily Herald* on July 7 through 9, but none registered outrage or even raised jurisdictional questions about whether Canadian sovereignty may have been breached. In Montana, the *Great Falls Daily Tribune* and the *Choteau Acantha* represented a good many local papers in that they too adhered to the Associated Press wire service story.

There were, however, notable exceptions. Dr. Arthur C. Hill, the Blackfeet Agency physician who had investigated Walmesley's death, was still living in Saint Paul, Minnesota. He objected strenuously to the reported facts in the wire service story of Spopee's presidential pardon that ran on one of the back pages of the *Minneapolis Journal* on July 8. Dr. Hill evidently had contacted the newspaper immediately to register his demur, for the next day, July 9, the *Minneapolis Journal* interviewed him on its front page and ran a photograph of Spopee that he provided, taken at the time of Spopee's trial in Helena, Montana. Wasting few words, Dr. Hill assessed the reputation of Walmesley, stating that "the man Spo Pee murdered was as fine a fellow as there was on the frontier." Nor was he having anything to do with the now frequent assertion that Spopee killed in self-defense. "He was murdered in cold blood by Spopee and a young Blackfoot called Good Rider." The *Minneapolis Journal* concluded that this was "a severe jolt" to the "romantic story sent from Washington." And to reinforce Dr. Hill's authority on this matter, the article ended with biographical information that should have squelched significant questioning. Dr. Hill, the reader was told, "spent twelve years in the Indian territory of Montana in the '70s and early '80s. He speaks several Indian languages."[3]

Others, especially in Montana, questioned the innocence of Spopee as well. Oddly enough, one of the few with a decided opinion was the Plains Cree leader Little Bear (Imasees). Then living on the Blackfeet Reservation, he was notorious for his involvement in the 1885 Frog Lake incident in Saskatchewan during the rebellion of Louis Riel, in which he and other Plains Cree had challenged the authority of his father, Big Bear. In the course of events, Big Bear's followers shot and killed a number of white inhabitants of the settlement, including clergy, in a drunken and bloody uprising that was independent of Riel's challenge but still fed into the general anxiety. Subsequently, Little Bear led a large number of his fugitive followers into Montana, claiming they had not made treaty with Canada and hoped to do so with the United States.[4]

When the news of Spopee's pardon and homecoming arrival in Browning reached Little Bear via a newspaper reporter in Great Falls, Montana, he was on his way back from Yellowstone National Park to the northernmost part of the Blackfeet Reservation. This was not far from the newly created Glacier National Park, where sympathetic officials in 1910 had temporarily placed the now-homeless Chippewa and Cree, under Rocky Boy and Little Bear, until a reservation could be established. When asked through an interpreter about the pardon, Little Bear said that he remembered perfectly well the killing of Walmesley. Then, with "many gestures and contortions," Little Bear "related a story that was almost identical with the testimony that convicted Spopee thirty four years ago." In Little Bear's version, Spopee and Good Rider "asked a white man for food, and virtually demanded it, and when refused started forward in a menacing manner. The white man seized an axe, when the Indians shot him and then helped themselves to his property, carrying the body away hidden in the blankets they were wearing."[5]

Little Bear's close description was impressive and carried authority. But how did he know? He knew, in all probability, because he had heard it firsthand while in the Judith Basin with his father, Big Bear, in the winter of 1880–81. James Willard Schultz, then trading with a welter of Native peoples, had reported on both Spopee and the forced removal of White Calf and his Southern Piegan, and while he did not mention Little Bear by name in those accounts, he had reported that Big Bear and his Cree were camping with the Piegan the following year, together with Crowfoot and his band of Blackfoot and buffalo-hunting Métis from the other side of the border. More than likely, Little Bear was with his father and in a position to know what he was talking about. He was thus credible, and his condemnation worthy of attention.[6]

Adding to Little Bear's authenticity, the *Great Falls Tribune* concluded its coverage by relating how he had yearned "to see wild

Little Bear (Imasees), Plains
Cree leader and son of Big
Bear. (Author's collection,
unnumbered.)

buffalo once again before he died." To do so he had gone to Yellowstone National Park, where remnants of wild buffalo still roamed,
somewhat protected. "The sight," reported the paper, "was too
much for him and he broke down and cried."[7]

In 1914 the national nostalgia for the West—for the emblematic
buffalo and his twin, the Plains Indian—fed a warm pathos. As seen
with Little Bear, this deep feeling was shared by older Indians as
well as whites. Prodded by the *Great Falls Tribune* reporter, Little
Bear became again a player, a credible authority who had "been
there." Spopee's pardon had been a mistake. He could vouch for
it. And the *Cut Bank Pioneer Press* noted that Little Bear's remem-
brances were at odds with the "Spopee fetish" or legend, which was
"being severely jolted these days."[8]

James Willard Schultz, too, must have gotten wind of Spopee's
pardon just before it came to pass. He related the remembered details of Spopee's capture in a story that appeared in the *Great Falls*

Daily Tribune on Sunday, July 5, two days before President Wilson signed the pardon into law in Washington, D.C. In a follow-up story on July 19, that paper featured the standard Washington photograph of Spopee in his pinstriped suit and vest, holding the American flag; beside him was Evelyn Finch, the young daughter of the U.S. pardon attorney, in her white dress. Overhead, in heavy black type inside an outlined black box, ran the headline "Innocence of Spo-Pee Questioned by Men Who Know Story of Crime." The focus of the story was that "Eastern newspapers for two or three weeks have made much ado over Spo Pee." But some people who were in Montana at the time of his conviction had not been taken in by the hoopla, and they believed that President Wilson had "been imposed upon." The two examples the newspaper extolled were the testimony of Dr. Hill to the *Minneapolis Journal,* which was reprinted word for word, and the July 5 story and rehash about the arrest of Spopee reported by Schultz. Actually Schultz had nothing to say about the issue of guilt or innocence. Instead he dealt with the details of Spopee's wintery arrest and capture in the Judith Basin by Sheriff Healy and the role played by the famous Joe Kipp, Indian trader. Nonetheless, the impression was left, as with the Little Bear interview, that Spopee's pardon involved more than a dash of western romance as understood and purveyed by the gullible East.

The *Choteau Montanan* expressed a similar opinion. The paper agreed that Spopee was an old man and unlikely to do any harm, and that it made no sense to keep him in prison. But it also pointed out that "the sentimental stuff the eastern correspondents are sending out concerning him and his brave deeds, that the Blackfeet mothers have been singing their babies to sleep with a song about him ever since he was taken to the penitentiary, that the murder had probably been committed in Canada . . . and that the murder is now believed to be have been committed in self-defense, etc. does not 'listen good' to the old time whites who were in this country when an Indian was a good Indian only after he was dead."[9] James Upson Sanders, son of Wilbur Fisk Sanders, Spopee's attorney at the Helena trial, confirmed such criticism of the "sentimentalist slant" when writing to George Bird Grinnell about the Society of Montana Pioneers. To his surprise, Sanders wrote, "a romantic story" had developed during the summer of 1914 about Spopee, or Turtle, whom his father had defended in Helena.[10]

These attempts to insert a bit of Montana realism into the growing legend of Spopee were mild, however, compared to the cynical fun-poking by the *Cut Bank Pioneer Press*, which evidently had had enough following Spopee's heroic arrival in the reservation town of Browning. One unnamed editorial writer backed into his tirade by drawing a long-winded comparison with "Blind Homer" of Ancient Greece, who, blessed with a vivid and hectic imagination, could put his gods to work, be they Achilles or Apollo. But even Homer, in their opinion, could not hold a candle to Great Northern Railway "press agents with bulging brows" once they got "a-going on this Indian Legend stuff." In their efforts to extol the newly created Glacier National Park these promoters did all they could "to revive and intensify that strange halo or aura that . . . has hedged the dusky native, and the jays back east have fallen for it in great shape."

First, according to the paper, "the Jim Hill press agency" had created the so-called "Glacier Park Indians"—colorful Blackfeet elders and their families who worked or performed at the park's hotels. The publicity department periodically sent contingents of these ambassadors east to generate interest in Glacier Park among tourists, under the corporate slogan "See America First." Then that same year came the eastern press, "reeking with this Spopee yarn, regaling their wondering readers with tales of fond mothers lulling their crooning babes to sleep with cradle-songs of Spopee's martyrdom." The newspaper's ironic, tongue-in-cheek conclusion was that "we don't want our beloved West to lose any of its magic and mystery, . . . and we hope that these unsentimental people with the good memories will quit 'busting' our most cherished traditions." It wasn't, after all, good for local business. With the one exception of the *Minneapolis Journal*, these critical responses came from Montana newspapers that bordered on the reservation, and like most border towns they lived up to their reputation for being, if not bigoted, then at least disparaging when it came to Indians.

Blissfully unaware of the buzz of the wire services following his pardon, Spopee, along with his escorts Robert J. Hamilton and Dr. John Daugherty, rode the Great Northern passenger train across

Montana on his way to the Blackfeet Agency and the little town of
Browning. It is hard to know what thoughts went through Spopee's
head as the Rocky Mountains came into view, a ragged edge on the
western horizon. I can imagine that it was comforting to see the
three conical buttes of the Sweet Grass Hills (Katoyissiksi) looming
to the north. The geography had to have again spoken to him, in
Blackfoot, reminding him of the eventful stories of Old Man, Napi;
of people gone, whose souls had migrated to the Sand Hills, that
bleak country south of the Saskatchewan; or of berry soup, pipe
bundles, and the entreating songs of the summer's medicine lodge.
Listening to the land, he knew he was home.

It had been an exciting trip. Everything had changed since the
last time he had seen the country. Then the huge Indian reservation
belonging to the Gros Ventre, Piegan, Blood, Blackfeet, and River
Crow, extending from the Rockies eastward to what would become
the border of North Dakota, had not yet been sold by executive
agreement and broken up into the isolated reservations known as
the Fort Peck, the Fort Belknap, and the Blackfeet. There were no
railroads then. And above all, this had been buffalo country. Now,
out the window, along the so-called Hi-line, the railroad tracks ran
uninterrupted through Wolf Point, Fort Belknap, Havre, Shelby, and
Cut Bank. It had become sod-buster country, punctuated by shiny
grain elevators, booming homesteader towns, claiming shacks, and
busy government land offices. The open prairies had been broken
up and fenced, and people and roads were everywhere. There were,
to be sure, vestiges of what it had been—places where the distinctive tracery of old buffalo trails could be seen meandering away
from the tracks or a pile of bleached buffalo bones were still visible.
These, however, were but ghostly reminders of what the place had
been like.

The Great Northern train pushed its way through the immigrant
towns, with European names such as Glasgow, Malta, and Havre,
and threaded its way past mountain island ranges like the Little
Rockies, Sweet Grass Hills, and the Bear's Paw, all well-known to
Spopee. Author William Atherton Du Puy, who penned a lengthy
newspaper account of Spopee and his homecoming, related how
upon reaching the plains "the old Indian began to take on a new

life." And when the passenger train left the little town of Cut Bank, named after a tributary of the Marias, Cut Bank Creek, and crossed the trestle bridging the deep, V-shaped creek bed to the west, Spopee immediately recognized it and said "Look! The Cut Bank. The body of the white man whose heart was bad lies there."[11] That he mentioned Walmesley, at least in Du Puy's telling, is not surprising. But if he said anything at all about the horrible events in January of 1870, when in Heavy Runner's camp he had been shot through the hips and his mother reportedly killed not far to the south, on the Marias River, it was either unspoken, unrecorded, or glossed over. That too, however, had to have been running through his mind as the land, however changed, still spoke to him.

Once on the Blackfeet reservation, it must have been easier to believe that the land had changed but little. There were no shelter-belts, few roads or buildings, and the unbroken grazing country rippled away in undulating waves as far as the eye could see. It looked open, free, and powerful. From a distance the poverty and distress were hidden away, sequestered in clustered shacks nestled among the same prairie swells that had harbored fugitive bison with their heads down, grazing. On reservation land it would not have taken much imagination to see those ghost buffalo out the window instead of the scattered groups of wind-blown horses and cattle.

The *Great Falls Daily Leader* reported that Spopee's homecoming was a great occasion. "When the train reached Browning, there were 500 Indians from the reservation in waiting. When the returning warrior stepped off they surged down upon him in a wave of cordial reception. For a moment Spope drew back in apprehension, but then grasped the idea that these were his own people. They gathered about him in vast handshakings and much demonstrative rubbing of his back. Long-Time-Sleep, one of the principal chiefs, owns and operates a handsome seven-passenger automobile and Spo-pe rode to the reservation in this."[12] The *Cut Bank Tribune,* via its community correspondent for Browning, "Aurum," covered the arrival as well, noting that "when our Indian exile stepped from the train and saw the crowd that had gathered to welcome him he said 'This is a great piegan welcome.'"[13] Spopee was described as looking "younger than we had supposed, and seems to be in good health. May his remaining days be many and happy. We were glad to clasp his hand!"[14]

The ride in Long-Time-Sleep's impressive limo was necessary because the Blackfeet agency, although visible on the treeless prairie, was on Willow Creek, two miles away to the north from the Browning train depot where all had gathered. With the three travelers, Spopee, Hamilton, and Dougherty, rode Spopee's daughter, Minnie Takes Gun. She had been but a baby when Spopee was imprisoned—now she was thirty-five and married, with children of her own, including The Star, or Mike, about fourteen; Agnes, ten; Rosa, seven; Mary Frances, five; Baby, three; and newborn Tom.[15]

Browning, home to fewer than two hundred souls, was a tangle of wooden shacks, raw buildings with false fronts, the trading posts of J. H. Sherburne, Willets and Scriver, and the Broadwater-Pepin Trading Company. It was primarily the home of the Blackfeet Indian Agency, with its square of government buildings, its wooden boardwalks, and its multiple buildings on or near Willow Creek. The agency had not been there long—only since 1895, when it had been moved from its former location on Badger Creek, some twenty miles to the south. The new community came to be called Browning, after the then commissioner of Indian Affairs, Daniel M. Browning. The Blackfeet, however, referred to the town as Ee-tun-yope, meaning "Where our Father is"—"Father" being the Blackfeet agent. Another common designation was Otach-kwis-ksisee-aetapisko, or "Light-brown-nose-town," after a horse that belonged to one of the first settlers there.

Whatever its name, the reason for moving the agency had been the arrival of the railroad across the empty center of the Blackfeet Reservation in 1893, more than ten years after Spopee had left. By relocating the agency, officials hoped to take advantage of better communications and more economic freight rates, and the move also dramatically shifted the reservation's center of gravity to the north away from its southern portions. The extreme isolation of the reservation as a whole became a thing of the past. Now many Blackfeet found themselves adjacent to the thoroughfare of the Great Northern, caring for their own cattle, digging irrigation ditches, cutting and raking hay meadows, living in log cabins, and experiencing

Browning, Montana, with agency in background on a busy Saturday, ca. 1910. (Author's collection, no. 1471.)

Blackfeet Agency, Browning, Montana, with Rockies in the background, ca. 1913. (Photograph by Thomas B. Magee. Courtesy Dorothy McBride, author's collection, no. 1469.)

almost daily contact with the world beyond the reservation boundaries. It was a very different world from the one Spopee had known.

Shortly before Spopee's expected arrival in Browning on July 12 and totally independent of his schedule, by happenchance alone, the Blackfeet had gathered for their Fourth of July celebration in Browning, although, in point of fact, the opening parade and the dancing began on Wednesday, the eighth. The celebration was something of a misnomer. By the beginning of the twentieth century, after strenuous agency efforts to discourage if not outright ban the tribe's most important religious and cultural event, the Blackfeet had decided to move the timing of what they called the Okan, or Medicine Lodge or Sun Dance, to coincide with the Fourth of July. Under the colors of this patriotic national holiday, the Blackfeet continued their sacramental assembly of sacrifice, blessings, and renewal without interruption and with less criticism. Before confinement to the reservation, the people had gathered when the grass was greenest, when the collective horse herds could be grazed and maintained in one spot, when the cow parsnip or Indian celery was at its highest, "when the service berries were ripe," and when the turbulent summer air drifted in sweet swirls. Now, blessed with the still rather unenthusiastic approval of the reservation agents and superintendents, the Blackfeet celebrated their most important religious celebration alongside American flags, fireworks, ice cream, parades, and social dances.

By 1914 the Fourth of July Sun Dance had become a major reservation and tourist event. Setting aside their everyday "civilized clothes" and leaving their frame or cottonwood log cabins behind, families and bands from every part of the reservation headed for Browning. They came by horseback or buggy and wagon, with a few automobiles thrown into the mix, and they camped in tepees and wall tents on the grounds to the west of the agency to renew themselves in the Okan, individually and as a people. It was like a medieval passion play—part secular and social, part religious and sacramental. There was feasting and drinking coffee, exchanging stories and gossiping, drumming and singing; the people gambled and they made offerings, with blessings and prayers. It would last for ten days.

The Fourth of July Sun Dance celebration in Browning accounted for the large number of Indians present at Spopee's arrival on the twelfth. The *Great Falls Daily Tribune* printed an account of the celebration on Saturday, July 11, noting, "This year was one of the most successful in attendance and interest for years."[16] On Friday, the celebrants had raised the annual "medicine lodge" or *okan*, the octagon tabernacle made of cottonwoods dedicated to the sacred sun. In the middle of the arbor, they had dug a hole to hold the center pole and connected it by means of rafters that were lashed to the outer perimeter. The sides of the resulting octagon or circle were covered with willows placed on end, with an opening left facing the west. Adding to this essentially religious occasion were the subsequent sham battles, staged by the older veterans of the intertribal wars. Using "real guns and loaded cartridges," they demonstrated and told the old, by now familiar stories of their generation's courage and adventure. The audience, noted the paper, was mixed, with "scores of visitors," including tourists from nearby Glacier National Park and young men associated with the U.S. Reclamation Service working on the St. Mary Project. The Methodist minister, W. W. Van Orsdel ("Brother Van"), who forty-two years earlier had preached "at their agency, near where Choteau now stands," was also there.[17]

No wonder that Spopee's homecoming seemed so glorious and celebratory, or that Spopee and his reimmersion into his unknown family was so easily lost in the shuffle of pageantry and holiness. Besides, it had been thirty-four years since Spopee had been with them—and even then, although he was one of the Real People, a Niitzitapi, he was a Blood, and not a Piegan. Now in Browning, still dressed in his pinstriped suit with vest, replete with a tie and black shiny shoes, Spopee must have been terribly out of place. As Joe Bear Medicine had remarked, "When he came home he was just like a white guy, he could even write."[18]

Taking advantage of the unusually large gathering in Browning, on Saturday, July 18, Blackfeet Superintendent Arthur McFatridge asked the Blackfeet General Council to meet at two o'clock in the afternoon for "the purpose of presenting the application of Spo-pee for enrollment with the Indians of this reservation." Chairman Wolf

Tail called the council meeting to order. Earlier discussions about Spopee's future had been initiated by Commissioner Sells. Prior to Spopee's departure from Washington, the Office of Indian Affairs, at Sells's prompting, had launched an investigation as to whether or not Spopee could be adopted by the Blackfeet in order to avoid legal complications regarding his tribal membership and "in order that he might fully share in the rights and privileges of the members of the tribe."[19]

Adoption, or the "making of relatives," had a long history with the Piegan and was accepted and practiced at a variety of levels, both personal and tribal. It was particularly common among the components of the Blackfoot-speaking peoples, north and south, and in an age of polygamy, warfare, frequent casualties, and multiple pairings, adoption made a good deal of sense. It had also been a common strategy with outsiders, even traditionally hostile groups, as individuals and bands attempted to gain additional power, influence, and access to wider networks of reciprocal support. Culturally, Spopee's adoption would pose no problems.[20]

Complying with Sells's interest, Superintendent McFatridge presented the case for Spopee's application to the assembled council. "Many of them made a talk with reference to the enrollment of Spopee, and stated that they were glad that he had been pardoned by the President, and were very anxious to have him enrolled with them." With the discussion out of the way, the council then voted on Spopee's application for membership, approving it by a unanimous vote. McFatridge went on to say that if Spopee's application had been presented to a general council of the whole of the tribal membership, in his opinion, it too would have received a unanimous vote of approval.

Considering that Spopee had been confined for the better part of his life and because he had "nothing with which to assist him in earning a living," the council, already attuned to the Indian Office's interest, decided to make a further request. It recommended that Spopee "be given an allotment, furnished with a team, wagon and harness, and such items as he may need to farm his land, free of cost and that it be charged against the Blackfeet Indian Funds."[21] This would have to be approved by the Office of Indian Affairs in Washington, but Superintendent McFatridge supported this additional request and willingly urged that the wishes of the council be approved in order that Spopee could be furnished with "the necessary implements at once, with which to make a living." There was no other business on the agenda, and the council adjourned. The minutes of the meeting were then signed by Wolf Tail with his mark, followed by James A. Perrine, secretary, with McFatridge certifying that the minutes were correct. The news was of such importance to Commissioner Sells that McFatridge wired Washington by telegram immediately after the adjournment of the council and later attached a copy of the minutes to his July 24, 1914, letter.[22]

The action of the tribe in adopting Spopee was approved formally by the Office of Indian Affairs on August 13, and the next day Superintendent McFatridge "was directed to assist Spo-pe in selecting suitable lands for allotment."[23] The *Great Falls Daily Tribune* broke the story with the headline "Spo-Pee Is Now a Blackfeet," while the *Washington Post* reported the adoption under the banner "Befriend Pardoned Indian."[24] Other papers too reported on what was referred to as "adoption" or "enrollment" in the tribal membership rolls.

Despite the turnout and the almost joyful celebration of Spopee's return, the Blackfeet reservation, from Heart Butte to Babb, and from Glacier Park Station to the experimental government farm at Seville, remained in truly desperate straits. These difficulties were so amply documented in the congressional hearings of February that the Joint Commission of Congress decided to continue these investigations in the following year. One result was a report by Harry Lane, senator from Oregon and member of the commission, who spent four days on the Blackfeet Reservation in late November 1914, following Spopee's return.[25] With devastating criticism Senator Lane found the situation of the Heart Butte community to be "pitiable," with six to eight persons living in single-room, overheated, underventilated shacks where contagious diseases such as tuberculosis and trachoma ran rampant. Dependent upon meager rations, "the Indians have no means of livelihood" and there was no game, "or at least not enough to afford them subsistence and I was informed that to keep from starving they had killed and eaten all the prairie dogs . . . and had resorted to eating skunks." Lane's conclusion was that "the condition of the full-blood Indians is deplorable, and if the present system is not improved it seems to be hopeless."[26]

The Joint Commission, meeting in February of 1915, also heard testimony from E. B. Linnen, chief inspector of the Office of Indian Affairs, and F. S. Cook, special agent, commenting on an investigative report they had previously submitted to Cato Sells. It confirmed the worse suspicions of mismanagement, nepotism, and graft, and at the center of it all was Superintendent McFatridge. Dr. John Dougherty, who had accompanied Spopee home from Washington, D.C., was so incensed at what he inadvertently found regarding the medical staff at the agency that he felt compelled to write a scathing, seven-page, unsolicited letter back to Washington, calling for the dismissal of the agency doctors for what he considered professional abuse. Three agency physicians had established rules governing their practice, he asserted, "which are absolutely opposed to the affording to the Indians a satisfactory medical attention."[27] The cumulative charges were so devastating that on January 18, 1915, the Office of Indian Affairs suspended McFatridge, handing over the supervision of the Blackfeet agency to Charles L. Ellis, and just a month later, on February 23, 1915, they dismissed Superintendent McFatridge from the Indian Service. Mercifully, Spopee was exempted from much of this subsequent turmoil.

Spopee's general acclimation to reservation life and his involvement with his daughter and the Takes Gun family received little formal attention or local mention. Nor does his file in the Indian Office in Washington, D.C., contain information or correspondence for the early weeks in Browning regarding contact with the Blackfeet Tribal Council or other entities, such as spiritual or band leaders or relatives from earlier days. Why, for example, had Spopee not looked for Painted Wing, who had helped his wife when she was desperate and still living on the reservation? Maybe he had, and there was simply no record. Some of this silence was probably due to his general inaccessibility while with his daughter, Minnie; some to the relentless interest of the press to find "new" news and, of course, their preoccupation with the coming war in Europe. The "guns of August" kept human interest stories like Spopee's to a minimum.

The first break in the silence came on August 14, when Commissioner Sells telegraphed McFatridge "to assist Spopee in selecting suitable lands for allotment and to forward the descriptions promptly." The superintendent did not respond, and nothing was done for close to two months. Exasperated, on October 17, the Washington office wrote another letter, again requesting such action.[28] At the very end of August, for whatever reason, the *Washington Post* momentarily recovered its interest, voicing to its eastern readership that Spopee was "content and happy in his new surroundings."[29] It did not reveal, however, the source of this information or the reason for this assessment.

Indeed, Arthur W. Brown of the Office of Indian Affairs in Browning flatly contradicted this cheerful assessment from the East Coast. In his report from the Blackfeet Reservation, dated September 2, he stated, "The case of Spo-pe, the Indian recently released from St. Elizabeth's in Washington and returned to the reservation, is really pitiful. It is reported that although he was offered a home with his daughter on the reservation, conditions are so changed that he is very much dissatisfied and unwilling to stay there." The specific causes of Spopee's dissatisfaction were elusive but not particularly mysterious. Following the Sun Dance, the *Cut Bank Tribune* had reported that Spopee "is at present living with his daughter in a tee-pee just north of town."[30] Undoubtedly this was on Cut Bank Creek, near what would become Starr School, where most of the poorer, full-blood families north of the tracks of the Great Northern Railroad were concentrated.

It must have been hard for the old man, so used to his own space, ample provisions, a clean bed in the "hospital," and an orderly, even palatial, institutional setting, to be stuck into a cramped canvas tee-pee without amenities and closely surrounded by eight people, including underfoot children and crying babies. He had not wanted to go back to the proverbial "blanket." He had made that clear in Washington, D.C., when asked if he would abandon his white man's clothes. His answer had been, no, never: "Never go back to Indian clothes." Then again, his difficulty may have been as simple as getting crosswise with an overburdened daughter who had not bargained for such a strange, balky father, who possibly had grown demanding with all of the recent attention or whose mental condition had worsened as a result of the move to Browning. Commissioner Sells's script may have called for a rosy Hollywood ending,

with father reunited with daughter, but such relationships, and particularly those unsupported by years of caring or contact, are seldom as sentimental or uplifting. For such scenes on the reservation,
there was only the Orpheum Theater in Browning.

Not knowing what to do with this unforeseen development, Superintendent McFatridge ordered that "quarters be provided for
him in the room occupied by the policemen, and that his needs in the
way of food and clothing be provided for." In other words, Spopee
returned to a structured world with beds, chairs, and routines, like
the one he had left. He was now provided for in the agency jail and
police quarters, where he was more comfortable.[31] That is not to say
he was happy or satisfied, for Brown's inspection report went on to
say that he was unwilling to stay in the jail "and spends part of his
time in the home of a friend living off the agency grounds in town."
It also speculated that Spopee's experience was not all that different from that of others who have been confined for years, including
whites. When these individuals return home, they find that "friends
have disappeared and surroundings are so changed that freedom
has no attraction for them. At best it will probably be very hard to
make arrangements for his needs so that he may be satisfied." And
in Spopee's case, the only suggestion that Inspector Brown could
come up with was that if he "could be provided with some small
tasks or a position where he could act as a janitor or some similar
capacity, at a very small salary, it would probably be a means of
helping him to be more contented with his lot."[32]

It was an awkward situation. In October, Robert Hamilton, cir-
cumnavigating Superintendent McFatridge as always, complained
directly to Senator Lane of Oregon regarding Spopee's physical
condition. As was so often the case, when McFatridge learned of
this, he immediately countered by wiring Washington that he had
provided Spopee with clothes and subsistence and there was no
cause for concern.[33] There must have been a problem, however, for
on November 14, Cato Sells, echoing Brown's written report, felt
he needed to intervene personally, writing to McFatridge: "My attention has been invited to the fact that Spo-pee . . . is dissatisfied
with his present manner of living on your reservation. This is not
surprising in view of the complete change his present manner of life

Jail and police headquarters at the Blackfeet Agency, Browning, Montana.
(Author's collection, no. 386.)

must be after his long years of imprisonment. I believe, however,
that we should do something to improve his condition, if practicable, and it has occurred to me that probably if he had some means
of employment fitted to his abilities which would occupy his time
he would gradually grow accustomed to his new life. Have you not
some minor employment at the agency or school, such as janitor
work or like service . . . and for which he could properly be paid a
small salary? Please submit your recommendations in this matter
immediately."[34] Clearly Commissioner Sells had followed Inspector
Brown's earlier suggestions.

On December 18, McFatridge replied, noting that "Spopee is
being cared for as well as it is possible to care for him. I have purchased clothing enough to keep him comfortable through the winter and am furnishing him subsistence. I undertook to keep him at
the police quarters at this Agency by giving him a room and a bed
where he could be comfortable, but this did not appear to suit him.
He appears to be very dissatisfied with his present condition which,

of course, is very natural after having been confined in prison the greater part of his life."[35] This solved the immediate problem and might work for a while—at least through the worst of the winter, but it was not a permanent solution. So Superintendent McFatridge had offered an alternative. One of the positions of laborer was vacant, and he had offered the job to Spopee, "intending to permit him to hold the position of laborer and use him as janitor and give him such light work as he was able to do." But this, too, proved less than satisfactory, for "he does not like to stay in one place long enough to hold a position. It is very difficult to do anything with him along this line." Not only was Spopee restless, in McFatridge's opinion, but "there was no question but what he is not mentally well-balanced, and, at times, he shows signs of insanity." Nonetheless, McFatridge recognized that something had to be done to avoid embarrassing Commissioner Cato and the Office of Indian Affairs, and he promised "to keep a careful watch of him and take as good care of him as is possible to do."[36]

It is not clear when Spopee took up residence at police headquarters or how long he remained there. The only notice of the arrangement outside of the agency correspondence was a cryptic note in the *Cut Bank Tribune,* in which the Browning correspondent "Aurum" noted that "Spopee wears a deputy sheriff's badge." The comment may have been facetious, or it may have been a way of addressing local questions as to why Spopee was being housed and supported in such a fashion.

After the Christmas holidays passed and the New Year rolled around, Spopee unexpectedly decided to take things in hand and make his own wishes heard. He did so by writing a personal letter to Commissioner Sells. The short, pencil-written letter on a piece of lined tablet paper was not only in a practiced cursive script but without spelling or grammatical errors; it was also properly punctuated and exhibited appropriate capitalization. Other than the above-noted statement of Joe Bear Medicine (and he may have been easily fooled), there is no indication from hospital authorities or others that Spopee had learned to write. Granted, he had copied or traced lines of print in newspaper advertisements, he had learned to write the prefix "Purifies" to his name, having learned that "purifies" has something to do with "keeping his heart clean." But this letter was significantly different. And yet it reflected a naïveté of expression that made it convincing.[37] Perhaps he had only dictated this letter to an acquaintance, in English or Blackfoot, as he had done long before when writing to his wife, or perhaps he had traced out a suggested English version in his own artistic hand. Or perhaps Bear Medicine was right after all, and he did know how to write. But if he could write, and given his complaining nature, there should be a larger number of letters to officials that survived, and there are not.

Whatever the case, Spopee began by announcing, "I need some help to build up my prospective allotment of land in severalty. I need a team, wagon, harness and a set of tools to develop my would be ranch. Now, Mr. Commissioner, what can you do for me along these lines?" Having made his appeal, Spopee then turned to his own situation. "I am getting along nicely," he wrote, "although I have no home of my own, but I enjoy the blessings under our destitute circumstances. Of course, you will understand the Blackfeet Indians are no means prosperous. Yours very truly, Spopee."[38] He did not have to wait long for a satisfactory reply from his benefactor. Sells informed Spopee: "I am writing the Superintendent to see you and talk the matter over, after which he will take it up with the Office in the regular way." After remarking that he was glad to hear that Spopee was getting along nicely, he signed off, "Your Friend."[39] Good to his word, Sells then wrote to the new superintendent, Charles Ellis, the same day, asking him to "Please see Spopee as soon as possible, talk the matter over with him, and then report with recommendations. If it is desirable and practicable to furnish any or all of the articles . . . you should accompany your report with proper requests, giving annual estimate numbers. Your prompt attention is requested."[40]

Spopee was concerned about his farming equipment in part because, with Superintendent McFatridge's support, he had already selected an allotment. But although the Office of Indian Affairs had correspondence with McFatridge regarding the selection, no description of the land selected had been received in Washington. Spopee, it appeared, was getting anxious. Chief Inspector Linnen confirmed this when appraising the Office of Indian Affairs. "Upon inquiry we found that a selection of land has been made for Spopee which is number 2645 on the schedule, and the same is described as follows: Lots 3 and 4, S/2, NW4, N/2 SW/4, and W/2, E/2 SW/4, Sec. 4, T.33, R.13 and E/2 E/2 SE/4, Sec.5, T.33, R.13." This tract consisted of 319.07 acres, which Superintendent McFatridge had stated, according to Linnen, was good land, "lying in one continuous body, that it is good grazing and hay land and that none of the same is irrigated."[41] It was north of Browning and the agency, between the North Fork of Cut Bank Creek and the upper reaches of the Milk River, about as far to the west as possible. It was surrounded by land belonging to the Madman family to the east and the Alice Three Guns family to the south, and best of all, a small stream ran through the property.

As with any real estate transaction, location was important. The criteria for the selection of such allotments are murky. In general the process was supervised by the agent, but to what degree were the individuals involved allowed to participate, particularly someone whose selection came as late in the process as Spopee's? This was also a time when families still thought of themselves in some lingering way as belonging to one of the earlier buffalo-hunting bands. As they settled down during the early reservation period, certain bands tended to dominate certain areas. In this case, it was the Buffalo Dung band that prevailed along the North Fork of Cut Bank Creek, and the families were Bear Child, Madman, and Bad Marriage. Spopee had an anonymous friend who was identified as a neighbor, although which neighbor (and there were four possibilities) was unclear. Generally family and band connections or neighbors were more important considerations in selecting an allotment than distance from Browning, or topography, or soils. Water for stock and human consumption was important, of course, but many families did not move to their allotments from where they already lived—in homes strung out along the streams and water courses that flowed east out of the mountains, be it Two Medicine Creek, Badger Creek, or Cut Bank Creek. Whether any of this figured in Spopee's case is an open question. Certainly Spopee's land was situated among prominent traditional (full-blood) people, indicating that by their standards, this was a good selection. On the other hand, the surrounding allotments were assigned much earlier, in the late 1880s, and it may have been that his allotment became available to Superintendent McFatridge because of a lack of heirs. In any event, it is doubtful that authorities really expected Spopee, already advanced in years and without farming experience, to "bust sod," when his neighboring allotees had not.

The inspectors, Linnen and Cook, perhaps knowing this and being concerned that it was only grazing land, promoted an alternative plan for Spopee's approval. Prior to sending in the tract information for formal approval, they suggested that Spopee "take out forty acres of the poorest land in said tract and substitute for same, forty acres of the best land that could be found in the irrigible district. This he said that he would do." As for Spopee himself, he was still living at Browning and appeared, wrote the inspectors, "to be well fed, well clothed and happy, but somewhat discontented and wants to return to Washington. As a matter of fact, Spopee is somewhat simple minded, but he is being well treated and is quite a favorite with everyone in the section."[42]

Writing from Browning on February 2, Special Indian Agent in Charge Charles L. Ellis reported that Spopee's earlier allotment selection had been sent to Washington with a supplemental schedule of allotments that had been forwarded on January 14. But now, with Spopee's agreement, Ellis wanted the previous selection "withheld," for he too agreed that it was a mistake to have allotted him "all grazing land, next to the mountains," even if it did "adjoin a friend." Ellis wrote that Spopee was anxious to raise a garden and seemed "pleased with my suggestion that he relinquish forty acres of the grazing land and take forty acres of irrigable land near the experimental farm, and, as soon as I receive a report from the farmer in charge as to the character and fitness of this land, I will submit formal request for the exchange, and report the articles needed by Spo-pee to farm thereon."[43] By the middle of March Ellis reported that Spopee had consented to the proposed changes in his allotment and that the superintendent was "getting a small tract of good irrigable land near one of the farmer's stations as site for his house, barn and garden. The buildings and team have been authorized and wagon, harness, and farm tools will reach here in a few days. He will be given seeds from the Agency supply. I expect to select the best land I can find on the reservation in lieu of that he now has, so that it can be rented and bring him a small income of which he will be in need balance of his life."[44] It all seemed to be coming together—at least as far as Ellis was concerned.

At the beginning of May, Spopee wrote or dictated another letter to his distant benefactor, Commissioner Sells. "Well I haven't heard from you for a while since January last and I have been writing to you for some money for you to sent to me and I have been writing down to Washington for some clothing and a pair of shoes and a watch. But ain't got no reply. Now I am sending you this letter so that you will answer soon. Well Sir you said you would sent me all my Clothing. So please tell Mr. C. L. Ellis to give me some money. I am yours trully, Francis Spopee." Sells answered on May 13, through the superintendent of the reservation: "My friend: I have received your letter of May 5, 1915, in which you say that you have written to me here in Washington and asked me for some money for clothing, shoes and a watch. You have no money here in Washington, so no money can be sent to you; neither is there money which could be used to purchase a watch for you. However, I will take up with Superintendent Ellis the question of getting you clothes if you need them. . . . I hope that you are well and enjoying being back among your own people. Your friend, Cato Sells"[45]

This was Spopee's last request. He died on the afternoon of Saturday, May 29, 1915. Two days later Superintendent Ellis informed Commissioner Sells of the occasion, adding that Spopee had been buried the previous afternoon in the Catholic Cemetery in Browning. "His death came unexpectedly to me," wrote Ellis, who at the time had been away from the agency, on a trip to the southern part of the reservation. Attempting to console, Ellis informed Sells that the unnamed Indian woman and her husband with whom Spopee boarded had "attended him faithfully to the last, and their kindness and devotion to his comfort are very commendable." Superintendent Ellis had ordered an autopsy and reported that it "revealed that the heart was affected by a fatty degeneration and myocarditis, and the gall bladder had acute inflammation. There was a gross enlargement of the liver and a chronic nephritis."[46]

The *Great Falls Daily Tribune* ran a special under the headline "Spopee Is Dead. Indian Who Served Nearly Two Score Years in Asylum Fades in Freedom."[47] In its reporting the paper pointed out that "although in extremely good health when he was released from the federal asylum," Spopee was "apparently unfitted for any other sort of life and he pined in the new environment until death came to release him from the cares and vicissitudes that had infected the greater part of his earthly existence." It had been less than a year since Spopee's release, but during the whole time he had been in Browning, "he was morose, despondent, and extremely retiring. He never mingled to any extent with the people of his race, and seldom uttered a word, even to his own child, a daughter." He had been ill, reported the paper, for only two days.[48] Other papers in Montana, such as the *Anaconda Standard*, ran Spopee's photograph and an accompanying story relating to his death, usually including a comment as to how he found it difficult to adjust to his new life.[49]

Cato Sells found the news of Spopee's death difficult, especially given his brief tenure among the Blackfeet. Sells did not, however, have any regrets regarding his efforts. In fact, in responding to Superintendent Ellis's letter he wrote that "it is comforting to know that he [Spopee] was restored to his people and to freedom for at least a few months preceding his death." Sells also took satisfaction in knowing, as he put it, "that since the return of Spopee to the Blackfeet reservation we have all exerted ourselves to the end that he might be so treated as to insure to him the privileges of tribal membership and the equipment for material advancement, together with the comforts of life so important to one of his age and under the conditions surrounding his later days."[50] Spopee's pardon and release may not have been one of the monuments of Cato Sells's administration, as he had anticipated when thanking Ella Clark for her involvement, but it had "given him a great deal of pleasure."[51] That would have to be enough.

EPILOGUE

Today Spopee is scarcely remembered on the Blackfeet Reservation. Even the local descendants of Minnie Takes Gun, Spopee's daughter, know little if anything about Old Turtle and his remarkable treatment by the American judicial system in the late nineteenth and early twentieth centuries. Here and among the other branches of the Blackfoot Nation, if Spopee's name comes up, it is often confused with the names of other men who bore the name of Turtle—some Blood, others on the North Piegan Reserve, in Alberta, others in Browning and on the Blackfeet Indian Reservation. Winold Reiss, the noted portrait artist of the American Blackfeet in the 1930s and 1940s, painted a well-regarded and popular figure by the name of Turtle, one of the so-called Glacier Park Indians, but he was of a different and later generation.

Then, in a recently collected story, there appeared a Blood who at times bore the name of Spopee, was present at the Baker massacre in 1870, and was also linked to a man named Good Rider at what may be about the same time as our Spopee, about 1880. This oral tradition sounds like an alternative telling, a variation on the story we already know. Here Spopee and Good Rider have broken away from a larger Kainai party on their way to capture mules that had been sighted among the Crow far to the south. There is not a lot of context in this handed-down story. There is no mention, for example, of the awful starvation in the area of Fort Macleod, or of how inexplicably the majority of the buffalo had left Canada. The two young men, according to Charles Crow Chief, contemporary Blood elder, had separated from the others and abruptly encountered a horse herd belonging to "the Many Wives," the Mormons, as they were moving toward the mountains north of the American-Canadian boundary and west of Cardston, Alberta. Cardston, however, was not settled until 1887, when ten families, members of the Church of the Latter-day Saints, came from Utah Territory in wagons, hoping to continue their religious practice of polygamy after it had been outlawed in the United States. In any case, the story continues: The Mormon ranchers thought the two Bloods were after their horses and began to shoot. Good Rider and Spopee shot back and, according to Crow Chief, "Spopee yelled for Good Rider to run for help, which Spopee couldn't do because he was crippled and walked crab-like—that is why he was called Turtle, but that is not his real name. I can't think of his real name. Anyway, one of the white men was killed by Good Rider, but they thought Spopee had done it. The ranchers captured Spopee and they brought him to a place, but instead of hanging Spopee then and there, the Mormon ranchers took him away." The Bloods thought Spopee was killed, said Crow Chief, remembering what he had been told at about the age of twelve by Spider and Bull Horn, "but afterwards it came out that Spopee was not dead."[1]

This Blood remembrance, passed on as it had been told, cannot be clearly dated or deciphered. The events resemble a cell phone communication that is breaking up because of distance or terrain—the fragments and scraps are tantalizingly close to making sense, but just when things are falling into place, when you think you are getting the message, there is only static, followed by a broken surge of new pieces of information that do not fit and seemingly cannot be squared with what was earlier related. The story is there, to be sure, but you have to know it already to get it, to understand it. Otherwise it makes no sense at all. Is this an undiscovered fragment of "our" story of Spopee and Good Rider that somehow escaped the evidentiary record as they ricocheted their way south from Fort Macleod? Or not? If the Mormons were involved, how could these be the same Spopee and Good Rider? The Mormons did not arrive until eight years after the killing of Charles Walmesley. Was this the same episode, or another one with another Spopee?

Other factors tear at the tissue of Spopee's remembrance as well. There had been reports, first in Montana newspapers in January of 1883 and then into Indian Country via the "moccasin telegraph," that Spopee had died in the Detroit House of Corrections in December of 1882.[2] That was not true, of course, but Spopee had not come home, nor had he responded to the letter that One-Who-Goes-Under-the-Water, his wife, had sent to him in Detroit on November 16, 1881. She had informed Spopee that she was "now with Painted Wing," that she could scarcely see to walk, and that she "would like to hear from him again."[3] There was no word from him, however, and there was no information that he was anywhere else. This kind of lack or shortage of information was all too common in the experience of those Blackfeet who had disappeared into distant jails or towns or later into "wild West shows," and also for those relatives and loved ones left behind.

Among the Kootenai in Canada, however, Spopee's fate was known—at least to one person—Chief Eustace. This was the same Eustace who, in a 1950 oral interview with the ethnographer Claude Schaeffer, had related how Spopee had been the last Blackfoot to kill a Kootenai in the area of Fort Macleod.[4] He also knew that in addition to the Kootenai, Spopee had killed again, he knew of Spopee's eventual release from the asylum in Washington, D.C., in 1914, which Eustace called a "jail," and he knew of Spopee's subsequent death. As Eustace related it, Spopee "had killed somebody and was sitting in jail for several decades but it seems he didn't die there. They say Spupe had been seen again after he got out; he had been a young fellow when he was arrested, now he was old. The man must have been a long time sitting . . . wherever he was sitting, about a year and a half after he got back he died." There was nothing about who had been killed, about the fact that he had been a white man, or that Spopee had been tried and convicted in Helena, Montana, or had been pardoned by the president of the United States. But Chief Eustace's description of what he did remember—the jail time, the decades, how Spopee left a young man and returned an old one—leaves little doubt as to the accuracy of Spopee's identity.[5]

There is nothing particularly mysterious about this lack of information regarding Spopee at the beginning of the twenty-first century. It has been almost one hundred years since 1915, when Spopee died and was buried in Browning. Moreover, it is important to remember how abruptly he arrived back in Montana—suddenly he was there, stepping off the train at the Browning depot. His people had little time to remember him or to create new memories of him; he was adopted into the Blackfeet tribe only a short time, less than a year, before he died. Before that he had been lost for more than thirty-four years—not only to those Piegans still alive who remembered him, but also to his Blood relatives in Alberta. Relationships had been simply severed. Spopee had disappeared. No one expected to see him again. And while his previous story and capture had been, for a short time, memorable enough, with people talking about it, once displaced, Spopee himself was not memorable. Once in Washington, D.C., he was forgotten, triply removed and estranged—by language, place, and time.

Then too, fresh events and more recent generations, like sediment, settled over and obscured or buried his memory. Blackfoot stories have to be repeated in order to breathe, to stay alive, to be heard. In doing so, they often compete with each other for notice and attention. One of the ways they accomplish this is to attach themselves to specific places or anchoring landmarks. The result is that the landscape itself helps preserve the stories, helps them live and compete by talking, whispering, or singing out loud. In doing so the rocks or buttes, buffalo jumps or prairie watering holes remind listeners, passersby, of what had happened there and to whom, or what could or could not happen—if only they would listen. As the elders say, "When the land no longer knows you, it won't speak to you, won't tell you its stories." For strangers there is only silence. And as for Spopee, most of his messy story had happened elsewhere—in Helena, in Detroit, in Washington, D.C. Those landscapes did not include Blackfeet except on the rarest occasions. Nor did those landscapes talk or pass on what they had seen, heard, or caused, for there the Niitzitapi were strangers and unrecognized—there was no occasion to tell and no one to hear. No wonder that Spopee's story was unknown or unremembered on the upper Missouri.

Even when the storied landscapes of home spoke out, more often than not they spoke in Blackfoot, and lamentably, with the steady slippage and outright loss of language fluency, the stories were not heard, or heard only in the most abbreviated form. If that were not enough, the middle and younger generations following Spopee lost interest in their own oral history as well as the ability to recognize the multiple Indian names of the men and women involved in their tribe's principal concerns and events. So, for example, when White Calf, or Onista-poka, the leader of the Southern Piegan, signed the Blackfeet Treaty of 1855, he did so as "Feather," his earlier name. Names were never considered indelible or permanent. And while White Calf's various names may have been known to contemporaries and noted, because of his prominence to the next generation, those of the majority of notable Blackfeet were not.

Identification can become questionable. So it was with Spopee. It was as if the scheduled program of an athletic event, where the names of the participants and their numbers are listed, was partial and incomplete. These shortcomings undermine the listener's recognition and make the story harder to follow, more difficult to remember, more susceptible to abridgment, and less likely to be repeated. Whatever muffled remembrance of Spopee there may have been at one time had faded away, and his name was no longer spoken around the cast-iron woodstove on cold winter nights on the reservation, when storytelling was the occupation of choice. Instead, new stories crowded in and crowded out old ones. Old favorites that were vividly recalled took precedence and took over. There was continuity and depth in these selections, but there was also attenuation—displacement and disappearance. There were inevitably losers and losses.

Spopee's unusual Blackfoot story was one of the losers "at home" because in its essence it was not an Indian story, not a Blackfoot story, not a culturally important account of counting coup, stealing horses, or benefiting from the intervention of one of the Spirit Beings. It did not need to be repeated. It took place elsewhere, far beyond the land of the Niitzitapi, and it primarily involved the activities and the aspirations of other Americans, both individuals and, above all, those collective abstractions called public or federal institutions.

As a result, I did not discover Spopee's story in the warm, welcoming space of the family, in the evening with the cold darkness pressing in from outside, just "before the kettle has boiled dry" (*A-ne'ma-ye ek'kotsis*). Instead it was found, as I had suspected from the outset, in the archival records of the territorial courts, the federal justice system, the Government Hospital for the Insane, the Blackfeet Agency, and the Office of Indian Affairs. Whether in Washington, D.C., Denver, or Seattle, these preserved writings and texts, notes and descriptions, collected and now housed in climate-controlled repositories far from the windy reserves and reservations of the northern plains, were the key. They did in fact harbor the detail and description necessary for a Spopee narrative. They were not easy to decipher or interpret, and they often raised more questions than they answered, as do most documents or tellings. But they had the capacity to give life, dimension, and even voice to what had been a silent Spopee and to shed welcome light on a few defining Blackfeet experiences, including their unjust tribal confinement to their reservation—more so than I had initially anticipated. The result, to my mind, is an extended Spopee narrative now complete enough and worthy enough to be repeated, like those stories of old associated with physical landmarks, be it a butte above the old Four Persons Agency outside of Choteau, Montana, on the Teton River, or on Red Blanket Hill to the west of Cut Bank Creek. Now Spopee's is a story big enough and memorable enough to be remembered and retold.

Beyond the issue of remembrance and documentation, however, looms a taller order—what to make of Spopee's whole dramatic story now that we know it? Are there parables or historical lessons to be taken from it? What is there to conclude, what is "the takeaway," as they say on the evening newscast? I have no doubt that Spopee's story will now "talk" to those who encounter it, but what does it say?

Unlike the somewhat parallel story of "the Trial of Indian Joe," so ably explored by Clare V. McKanna, Spopee's story is not limited to the trial, conviction, and execution of an impoverished Indian, who spoke little or no English, by a judicial system infected by racism. We know little of the laborer Indian Joe, also known as José Gabriel, other than that in 1892, already in his sixties, he was tried for the double murder of a farm couple near San Diego, California. Like Spopee's, his case was terribly flawed by legal missteps, misunderstandings due to language and culture, and prejudicial stereotyping. As a result, neither José Gabriel nor Spopee received a fair trial.

But while Spopee's story shares much with his counterpoint in California, it is also very different. Spopee's experiences, for example, are emblematic of the "Starvation Year of 1879" among the confederation of tribes known as the Niitzitapi. He stood in for so many as they coped with the near extinction of the buffalo on the northern plains; he shared their desperate need to leave their home territories to feed themselves and their families, and he experienced their subsequent confinement to restricted reservations. Spopee's story is a small story telling a larger one. It is not only about an erratic killing and its repercussions for an individual, including years of distant, demeaning confinement, but also about what happened to a buffalo-hunting people on the northern plains at a time of critical transition, when they were bewildered by the disappearance of the buffalo, confused by drink and change, confined to a reservation, and subjected to agency management. Spopee's individual story inadvertently interacts with and mirrors this larger tribal experience. Here are parables exposing parallels, big and little.

Here are also small shards of information involving a surprising number of events and people involved in the dazed tribal transition to a reservation reality. These contributions range from Spopee's involvement at the 1870 Baker massacre on the Bear or Marias River—when his mother, Antelope Woman, supposedly was killed and he was shot through the hips, thereafter walking with the crabbed, stiff-legged gait that gave him the name Turtle—to details about his personal travel on the Whoop-Up Trail and its feeder routes, as well as his involvement with the Piegan in the Judith Basin, prior to both his and their confinement. Spopee, for example, had worked with and for white traders such as Fred Kanouse in the early days of Fort Macleod; he had experienced the growing reputation, even fearsomeness, of the NWMP among the Canadian tribes prior to Treaty 7 in September of 1877 at Blackfoot Crossing on the Bow River.

Treaty 7 was in part occasioned by the unexpectedly premature disappearance of the buffalo and Canadian concerns about immigration, tribal unrest, and political upheaval. By 1879 starvation was indeed widespread; most of the Bloods, Siksika, and Northern Piegan, to say nothing of Cree, Sarcee, and Assiniboine, were desperately threading their way south across the Medicine Line in hopes of finding buffalo beyond the Missouri River. Spopee had joined this exodus, so driven by hunger that he choked down the strychnine-laced meat that "wolfers" had left out on the open, now empty land. And it was his and Good Rider's gnawing hunger that had initiated their fateful decision to follow the wagon tracks of the white man, Walmesley. Spopee had this knack for cropping up at critical junctures or for participating in a common experience—squeezing into a ragtag line of Piegan awaiting rations, following White Calf and his bands into the Judith Basin.

Like others, Spopee experienced the growing importance of the Medicine Line, both in how the border was viewed and exploited by Indian people and in how it was becoming subtly less imaginary, less fluid, less a source of hope. Spopee knew first-hand the loss of personal freedom and the growing confinement to ever-shrinking reservations—the hemmed in, closed-off feeling that led some leaders to declare that after the buffalo were gone, there was nothing. Equally, the correspondence between Spopee and his wife, however mediated, constrained, and limited, illustrated in some small way what could happen to wives and infant children when their men, for whatever reason—death or prison—failed to come home and the sweet taste of berries was absent. Falling into dependence, reduced to rags, poverty, and drudgery, these women handed over their children, letting others raise them—if they were lucky, more capably than they could, but just as likely, leaving the children vulnerable to neglect and abuse.

Spopee bore testimony to many of these historical events, perhaps not directly or as eloquently as other witnesses, but with his own experience and in his own mediated words, whether by letter or at court. He was not a political leader like White Calf or Three

Suns, he was not Running Crane or a famous warrior like Little Dog or White Quiver, engulfed in a nimbus of acclaim for his special gifts when it came to stealing horses and mules from enemies. He did not have the presence or the extraordinary spiritual "powers" of Red Old Man or, more recently, the impressive weather dancer Bull Child. But simply by becoming enmeshed in the jurisdiction and record keeping of the *napikwan,* Spopee, mute as he often was, left behind relics of his behavior and revelations as to how the Blackfeet were attempting to respond to the changes being thrust upon them.

Spopee also became a small conduit for specific information about tribal movements and territorial relationships that were by chance caught and preserved. As a result of this inadvertent institutional record keeping, Spopee avoided the fate of those mentioned in the Ecclesiasticus, who "have no memorial, who have perished as though they had not lived; . . . have perished as though they had not been born, they and their children after them."[6] In short, Spopee's story reveals a good deal about the Niitzitapi, a people about to become bereft of their life-sustaining buffalo, separated by an international boundary, by different treaties, laws, and political allegiances, confined to shrunken reservations of land, and controlled by white men and their dominating institutions. They were a people forced to change from what they had been but given little to help them understand what they could be.

In the chase, arrest, and murder trial of Spopee, we also come to learn a great deal about Montana Territory and its criminal justice system. It is here that a comparison with the Trial of Indian Joe is most appropriate, although even here there are substantial differences. As with Indian Joe, Spopee did not have a fair trial, either by our standards or those of Montana Territory. Yet his experience is not always what one might expect in terms of nineteenth-century prejudice or racial injustice toward Indians, in or out of the courts. Spopee's story unexpectedly challenges the modern view that ideas of fairness were largely absent when Indians became involved in the criminal justice system or when they became "wards" in the hands of the distant bureaucrats in the Office of Indian Affairs. Spopee's experiences do not belie the stereotypes, but neither do they fit them. Sheriff Healy "drunks Spopee up" and attempts to trick him with a "medicine paper," but he did not beat him up or mistreat him. In territorial federal court in Montana, Spopee and Good Rider were well represented by more than competent attorneys exercising "due diligence." Unlike Indian Joe, who "was deprived of any interpreter at the preliminary inquiry or effective interpretation throughout the trial," Spopee had three interpreters—two official interpreters, one from the Blackfeet Agency and a court-appointed one, and one, John V. Brown, that he found himself. Yet, although there were three interpreters, none was available to the defense attorneys as they prepared or defended their case as a fair trial would have required, and the defense attorneys complained bitterly about their absence.

Another difference between the two cases for murder has to do with the matter of appeal. There was none for Indian Joe. In Spopee's case, following his conviction and sentencing, his defense attorneys, when rebuffed, initiated an unorthodox and creative appeal that went around the territorial appeal process and relied instead upon political intervention in distant Washington, D.C. This should not have happened, but it did. Consequently, although Spopee's trial was anything but "fair," he enjoyed a range of procedural protections and a surprising degree of support, without blatant and obnoxious prejudice, on the part of the jury and the court. Even Judge Conger "cheerfully" signed the request for presidential clemency.

Spopee's odyssey was by no means over. In a sense it had just begun. After the trial in Helena came years of imprisonment and decades within the institutional bedlam of a mental asylum. Here Spopee cropped up in a most unexpected place, opening a small but important window on American institutions for the insane and mental illness in general. Considered crazy because he did not speak English and did things that were considered normal in his own culture, but thought odd or bizarre among non-Indians, he left hospital authorities at a loss in diagnosing him or providing effective therapy.

Among Spopee's responses was a tool always available to the weak and the vulnerable—to fall silent, to go mute, and turn away, retreating to an interior world. Abandoning speech was an attempt to reduce the elements of mutual confusion and misunderstanding, whether these were due to language, cultural life ways, or mental challenges. This passive, if unnerving, approach became a fallback position at the beginning of his incarceration and later, in Browning, at the end of his life, when once again the fog rolled in and he was once more lost and unable to see. There are multiple examples of Native Americans seeking refuge in muteness and silence while in captivity. Perhaps the most familiar example in the popular culture is that of "Chief" Bromden in Ken Kesey's *One Flew Over the Cuckoo's Nest*, published in 1962, and the Academy Award–winning film based on it and released in 1975.

Throughout these experiences, Spopee nonetheless enjoyed a surprising degree of fairness. Not just at the trial in Helena, but also at St. Elizabeths Hospital. The treatment, housing, work assignments, and attention were, as far as we can tell, even-handed, benign, and well-meaning. They may also have been condescending and paternalistic, but it was seemingly without overt and malicious racism. Spopee did what he could to return the friendly regard by reciprocating with favors in the shape of "made money" and his carefully crafted form of bank drafts. Americans valued both money and paper, so he thought, "I will make them some." His may have been an extravagant charade, but valuing money was their conviction, not his, and he gave them his favor.

Finally, upon Spopee's discovery at the Government Hospital for the Insane in 1914, the commissioner of Indian Affairs quickly decided to right a wrong and to seek via a presidential pardon Spopee's release. Commissioner Sells promised that Spopee would "have a 'square deal.'"[7] Could the authorities have done more, as the newspaper columnist Herbert Quick had suggested, with compensation for a life lost to an injustice? Yes, of course they could have done more. Still, Spopee became Commissioner Sells's personal pet project, and he orchestrated the multiple efforts to achieve the promised "square deal," including the presidential pardon. Even after Spopee's sudden death, Sells saw to it that the wagon, harness, and agricultural implements that were to have gone to Spopee were transferred to his designated heir, his daughter, Minnie Takes Gun.

Throughout, this protective interest in Spopee's welfare, this indulgent regard for his shortcomings, and the subsequent efforts at accommodation, were noteworthy. Part of this came about because

Spopee was so visibly vulnerable. Had he been rebellious, belliger-
ent, resentful, or simply demanding, there might well have been a
different response. Naturally this more tolerant approach became
more common as Indians and their "primitive culture" became less
threatening and more appreciated among the American public after
1900. Nonetheless, Spopee seemed to have enjoyed such solicitude
long before, going all the way back to Judge Conger's courtroom
in Helena. This does not fit the stereotype—but then Spopee didn't
either.

On the other hand, it is fair to note that much of this response
was the equivalent of what the German theologian and Nazi re-
sister Dietrich Bonhoeffer has termed "cheap grace" in that these
institutional responses were relatively easy to do—they made few
demands, they challenged no institutional authorities or preconcep-
tions, and they compelled no sacrifice. The two presidential pardons
were good examples. There were serious legal problems with the
territorial trial, so serious that Wilbur Fisk Sanders was convinced
that had Spopee been a white man he would never have been tried,
much less convicted. The commutation of Spopee's sentence to life
in prison from death by hanging covered a multitude of sins and
stilled a number of consciences. It was an easy call and a political
one.

Finally, Spopee's story is about the individual persistence and
durability of this Blackfoot speaker at a time when, because of in-
fectious diseases, pent-up violence, and sheer callousness, most Indians in such institutional circumstances did not survive, let alone
come home. Following his return after thirty-four years, Spopee
participated in the latest tribal crisis in 1914, the belated allotment
of the Blackfeet Reservation, the controversial sale of surplus lands,
and the dismissal of Superintendent Arthur McFatridge from the
Indian Service.

As for President Wilson's second pardon, some argued that
Spopee was innocent by reason of self-defense. An alternative story
had emerged, one that had been suppressed and unrecognized
because of Judge Conger's unwillingness to admit Spopee's post-
trial testimony. In 1914, a now harmless old man who had exempli-
fied good conduct over the years in St. Elizabeths, who had spent

thirty-four years behind bars, "among lunatics," under conditions that compensated for whatever crime he had committed, was exonerated. This too was easy to do, without the danger or cost of embarrassment or political repercussion. Moreover, such a redeeming presidential act demonstrated the superiority of the American legal system; when mistakes were made, they were recognized and righted. (Well, kind of.) Besides, the presidential pardon of an Indian made for good news and good publicity, particularly valuable in 1914 when Indian valences had dramatically shifted to the positive side, when conditions on Indian reservations were overwhelmingly negative, and when the Indian Office suffered from internal policy contradictions and was subject to congressional hearings. Spopee's case appeared at an appropriate time, when Sells could take the "high road" by acknowledging that when a mistake had been made, for whatever reason, even for a poor, mentally challenged Indian, averred to be a bit crazy, the American system was self-correcting and provided for relief. Such expiation was "cheap."

Whatever the motivations may have been, however limited Spopee's agency may have been in this redemptive drama, Spopee resorted to a cultural solution in the end. This came, according to Charles Crow Chief, when Spopee left a "spirit message" and did so upon a significant landmark that had long been a place for such communications. This comes as a surprise. Spopee was not known in the surviving records to have been a particularly spiritual man. There was no indication that Spopee had been blessed with or owned medicine bundles or pipes. There were no stories of his seeking powers or protection from the spirit beings, of sleeping and fasting atop an isolated butte in a rocky "dream bed," or exercising remarkable power in difficult and dangerous situations as a result of war medicines he had purchased or borrowed. At the same time, he belonged to a cultural tradition where the unseen spiritual world held more power than the visible, and where people and animals not only talked to each other but negotiated and exchanged gifts and identities.

This spiritual visit occurred when Spopee was morose, despondent, and confused, living in the community of Browning, huddled around the Blackfeet Agency buildings. Somehow his relatives in

Canada across the Medicine Line had learned the news of his miraculous return, itself a revelation of the involvement of the spirits. But agency officials had told Spopee that for some reason, probably relating to his adoption by the Blackfeet and his new legal status, he could not leave the reservation—no necessary permit would be issued, not even to visit the Blood reserve just across the border. Confinement would be enforced by the tribal police. Given this situation, in which he could not come to them, his Blood relatives decided they would have to go to him. Making their way south across the checker-boarded and recently homesteaded land off the Blood reserve, they reached the winding Milk River valley immediately north of the Canadian border. Following the river downstream, they reached what was known as Writing-on-Stone. It was and remains an eerily spiritual place—a sacred place, an ancient place, a place "where the ghosts live" for the "Real People" and where they "talk." Marked by tall, broken sandstone cliffs at the north edge of the river bottom and weird vertical erosions called hoodoos, this torn edge of the prairie occupies a significant place in the sacred geography of the Niitzitapi. Over generations, the spirit beings, the *naa-to-yi-ta-piiksi,* had left messages in the form of cryptic symbols or petroglyphs, carved into the protected rock faces and overhangs along this twenty-mile stretch of breaks. Sometimes this ancient rock art warned of nearby enemies, forecast future events or choices, or revealed the location of buffalo herds. New carvings appeared from time to time to join the old. Here the unseen powers were particularly accessible and active.

When Spopee's Blood relatives reached this magical place, to their surprise they found that Spopee, his spirit helper, or his ghost had already been there. They could tell because the marks, etched in the soft stone, indicated as much. As Crow Chief put it in the fall of 2009, "Spopee had been through—coming here or whatever."

But as with Spopee's narrative as a whole, an exact message was hard to decipher. What did it mean? Petroglyphs and paint might be more informative than a rock cairn, as my friend and philosopher Albert Borgmann has pointed out, but both still have to struggle mightily to communicate, especially to those who need more than a suggestive reminder. Too often, rock paintings or carvings

Writing-on-Stone, Milk River, Alberta, with Northwest Mounted Police Post. (Glenbow Archives, Calgary, Alberta, NA-2257-5.)

are shrouded in ambiguity. And so it was with the marks indicating that "Spopee had been through." There is no clue as to the shape of those marks—there is no turtle, no big-shielded warrior, no bird winging its way somewhere—much less do we know what message Spopee's marks were meant to convey. As Borgmann has observed about cairns in his book on the history and nature of information, "since the informational capacity of cairns is so small, large tasks remain for the people to whom the cairn is significant."[8]

And so it has been for us, both in terms of Spopee's marks at Writing-on-Stone and of his narrative, whether the source be Indian or non-Indian. Spopee's "marks" were there in the historical record, even in abundance, etched in the official language of presidential pardons and the chance discovery of Spopee in the Government Hospital for the Insane. But as with the rock art or the cairn, there was not sufficient information to tell a whole story or to understand immediately what was being said. The necessary elaborating details, the vocal stories of landmarks, geographical, cultural, and personal, were missing; the story needed the scaffold of a chronology and a detailed program of personal names, both Indian and white. In time, these were more or less found in the extant archival record, and when informed by a limited but crucial oral tradition, they permitted an expanded telling of Spopee's story, the narrative instruction that cairns or glyphs, scratched on sandstone cliffs, both lack and require. But for the story to retain its message in the future, it also has to be memorable, it has to repeated, and it has to be told to others. Then Spopee and his story will be remembered and "talked about" on long winter nights, when windy gusts swirl around the isolated cabin or house, when elders tell such stories and children sit and listen.

As we go further into the twenty-first century, a modern alternative is for people, Indian and non-Indian alike, on or off reserves and reservations, to ignore the blather of the television set or the e-mails that pepper our computer screens, and to turn to a book, as they once turned to prominent landmarks in order "to hear" or "to read" about the Blackfoot past. It has happened before. So it was that when young Blackfoot traditionalists attempted to recover the ceremonial heritage of their forebears in the 1980s and 1990s, they not only relied upon revered elders in their midst, but they poured over such books as those of George Bird Grinnell and Walter McClintock, using a written literature as a means to augment, in word and photograph, the rich oral tradition that had been forgotten or had become increasingly fragmented. The welcome result of this common effort was a flourishing of a ceremonial and historical heritage where practices and stories, like that of Spopee, became to both Indians and whites more accessible and therefore at once memorable and worth repeating.

Early on, at Spopee's trial, and later, with his presidential pardon, newspapers in the East and then across America struggled to tell Spopee's story, to capture its essence. People wanted to make sense of the story by making Spopee a hero; but he was not and is not. There were references to the infamous Baker massacre on the Bear or Marias River, there were references to Blackfoot songs about Spopee and his bravery, references to Ella Clark singing to him, references to his own words as he reacted to the prospect of freedom and home. But against these romantic inclinations runs the heavy realism of trial, prison, mental institution, dependency, and Spopee's inability to adapt to his daughter's contemporary reality. Spopee had to get and to keep "his heart clean." It was a constant struggle.

In the end, it is not romanticism *or* realism that wins our attention with Spopee. Nor is it the jolt of his coming alive in the modern world of the twentieth century. It is not even Spopee's own acknowledgement that he needed a new name, "Purifies," to express his redemption. What is so memorable, for Indian and white alike, is the mysterious, quicksilver alchemy of each human life. In the Blackfoot tradition, stories carry "messages." Spopee's story reminds us again and again how unpredictable and coldly random ordinary life can be and how emblematic insignificant people and their small dramas can be. To my mind, this is the "message" of the Spopee Blackfoot story, the "mark" he left behind.

Notes

PREFACE AND ACKNOWLEDGMENTS

1. McKanna, *The Trial of "Indian Joe,"* p. 94.

INTRODUCTION

1. See Sackman, *Wild Men,* which includes an extensive bibliography.

2. Government Hospital for the Insane, Synopsis of Record, lists Spopee's age in 1882 as thirty-three years. Records of St. Elizabeths Hospital (RSEH),

file #5445, Record Group (hereafter RG) 418, National Archives and Records Administration (hereafter NARA).

3. Sometimes termed the Blackfoot Nation because they spoke the same language, Blackfoot, this extended family was made up of two branches of Piegan, or Piikuni, Northern and Southern, the Bloods, and the Blackfoot proper, or Siksika. Together, these tribes constituted the "Niitzitapi;" they were relatives—not only speaking the same language but sharing an elaborate common culture and history, enjoying the same sacred places, and subject to the same intervening supernatural powers. Although these peoples intermingled and intermarried, they also fought and killed each other, as relatives often do. And while they banded together to keep common enemies from entering their hunting territories and lands east of the Rocky Mountains, over time concentrations also came to live in different parts of their common territory—the Siksika to the north on the Bow River, the Bloods in the middle on the upper reaches of the South Saskatchewan River, and the Piikuni, west and south, along the foothills of the Rockies. See the Blackfoot Gallery Committee, *The Story of the Blackfoot People*.

4. Sherry L. Smith's *Reimagining Indians: Native Americans through Anglo Eyes, 1880–1940* is an insightful study of some of these "popularizers" and their impact. Particularly helpful for the study of the Blackfeet are the popular works of James Willard Schultz, including his books for boys about the Blackfeet in pre-reservation days.

5. Hutchinson, *The Indian Craze*.

6. See Viola, *Diplomats in Buckskins*.

7. RSEH, file #5445, RG 418, NARA.

8. Hugh A. Dempsey, *The Vengeful Wife*, pp. 74–76.

9. *Washington Evening Star*, April 18, 1914.

10. Rosier, *Rebirth of the Blackfeet Nation*, pp. 14–17.

11. Hugh A. Dempsey, *Firewater*, pp. 42, 211. See DeMarce, *Blackfeet Heritage*, p. 45, for a genealogy of Grace Hamilton Brown and p. 68, under Malcolm Clark, for information regarding the relatives of his wife, Ella Hamilton Clark. See also *Montanian*, March 10, 1899, and *Benton Record*, June 28, 1878, p. 3, which reads: "Mr. A. B. Hamilton, whose Indian title is 'Long Hair,' but whose hair is now remarkably short, is in from Fort Conrad, looking as well and hearty as he ever did in the old time Whoop Up days."

12. *Washington Evening Star*, April 18, 1914, p. 1; among others, see also *Daily Missoulian*, April 28, 1914, p. 4.

13. *Washington Evening Star*, April 18, 1914, p. 1.

14. Ibid.

15. Hugh Dempsey, *Red Crow*, p. 69.

16. Catholic census files for 1874 provided by Hugh A. Dempsey, personal correspondence, August 13, 2008. Comes in the Night may have been Spopee's father, but there is no direct evidence either way. Five days after his capture in 1880, Spopee related to Sheriff J. J. Healy, who knew the Bloods and Whoop-Up

Country well: "I am a blood Indian, and my friends belong to Ne-kas-toes [Red Crow's band]." *Benton Record,* Friday, January 9, 1880, p. 3.

17. Morris, *The Treaties of Canada,* p. 248.

18. On Red Crow, see Dempsey, *Red Crow,* pp. 75–76; Dempsey, *Firewater,* p. 2n4. See as well Sharp, *Whoop-Up Country.*

19. Friesen, *The Canadian Prairies,* p. 166.

20. Blood annuity books, courtesy of Hugh A. Dempsey, personal correspondence, 2005.

21. See especially the insightful study by Dobak, "Killing the Canadian Buffalo," where the problem is addressed and the appropriate literature is reviewed. In addition, see Flores, "The Great Contraction," as well as Hogue, "Disputing the Medicine Line" and Daschuk, Hackett, and Macneil, "Treaties and Tuberculosis," especially pp. 315–18.

22. Hugh A. Dempsey, *A Blackfoot Winter Count,* p. 17.

23. Morris, *Treaties of Canada,* p. 268. On the estimated ten years, see David Laird, Lieutenant-Governor and Special Indian Commissioner, in Morris, *Treaties of Canada,* p. 262.

24. Hugh A. Dempsey, ed., "The Starvation Year," part 1, p. 9.

25. For more on the situation around Fort Macleod, see *Saskatchewan Herald* (Regina), November 3, 1879, as quoted in Ewers, *The Blackfeet,* p. 279; on Edgar Dewdney, see Edgar B. Dewdney to D. L. McPherson, August 4, 1881, in the Macdonald Papers, vol. 210, pp. 242–43, as quoted by Hugh A. Dempsey in *Crowfoot,* p. 115, and Paul F. Sharp, *Whoop-Up Country,* p. 155.

26. Report of the North-West Mounted Police (hereafter NWMP) for 1879 by Captain William Winder, Canada, Parliament, Sessional Papers, vol. 3, session 1880, Paper no. 4, p. 10.

27. For a list of Indians at the Blackfeet Agency, including number 602, Spopee, see microcopy 234, Letters Received, 1824–81 (hereafter LR), roll 515, frame 1098, RG 75, NARA. See also microfilm I-16, Records of the Blackfeet Agency (hereafter I-16, RBA), roll 22, beginning on December 21, 1878, has the weekly ration record of Spopee, or Turtle. This continues through March 18, 1879.

CHAPTER 1

1. The literature on the Nez Perce and 1877 is voluminous. Three important studies are Hampton, *Children of Grace;* Greene, *Nez Perce Summer;* and most recently, with an extensive bibliography, West, *The Last Indian War,* especially pp. 101 and 113.

2. For a fuller treatment, see West, *The Last Indian War,* especially ch. 16, "Under the Bear's Paw," pp. 267–82.

3. Hugh A. Dempsey, *Firewater,* p. 55, quoting George Houk from the *Lethbridge Herald,* November 15, 1924.

4. As quoted in Hugh A. Dempsey, *Crowfoot*, p. 78.

5. Howard Palmer with Tamara Palmer, *Alberta*, p. 31.

6. George Munro Grant, a member of Sanford Fleming's 1872 Pacific Railway expedition, described one concoction peddled by American traders to the Blackfoot. It was "a poisonous stuff, rum in name, but in reality a compound of tobacco, vitriol, bluestone and water." See Grant, *Ocean to Ocean*, p. 190. A more colorful recipe was attributed to the famous NWMP scout Jerry Potts. In this version of "firewater," as cited in LaDow, *The Medicine Line*, p. 38, the ingredients were one quart of alcohol, one pound of overripe black chewing tobacco, one large handful of red peppers, one bottle of Jamaica ginger (or failing that, a bottle of mare's sweat), one quart of black molasses or red ink, poured slowly, and water (to taste). For other common formulas, see Sharp, *Whoop-Up Country*, pp. 43–44.

7. See Dempsey, "The Wolfers and the Cypress Hills Massacre," chap. 8 in *Firewater*, pp. 109–23; also Sharp, *Whoop-Up Country*, pp. 55–77.

8. Graybill, *Policing the Great Plains*, p. 3.

9. Dempsey, *Firewater*, p. 186.

10. Annual Report of the Secretary of Interior, U.S. Department of Interior, 41st Cong., 3rd sess., 656, as cited and quoted in McManus, *The Line Which Separates*, p. 66.

11. Ibid.

12. Agent John Young to Benjamin F. Potts, November 18, 1879, as cited in the *Madisonian* (Virginia City), on November 29, 1879, p. 2; Blackfeet Agency, Monthly Reports (hereafter MR), December 1, 1879, Copies of General Letters Sent (hereafter CGLS), 1875–1915, entry 3, vol. 4B, RBA, RG 75, NARA, Rocky Mountain Region Archives, Denver (hereafter NARA-D).

13. John Young, MR, December 1, 1879, CGLS, 1875–1915, entry 3, vol. 4B, RBA, RG 75, NARA-D.

14. Ibid. For the identity of the agency personnel, see *Helena Weekly Herald*, October 16, 1879, p. 4, and for A. C. Hill's supervision of the agency police, see microcopy 234, roll 515, frames 1129 and 1130, RG 75, NARA. Dr. Hill had been appointed resident physician on April 19, 1875, and was, in the words of Agent John Wood, "a regularly educated physician thoroughly competent to perform his duties." See Blackfeet Correspondence, I-16, RBA, roll 45, NARA-D.

15. John Young, MR, December 1, 1879 (see note 13); Agent John Young to Commanding Officer, NWMP, Fort McLeod, NWT, November 18, 1879, I-16, RBA, roll 56, Letter Press Book, pp. 107–10, RG 75, NARA-D.

16. Young to Commanding Officer, NWMP, November 18, 1879 (see note 15).

17. Ibid.

18. Ibid.

19. *New North-West*, November 28, 1879, p. 3. Later Governor Potts again offered a one-thousand-dollar territorial reward in the case of the murder of Charles Tacke on August 30, 1880. For the legal foundation of these rewards,

see 1872 Laws of Montana Territory, Sec. 190. The first alleged and then convicted killer, Peter Pelkey, was tried at the same time as Spopee, and both were sentenced to hang on the same day. See Donovan, *Legal Hangings*, p. 71.

20. See W. F. Sanders, letter to the editor, *Helena Independent*, July 8, 1914, p. 8.

21. Hunt, *Whiskey Peddler*, p. 76.

22. Ibid., p. 94.

23. John Young to Commanding Officer, NWMP, November 18, 1879 (see note 15).

24. Ibid. See also Major J. T. Winder to Agent John Young, November 28, 1879, I-16, RBA, roll 46, RG 75, NARA-D. The initials "J. T.", indicating Major Winder's first and middle name, were made in error. Winder's first name is William. See Dempsey, *Firewater*, p. 194. For wolfers and wolfing, see Dempsey, *Firewater*, pp. 109–14.

25. Major J. T. Winder to Agent John Young, November 28, 1879 (see note 24).

26. Major J. T. Winder to John Young, November 25, 1879.

27. Ibid. For the colorful career of Henry Alfred "Fred" Kanouse, Chouteau County deputy sheriff, whiskey trader, murderer of Jim Nabors, and the second husband of Natawista or Mrs. Alexander Culbertson and aunt of Spopee, see Dempsey, *Firewater*, pp. 213–14 and passim as well as Dempsey, "Fred Kanouse: Calgary's First Businessman," *Calgary Herald*, May 31, 1957. See also Wischmann, *Frontier Diplomats*.

28. Major J. T. Winder to Agent John Young, November 28, 1879 (see note 24); John Young to Governor B. F. Potts, December 9, 1879, I-16, RBA, roll 56, Letter Press Book, p. 132, RG 75, NARA-D.

29. *Saskatchewan Herald*, December 29, 1879 (remarks dated December 1, 1879).

30. All quotations are identical to the original source, including misspellings, which shall go unnoted except where egregious or potentially confusing.

31. *Helena Daily Independent*, December 3, 1879, p. 3.

32. John Young to Major J. T. (read "William") Winder, Fort McLeod, NWT, December 9, 1879, I-16, RBA, roll 56, Letter Press Book, pp. 136–38, RG 75, NARA-D. For the December 9, 1879, letter to Governor Potts and the December 16, 1879, letter, see *Helena Daily Independent*, December 23, 1879, p. 3; see also John Young, MR, January 2, 1880 (see note 13). Many years later, in 1914, Dr. A. C. Hill, writing in the *Minneapolis Journal*, offered conflicting testimony, reporting that Spopee had killed Walmesley's dog at the time he had shot and killed the trapper.

33. John Young to Major J. T. (should read "William") Winder, Fort McLeod, NWT , December 9, 1879 (see note 32); John Young to Governor B. F. Potts, December 9, 1879 (see note 28). On the identity of Thomas Davis, see Young to Marshall Alex C. Botkin, January 27, 1880, I-16, RBA, roll 56, Third Letter Book, pp. 177–78, RG 75, NARA-D.

34. John Young to Major J. T. Winder, December 9, 1879 (see note 28).

35. Wischmann, *Frontier Diplomats*, p. 364.

36. John Young to Marshall Alex C. Botkin, January 27, 1880, I-16, RBA, roll 56, Third Letter Book, pp. 177–78, RG 75, NARA-D.

37. Agent John Young to Major J. T. Winder, December 10, 1879, I-16, RBA, roll 56, Third Letter Book, pp. 139–45, RG 75, NARA-D.

38. John Young, Annual Agent's Report, August 6, 1880, to R. E. Trowbridge, Commissioner of Indian Affairs, Blackfeet Agency, CGLS, 1875-1915, entry 3, vol. 4B, p. 78, RBA, RG 75, NARA-D. For the date of December 15, see *Helena Daily Herald,* January 15, 1880, p. 3.

39. *Helena Daily Herald,* December 23, 1879, p. 3. For the August 13, 1877, Indian census, see microcopy 234, LR, Office of Indian Affairs (hereafter OIA), 1824–81, roll 506, 1877, frame 206, RG 75, NARA.

40. For the Sioux refugees, see MacEwan, *Sitting Bull,* pp. 90–91; for the Canadian tribes who had taken treaty and their southern migrations, see Tobias, "Canada's Subjugation of the Plains Cree," p. 215.

41. Commissioners of the NWMP, *Opening the West,* Report of Commissioner James Walsh, 1877, p. 20, as quoted in Daschuk, Hackett, Macneil, "Treaties and Tuberculosis," p. 317.

42. Report of the NWMP for 1879 by Superintendent William Winder, Annual Reports for the Department of the NWMP, Canada, Parliament, Sessional Papers, 1880, vol. 3, second session of the fourth Parliament, pp. 8–9.

43. As quoted in Treaty 7 Elders and Tribal Council with Hildebrandt, Carter, and First Rider, *The True Spirit and Original Intent of Treaty 7,* p. 259.

44. Hugh A. Dempsey, "The Starvation Year," part 1, p. 10.

45. For more on the situation around Fort Macleod, see *Saskatchewan Herald,* November 3, 1879, and especially, December 29, 1879. On Edgar Dewdney, see Edgar B. Dewdney to D. L. McPherson, August 4, 1881, in the Macdonald Papers, vol. 210, pp. 242–43, as quoted by Hugh A. Dempsey in *Crowfoot,* p. 115, and Paul F. Sharp, *Whoop-Up Country,* p. 155.

46. *Saskatchewan Herald* (Regina), December 29, 1879.

47. Report of William Winder, NWMP, Canada, Parliament, Sessional Papers, 1880, vol. 3, second session of the fourth Parliament, part III, "North-West Mounted Police Force, Commissioner's Report 1879," appendix, p. 9. For selling horses and pawning guns, see Hugh A. Dempsey, "The Starvation Year," part 1, p. 8. For Macleod's report, see Macleod to Dewdney, Ft. Macleod, December 29, 1880, Canadian House of Commons, Annual Report of the Department of Indian Affairs, 1880, Sessional Papers (1881), as quoted in McCrady, *Living with Strangers,* p. 90.

48. Hugh A. Dempsey, *The Vengeful Wife,* p. 220.

49. Dewdney to Superintendent General of Indian Affairs, Ottawa, December 31, 1880, Canadian House of Commons, Annual Report of the Department of Indian Affairs, 1880, Sessional Papers (1881), p. 81, as quoted in McCrady, *Living with Strangers,* p. 90.

50. Jean L'Heureux to Dewdney, Ft. Walsh, September 29, 1880, National Archives of Canada, RG 10, vol. 3771, file 34527, microfilm reel C-10135, as quoted in McCrady, *Living with Strangers*, p. 90.

51. I-16, RBA, roll 56, October 21, 1879, Letter Press Book, note 85, RG 75, NARA-D.

52. John Young to Major J. T. Winder, December 10, 1879 (see note 36), pp. 139–45.

53. John Young, MR, January 2, 1880 (see note 13). See also *Madisonian*, December 27, 1879, p. 3. Interestingly, the agency physician, A. C. Hill, recollected that he was the one who had wrung a confession out of Good Rider: "He told me everything." See *Minneapolis Journal* and *Great Falls Tribune*, July 19, 1914.

54. John Young to B. F. Potts, December 16, 1879, I-16, RBA, roll 56, Third Letter Press Book, pp. 146–52, RG 75, NARA-D.

55. Ewers, *The Blackfeet*, pp. 279–80. The Piegan term comes from a personal conversation with Earl Old Person, 2008.

56. Dempsey, *Firewater*, p. 96. Riplinger Road is named after John Riplinger, post trader on the Teton, who in the winter of 1869–70 built another post on the Marias.

57. For the Riplinger Road, see U.S. Army Corps of Engineers Map of Northern Montana, as well as Kennedy, "Whoop-Up Trail of Northcentral Montana," and Wright, Dorius, Innes, and Lowry, "Mapping the Alberta Route," p. 2–5. For the Blackfoot reference to the Livingston Range as "tipi liners," see Blackfoot Gallery Committee, *The Story of the Blackfoot People*, p. 4.

58. For the December 9, 1879, letter to Governor Potts and the December 16, 1879, letter, see *Helena Daily Independent*, December 23, 1879, p. 3; see also John Young, MR, January 2, 1880 (see note 13).

59. Information on the rifle came from Dr. A. C. Hill, *Great Falls Daily Tribune*, July 19, 1914.

60. *Helena Daily Independent*, December 23, 1879, p. 3; see also John Young, MR, January 2, 1880, p. 62 (see note 13).

61. For a welcome discussion of war honors among the Blackfoot-speakers, see L. James Dempsey, *Blackfoot War Art*, p. 14.

62. John Young, MR, January 2, 1880, p. 62 (see note 13).

63. For the December 9, 1879, letter to Governor Potts and the December 16, 1879, letter, see *Helena Daily Independent*, December 23, 1879, p. 3; see also John Young, MR, January 2, 1880 (see note 13). For Hamilton and Hazlet's trading post, see *Benton Weekly Record*, January 9, 1880, p. 3.

64. *Benton Record*, November 7, 1879, p. 3; see also *Helena Weekly Herald*, October 16, 1879, p. 4.

65. *Helena Weekly Herald*, October 16, 1879, p. 8.

66. *Helena Weekly Herald*, October 23, 1879, p. 7.

67. E. J. Brooks, Acting Commissioner of Indian Affairs, to John Young, Blackfeet Agency, December 27, 1879, I-16, RBA, roll 46, RG 75, NARA-D.

68. *Helena Daily Independent,* December 23, 1879, p. 3.

69. Ibid. See also John Young, MR, January 2, 1880 (see note 13).

70. Chief Eustace interview, January 27, 1950, Claude Schaeffer papers (M-1100-88). In this interview Eustace is reminiscing about events of his youth during the 1870s and 1880s. See also Reeves and Peacock, *Our Mountains Are Our Pillows,* p. 40, where the authors reference an interview with Chief Eustace, July 27, 1950, done by Claude Schaeffer, f: 88.

71. Chief Eustace interview; Reeves and Peacock, *Our Mountains Are Our Pillows,* p. 40.

72. Hugh A. Dempsey, "The Starvation Year," part 2, p. 11.

73. Chief Eustace interview, Claude Schaeffer papers.

74. The Issue Reports for January, February, and March of 1879, I-16, RBA, roll 22, "Issues to Indians," RG 75, NARA-D.

75. John Young to Major J. T. Winder, December 10 (see note 36), pp. 141.

76. Annual Report of Superintendent L. N. F. Crozier, 1880, pp. 30–34, in Walsh Papers, Provincial Archives of Canada, microfilm box M705, Public Archives of Manitoba collection 333-41, as quoted in LaDow, *The Medicine Line,* p. 41.

CHAPTER 2

1. *Helena Daily Herald,* December 23, 1879, p. 3.

2. Ibid.

3. See A. B. Hamilton's letter of December 17, 1879, which was printed in the *Helena Daily Herald,* December 22, 1879, p. 3; see also *Helena Daily Herald,* December 25, 1879, p. 2.

4. *Helena Daily Herald,* December 22, 1879, p. 3.

5. *Benton Record,* December 26, 1879, p. 3.

6. For the distances, round trip, see "A Wild 400 Mile Ride through the Indian Country," *Helena Daily Independent,* January 16, 1880, p. 3.

7. *Helena Daily Herald,* August 1, 1879, p. 2.

8. Ibid.

9. Ibid.

10. Ibid.

11. *Helena Daily Herald,* March 10, 1879, p. 3.

12. Governor B. F. Potts to John Young, Blackfeet Agent, December 20, 1879, I-16, RBA, roll 46, RG 75, NARA-D.

13. Alexander C. Botkin, U.S. Marshal, to Agent John Young, January 3, 1880, I-16, RBA, roll 46, RG 75, NARA-D.

14. *Helena Daily Herald,* January 15, 1880, p. 3.

15. *Benton Record,* December 19, 1879, p. 3; for the buggy, see *Benton Weekly Record,* January 2, 1880, p. 3.

16. *Benton Record,* December 19, 1879, p. 3.

17. Blackfeet Agency, MR, February 2, 1880, p. 64, CGLS, 1875–1915, entry 3, vol. 4B, RBA, RG 75, NARA-D.

18. Alex C. Botkin, U.S. Marshal, to Chas. Devens, Attorney General, November 23, 1879, Montana Historical Society (hereafter MHS), vertical file, copies from the Department of Justice, Washington, D.C.

19. Ibid.

20. Ibid.

21. Alex C. Botkin, U.S. Marshal, to Chas. Devens, Attorney General, January 5, 1880, MHS, vertical file, copies from the Department of Justice, Washington, D.C.

22. For the complete story of the killing and trial of Star Child, see Hugh A. Dempsey, *The Vengeful Wife*, pp. 157–72.

23. Denny, *Riders of the Plains*, pp. 132–33.

24. Hugh A. Dempsey, *The Vengeful Wife*, p. 163.

25. *Helena Daily Independent*, January 16, 1880, p. 3.

26. *Helena Daily Independent*, January 16, 1880, p. 3; for the buggy, see *Benton Weekly Record*, January 2, 1880, p. 3.

27. Schultz, *Blackfeet and Buffalo*, p. 27.

28. Ibid.

29. Eli Guardipee's Story, p. 11, MHS.

30. Schultz, *Blackfeet and Buffalo*, p. 33.

31. Ibid., p. 36.

32. Eli Guardipee's Story, p. 12, MHS.

33. *Benton Weekly Record*, January 2, 1880, p. 3.

34. Ibid.

35. Schultz, *My Life as an Indian*, pp. 370 ff.

36. For the Christmas Eve date, see *Helena Daily Herald*, January 15, 1880, p. 3.

37. For the winter count of Bad Head, a minor chief of the Bloods, see Hugh A. Dempsey, *A Blackfoot Winter Count*, p. 17; and Racska, *Winter Count*, p. 69.

38. *Helena Daily Herald*, January 15, 1880, p. 3; and *Helena Weekly Herald*, January 22, 1880, p. 8.

39. *Helena Daily Herald*, January 16, 1880, p. 3.

40. Schultz, *My Life as an Indian*, p. 370. Schultz gave much the same account in the memorial of Joseph Kipp published in the *Great Falls Daily Tribune*, July 5, 1914, and reprinted there as well on July 19, 1914, in an article titled "Innocence of Spo-pee Questioned by Men Who Know Story of Crime."

41. Schultz, *My Life as an Indian*, p. 370.

42. Ibid., p. 371.

43. Ibid.

44. Schultz, "Joseph Kipp," *Great Falls Daily Tribune*, July 5, 1914, p. 4.

45. Schultz, *My Life as an Indian*, p. 372.

46. *Helena Daily Herald*, January 16, 1880, p. 3.

47. Hugh A. Dempsey, *Firewater*, pp. 47–48.

48. See Hugh A. Dempsey, *Red Crow*, p. 68; and Schultz, *My Life as an Indian*, p. 371. Information on Healy's Blackfoot name stems from personal communication with Hugh Dempsey, June 12, 2009. For the fracas with The Weasel Head, see Tappen Adney Papers, microfilm, "The Weasel Head," chap. 6, pp. 90–96, MHS. This account was written in Seattle, August 25, 1905, in reply to a request for certain details, previously related.

49. Tappen Adney Papers, microfilm, "The Weasel Head," chap. 6, pp. 90–96, MHS.

50. Schultz, *My Life as an Indian*, p. 370. Healy was to make a career of hauling Indians out of their camps. See the 1882 arrest of Mountain Chief's son, The Rider, related in the *Daily Helena Independent*, November 1, 1882, p. 3.

51. See "Report J. M. J. Sanno, Capt. 7th Infantry of His Inspection of Indian Supplies at the Blackfeet Indian Reservation, M.T.," sent to Lieut. L. F. Burnett, A.A. Adjt. General District of Montana, in microcopy 234, LR, OIA, 1824–1881, 1877, roll 508, 1877, frame 0964, RG 75, NARA.

52. Agent John Young to E. A. Hayt, August 5, 1878, microcopy 234, LR, OIA, roll 512, frame 613, RG 75, NARA.

53. *Helena Weekly Herald*, February 7, 1878, p. 4.

54. Agent John Young to E. A. Hayt, August 5, 1878, microcopy 234, LR, OIA, roll 512, frame 613; and John Young to E. A. Hayt, June 2, 1879, microcopy 234, LR, OIA, roll 512, frame 1057—both in RG 75, NARA. For the number of police (thirty), see Blackfeet Agency, CGLS, 1875–1915 (entry 3), vol. 4B, August 20, 1880, p. 81, RG 75, NARA-D.

55. A. C. Hill, Chief of Police, to John Young, Blackfoot Agent, July 15, 1879, microcopy 234, LR, OIA, roll 512, frames 1073–74, RG 75, NARA.

56. Chas. A. Coolidge, Capt. 7 Infantry, Inspector Indian Supt., to Commissioner, OIA, May 14, 1879, microcopy 234, LR, OIA, MS, roll 513, frames 483–92, RG 75, NARA.

57. Author's interview with Earl Old Person, September 24, 2005.

58. A. C. Hill, Chief of Police, to John Young, Blackfoot Agent, October 15, 1879, microcopy 234, LR, OIA, roll 515, frames 1129–30, RG 75, NARA.

59. *Helena Daily Herald*, October 11, 1879, p. 3; *Helena Weekly Herald*, October 16, 1879, p. 8.

60. *Benton Weekly Record*, January 2, 1880, p. 3.

61. *Helena Weekly Herald*, January 6, 1881, p. 1.

62. *Benton Weekly Record*, January 2, 1880, p. 3.

63. Ibid.

64. John J. Donnelly was a fiery Irishman born in Rhode Island who led Fort Benton volunteers against the Nez Perce at Fort Claggett and Cow Island; see Sheriff John Healy to Agent Young, Blackfeet Agency, January 5, 1880, LR, RBA, RG 75, Set 2, NARA-D. Also found in I-16, RBA, roll 46, RG 75, NARA-D.

65. John Young to Governor B. F. Potts, December 16, 1879, as cited in the *Helena Daily Independent*, December 23, 1879, p. 3, and referred to in the *Helena Daily Independent*, January 16, 1880, p. 3. Healy's use of the "medicine paper" is related in the newspaper on January 16 as well.

66. This should be "Mekaisto." See Hugh A. Dempsey, *Red Crow*, p. 17.

67. H. A. Kanouse had been employed as a trader for the I. G. Baker & Company on the Marias River but had concentrated his efforts in Whoop-Up Country after he had killed Jim Nabors on American territory in 1872. He later built a fur-trading post in partnership with George Houk at the north end of Waterton Lake, "half way up from the Big Lake, just where the trail started." See Hugh Dempsey, *Firewater*, p. 160.

68. "Dutch Fred" was Alfred H. Wachter. See the *Benton Weekly Record*, January 9, 1880, p. 3.

69. See Hugh A. Dempsey, *Firewater*, p. 96.

70. *Benton Weekly Record*, January 9, 1880, p. 3.

71. Ibid.

72. Ibid.

73. Ewers, *The Blackfeet*, p. 250.

74. *Benton Weekly Record*, January 9, 1880, p. 3.

75. Ibid. The information on kissing was given to me by Earl Old Person in a conversation I had with him on August 20, 2008. In another example, George Bird Grinnell reported how the leader of the Crows came out to meet Bear Chief, kissed him, and took him to the middle of the group and sat down. See Grinnell, Letters, reel 35, heading "Glacier National Park," August 10, 1928, p. 37.

76. *Benton Weekly Record*, January 9, 1880, p. 3.

77. John Young to John J. Healy, from Piegan, Mont., January 20, 1880, I-16, RBA, roll 56, RG 75, NARA-D; Young to Winder, January 20, 1880, I-16, RBA, roll 56, RG 75, NARA-D.

78. *Helena Daily Herald*, January 13, 1880, p. 3.

79. Alex C. Botkin, U.S. Marshal, to John Young, U.S. Indian Agent, January 8, 1880, I-16, RBA, vol. 56, RG 75, NARA-D.

80. John Young to Alex C. Botkin, January 14, 1880, I-16, RBA, roll 56, RG 75, NARA-D.

81. Ibid., January 27, 1880.

82. Special to the *Benton Weekly Record*, February 6, 1880, p. 3. Isaac R. Alden was listed as the clerk of the Montana Territorial Supreme Court; see *Helena Daily Independent*, November 19, 1880, p. 1.

83. *Helena Daily Herald*, January 16, 1880, p. 3.

84. Ibid.

85. *Benton Weekly Record*, February 6, 1880, p. 3. See also John Young to the Commissioner of Indian Affairs, February 2, 1880, Blackfeet Agency, MR, CGLS, 1875–1915, entry 3, vol. 4B, RBA, RG 75, NARA-D.

86. Clark C. Spence, *Territorial Politics and Government*, p. 221.

87. U.S. Attorney, Helena, Montana, J. W. Andrews, to Agent John Young, Blackfeet Agency, March 8, 1880, LR, RBA, box 5, entry 2, file 34, RG 75, NARA-D.

88. *Helena Daily Independent*, February 5, 1880, p. 3. A possible copy of Bundy's photo of Spopee appeared in the *Minneapolis Journal*, July 9, 1914, p. 1, on the occasion of his pardon and release. (See photograph on page 67.)

89. Spopee to Agent John Young, October 10, 1880, LR, RBA, box 5, entry 2, folder 37, RG 75, NARA-D.

90. Ibid., October 18, 1880.

CHAPTER 3

1. Everton J. Conger file, July 5, 1883, Appointment Papers, Department of Justice, NARA, as quoted in Clark C. Spence, *Territorial Politics and Government*, p. 214.

2. *Helena Weekly Herald*, Thursday, July 22, 1875, p. 5.

3. See Reid, *Law for the Elephant*; and Reid, *Policing the Elephant*, as well as Ellis, "Legal Culture and Community," p. 187.

4. Montana Laws, 1872, p. 220, sec. 196.

5. Wunder, "Persistence and Adaptation," p. 115. In 1876, the Flathead agent, Charles S. Medary, wrote to the commissioner of Indian Affairs complaining about the Flathead chief, Arlee. Together with Michelle, the Pend d'Oreille chief, Arlee had been absent in Deer Lodge "as witnesses, I believe against the Government" in a case involving the sale of whiskey by a trader named T. J. Demers. "If it be true," he wrote, "that they are his witnesses of course they are there to testify that they gave him [Demers] permission to have his cattle on the reservation. They must therefore perjure themselves, as they, twice at least, denied to me that they had given him authority." Chas. S. Medary, Flathead Agent, to J. Q. Smith, Commissioner of Indian Affairs, December 8, 1876, microcopy 234, LR, OIA, 1824–81, roll 505, 1864–1880, frame 702, RG 75, NARA.

6. Wunder, "Persistence and Adaptation," p. 115.

7. Daschuk, Hackett, and Macneil, "Treaties and Tuberculosis," p. 308.

8. The so-called Cypress Hills massacre in the spring of 1873, in which a camp of Assiniboine Indians was attacked by a group of "wolfers" from Fort Benton, resulted in a protracted effort on the part of the British minister in Washington to request warrants and extradition. When on June 21, 1875, seven of the wanted men were arrested in Fort Benton by federal marshals, there was great public outrage, and the uproar continued with an extradition hearing in Helena. This was deemed "a British invasion" of American rights, causing an immense brouhaha, fueled in part by the Irish Fenians of Fort Benton. Public sentiment also was of the opinion that Indian "outlaws" had to be "pursued and punished according to their own method of warfare." This was considered,

as historian Paul Sharp has written, "a positive good, insisting that it was not a crime but . . . a salutary lesson to the red men." Sharp, *Whoop-Up Country*, pp. 70–71.

9. For Nebraska, see Ellis, "Legal Culture and Community on the Great Plains," p. 191, where "indigent affidavits" were filed.

10. For more on whether or not Indians were legally persons, see Mathes and Lowitt, *The Standing Bear Controversy*, p. 69.

11. For an example of the calls for confinement of Indians to their reservations in Montana Territory, see Granville Stuart's letter to Martin Maginnis, *Helena Weekly Independent*, September 8, 1881, as well as Stuart's petition to the secretary of the Interior, Samuel J. Kirkwood, April 18, 1881, found reprinted in the *River Press* (Fort Benton, Montana Territory), May 4, 1881, p. 4. "All these Indians have large reservations set apart for their sole use and benefit, and it is rank injustice to the whites, and a positive injury to the Indians, to allow them to roam uncontrolled over all the territory."

12. As noted in the preface and in an insightful review by Gilles Renaud, Clare V. McKenna's recent study, *The Trial of "Indian Joe,"* provides a provocative parallel description in California of the judicial consequences of such racial public bias a decade later than Spopee.

13. United States v. Spo-pe alias Turtle, box 28, folder 425, Records of U.S. District Courts, Territorial Court Montana, Third Judicial District, Helena, case files 1867–89, RG 21, National Archives, Pacific Alaska Region, Seattle, Washington (hereafter NARA-PAR).

14. Ibid.

15. Agent John Young, Blackfeet Agency, MR, December 25, 1880, p. 88, CGLS, 1875–1915, entry 3, vol. 4B, RBA, RG 75, NARA-D.

16. Ibid. For Young's appearance, see *Helena Daily Herald*, November 29, 1880, p. 3.

17. John Young, MR, December 25, 1880, p. 88, CGLS, 1875–1915, entry 3, vol. 4B, RBA, RG 75, NARA-D. See also Register of Actions, *U.S. v. Spo-pe*, box 28, folder 425, Records of U.S. District Courts, Territorial Court Montana, Third Judicial District, Helena, case files 1867–89, RG 21, NARA-PAR.

18. *Helena Daily Herald*, December 11, 1880, p. 3; see also December 12, 1880, p. 3. Attorneys Sanders and Chumasero, in their later appeal to President Garfield to commute Spopee's death sentence to life imprisonment, also stated that "Upon his [Spopee's] arraignment, Hon. E. J. Conger, Associate Justice of this territory appointed us to defend him [Spopee] as his attorneys which we did." Records of the Office of the Pardon Attorney (hereafter ROPA), pardon case files, 28-692, New Year's Day, 1881, RG 204, NARA.

19. ROPA, pardon case files, 28-692, Plea for Clemency, New Year's Day, 1881, RG 204, NARA.

20. For Sanders as "Pericles," see Pemberton, "Montana's Pioneer Courts," p. 104; for "keenest blade," see McClure, "Wilber Fisk Sanders," p. 29.

21. Allen, *A Decent Orderly Lynching*, p. 166.

22. Ibid., p.183.

23. Malone and Roeder, *Montana*, pp. 150–51.

24. Clark C. Spence, *Territorial Politics and Government*, p. 96.

25. Sharp, *Whoop-Up Country*, pp. 71–72.

26. Guice, *The Rocky Mountain Bench*, p. 76.

27. Various documents, Western Law and Order, University Publications of America, reel 3, LR, Attorney General, 1871–84 (e.g., see frames 302, 308, 323, 375, 434).

28. Clark C. Spence, *Territorial Politics and Government*, p. 227. See also Criticism of W. F. Sanders in various documents, Western Law and Order, reel 3, LR, Attorney General, 1871–84.

29. *U.S. v. Spo-pe* (see note 13).

30. *Helena Daily Herald*, December 16, 1880, p. 3.

31. See Wunder, "Persistence and Adaptation," pp. 112–15.

32. *Helena Weekly Herald*, December 23, 1880, p. 4.

33. For an account of the events of December 16, 1880, see *Helena Weekly Herald*, December 23, 1880, p. 4, including the swearing in of A. B. Hamilton as interpreter. For an additional citation for the swearing in of A. B. Hamilton on December 16, 1880, see *Helena Daily Independent*, December 17, 1880, p. 3.

34. *Helena Daily Herald*, December 16, 1880, p. 3.

35. *Helena Weekly Herald*, December 23, 1880, p. 4.

36. *Helena Daily Herald*, Thursday, December 16, 1880, p. 3.

37. *U.S. v. Spo-pe* (see note 13).

38. *Helena Daily Herald*, December 16, 1880.

39. *U.S. v. Spo-pe* (see note 13). See also Record of Journal of Proceedings, Records of U.S. District Courts, Third Judicial District, Territorial Court, Helena, Montana, pp. 196–201, RG 21, NARA-PAR; and *Helena Weekly Herald*, January 6, 1881, p. 1.

40. *U.S. v. Spo-pe* (see note 13).

41. Ibid.

42. Ibid.

43. Ibid. For date of conviction, see box 6, Register of Actions, 1873–1889, p. 203.

44. *Helena Daily Herald*, December 17, 1880, p. 3.

45. *New North-West*, Friday, December 17, 1880, p. 3.

46. *Helena Daily Herald*, December 21, 1880, p. 3.

47. Record of Journal of Proceedings (see note 39), pp. 199–200. I. R. Alden was the Clerk of the Third Judicial District. See *Helena Daily Independent*, November 19, 1880, p. 1.

48. *Helena Weekly Independent*, December 22, 1880.

49. *Helena Daily Independent*, November 19, 1880, p. 1. For the ten o'clock hour, see *Helena Daily Herald*, December 20, 1880, p. 3.

50. *Helena Daily Independent,* November 19, 1880.

51. See *Fort Benton River Press,* December 22, 1880, p. 8; and *Madisonian,* December 25, 1880, p. 2. "Spo-pee, the Indian charged with the murder of Charles Walmsley, near the British line, was also found guilty. Good Rider, the other Indian implicated in the last-named crime, was acquitted." See also *Benton Weekly Record,* January 7, 1881, p. 5.

52. *Helena Daily Herald,* December 27, 1880, p. 3.

53. Ibid.

54. *Helena Weekly Herald,* Thursday, January 6, 1881, p. 1.

55. *Helena Weekly Herald,* Monday, December 27, 1880, p. 3.

56. *Helena Daily Herald,* December 21, 1880, p. 3.

57. *Benton Weekly Record,* January 7, 1881, p. 5.

58. *Helena Daily Herald,* December 27, 1880, p. 3.

59. Record of Journal of Proceedings (see note 39). See also the account in the *Helena Weekly Independent,* December 30, 1880.

60. Hugh A. Dempsey, *Jerry Potts,* pp.–17.

61. *Benton Weekly Record,* January 9, 1880, p. 3.

62. See transcript of author's interview with Charley Crow Chief, Great Falls, Montana, in author's possession.

63. Ewers, *The Blackfeet,* pp. 249–50.

64. For the sign to shake hands, see J. J. Healy, "The Weasel Head," in Healy Reminiscences, microfilm 95, p. 94, MHS.

65. *Helena Weekly Herald,* Thursday, January 6, 1881, p. 1.

66. Ibid. For the Iron Line, see Sharp, *Whoop-Up Country,* p. 155, quoting from *Fort Benton Record,* July 19, 1878; see also Hugh A. Dempsey, *Firewater,* p. 80.

67. See Hugh A. Dempsey, *Firewater,* p. 80, for the remembrance of this incident by a Blood chief.

68. Hugh A. Dempsey, *Red Crow,* p. 83.

69. Hugh A. Dempsey, ed. *A Blackfoot Winter Count,* p. 16.

70. *Helena Weekly Herald,* January 6, 1881, p. 3.

71. Ibid.

72. A special report for the *Fort Benton Record* from Helena substantiated Spopee's reference to a "Commissioner" and the "squaw interpreter." On February 3, 1880, nine months earlier, the newspaper had reported, "Spopee and Good Rider, the Indians who murdered Charles Walmsbury, on Cut Bank River, in October last, had their examination before U.S. Commissioner Alden today. Both Indians confessed to having murdered Walmsbury."

73. For the Court Directory, see *Helena Daily Independent,* November 19, 1880, p. 1.

74. For Wren as farmer, see *Helena Weekly Herald,* October 16, 1879, p. 4. For the account of their expenses, see Alex C. Botkin, U.S. Marshal, to John Young, Blackfeet agent, June 6, 1881, I-16, RBA, roll 46, RG 75, NARA-D.

75. *Helena Daily Herald,* December 28, 1880, p. 3.

76. Letter from Spopee or Snake in St. Elizabeths Hospital to his wife, June 27, 1884, RSEH, file 5445, RG 418, NARA.

77. See Brown and Peers, *Pictures Bring Us Messages,* p. 111.

78. In Appendix 2 of De Jong's *Blackfoot Texts,* Mountain Chief, or Ninastako, relates how and why he gave his children their names.

79. Record of Journal of Proceedings (see note 39), box 6, p. 425.

80. *Helena Daily Herald,* December 27, 1880, p. 3.

81. *Benton Weekly Record,* January 7, 1881, p. 5.

82. *Helena Daily Herald,* December 27, 1880, p. 3.

CHAPTER 4

1. The Revised Statutes of Montana, Twelfth Legislative Assembly of Montana, 1879, Sec. 377, p. 336.

2. *Benton Weekly Record,* January 7, 1881, p. 3.

3. Ibid.

4. Ibid., p. 4.

5. *Helena Daily Herald,* February 3, 1881, p. 3.

6. Ibid.

7. Ibid.

8. Ibid.

9. Ibid.

10. *Helena Daily Herald,* February 3, 1881, p. 2.

11. See writs of error and appeals from the final decisions of the supreme court of either of the Territories of New Mexico, Utah, Colorado, Dakota, Arizona, Idaho, Montana, or Wyoming in *Revised Statutes of the United States,* title 23, chap. 2, p. 336.

12. *Helena Daily Independent,* Montana, January 10, 1881.

13. Morriss, "Judicial Removal," p. 88.

14. Clark C. Spence, "The Territorial Bench in Montana," p. 26.

15. Richard Kluger, in his *The Bitter Waters of Medicine Creek,* has explored the trials of the Nisqually leader Leschi, accused and then convicted by Washington Territory of murder in 1857. Although Spopee's case is much later, there are many similarities between it and Washington Territory v. Leschi, an Indian. These included a public sentiment that was openly racist in tone, a developing territorial judicial system, numerous legal shortcomings in spite of claims to the contrary, and, after conviction and appeal, the decision to seek executive clemency from either the president of the United States or the governor of Washington Territory. Yet while Leschi's case was notorious and well known, in part because of the animus of Governor Isaac Ingalls Stevens and in part because it concluded with the hanging of Leschi, I am doubtful if Sanders and Chumasero were aware of it in their own deliberations in Helena, Montana, specifically

regarding how to overcome the prejudicial decisions that they encountered in their own territorial court.

16. Holmes and Garfield, "Peregrinations of a Politician," p. 39.

17. Clark C. Spence, "We Want a Judge," p. 7.

18. For a report of pardons granted by Governor B. F. Potts, see *Helena Daily Independent*, January 15, 1881.

19. Clark C. Spence, *Territorial Politics and Government*, p. 74.

20. Ibid., p. 85.

21. Ibid., p. 88.

22. Ibid., p.148.

23. Petition for Clemency, Sanders and Chumasero, Helena, Montana, ROPA, pardon case files, 28-692, New Year's Day, 1881, RG 204, NARA.

24. Ibid.

25. Ibid.

26. Ibid.

27. Ibid.

28. Ibid.

29. Ibid.

30. Wunder, "Persistence and Adaption," p. 115.

31. For instances of this public sentiment, see Sharp, *Whoop-Up Country*, pp. 70–71, quoting from territorial newspapers.

32. ROPA, pardon case files, 28-692, RG 204, NARA.

33. Ibid. See also *Helena Daily Herald* for the reprieve.

34. Alexander T. Gray, Clerk of Pardons, Department of Justice, to Attorney General [Wayne MacVeagh], April 9, 1881, ROPA, pardon case files, 28-692, RG 204, NARA.

35. Telegram sent from Helena, Montana, March 29, 1881, at 10:26 from J. L. Dryden, U.S. Attorney, to Alex T. Gray, Pardon Clerk, Washington, D.C. Copy found in RBIA, Central Classified Files (hereafter CCF), 1907–39, Series E: Law and Order, Records of the OIA, file 41522-14-175.5, U.S. v. "Spopee" or "Turtle," a Piegan Indian, RG 75, NARA.

36. *Benton Weekly Record*, June 16, 1881, p. 5.

37. McClure, "Wilbur Fisk Sanders," p. 29.

38. ROPA, pardon case files, 28-692, RG 204, NARA.

39. Ibid.

40. *Helena Daily Herald*, April 15, 1881. See also *Helena Weekly Herald*, April 21, 1881, p. 8.

41. Ibid.

42. Edgerton, *Montana Justice*, p. 35.

43. Ibid., pp. 35–41.

44. Ibid.

45. *Helena Daily Independent*, January 12, 1881.

46. *Helena Daily Herald*, April 15, 1881.

47. Ibid. For Botkin in a wheelchair, see Clark C. Spence, *Territorial Politics and Government*, p. 96.

48. *Helena Daily Independent*, May 5, 1881, p. 3.

49. Woodford and Woodford, *All Our Yesterdays*, p. 178, as quoted in Keve, "Building a Better Prison," footnote 9.

50. Keve, "Building a Better Prison," footnote 69.

51. Alex. Botkin, U.S. Marshal, to Attorney General of the United States, "Warrant for the Pardon of the following-named person, to wit Spo-pee or Turtle, was this day executed by his delivery at the Detroit (Mich.) House of Correction, as therein directed." See Copies of Pardon Attorney, Dept. of Justice, that were copied in 1914 and found in CCF, 1907–39, Blackfeet Agency, file 41522-14-175.5, Records of the OIA, RG 75, NARA.

52. See Botkin to John Young, June 6, 1881, I-16, RBA, roll 46, RG 75, NARA.

53. *Helena Daily Herald*, January 6, 1883, p. 3; *Fort Benton River Press*, Wednesday, January 17, 1883, p. 7.

54. J. L. Dryden, Jr., U.S. Attorney, to Major John Young, Agent, March 3, 1881, LR, 1873–1909, box 5, entry 2, file 38, RG 75, NARA-D.

55. I-16, RBA, roll 56, Letter Press Book, p. 2, RG 75, NARA-D. Painted Wing was still alive in October of 1914. See complaint about Superintendent A. E. McFatridge in Thomas R. Straw to the Commissioner of Indian Affairs, October 20, 1914, CCF, 1907–39, Blackfeet Agency 154, RG 75, NARA. For the spelling of Painted Wing's Blackfoot name, see I-16, RBA, roll 22, March 18, 1879, RG 75, NARA-D, where Painted Wing is number 106 with a family of six.

CHAPTER 5

1. *Benton Weekly Record*, January 2, 1880.

2. James Willard Schultz, Joseph Kipp obituary, *Great Falls Daily Tribune*, July 5, 1914.

3. Only some 10 months later, Jeff Talbert returned from the Musselshell Country, where he had tried to arrest a horse thief in a camp of one hundred and fifty lodges of Bloods and Piegan. Talbert failed to get his man because the Indians surrounded him with cocked guns and told him their "hearts were getting bad in consequence of two of their men being taken last winter whom the whites were going to hang." *Helena Weekly Independent*, October 14, 1880.

4. For the troops leaving Fort Benton, see *Helena Daily Herald*, February 7, 1880, p. 3.

5. Prucha, *American Indian Treaties*, pp. 310–13.

6. Ibid., especially pp. 6, 63–68, 100–103. See also Wilkenson, *American Indians, Time, and the Law*.

7. Prucha, *American Indian Treaties*, p. 312.

8. For a full discussion of these administrative decisions, see Farr, "Going to Buffalo," pp. 31–35.

9. Ibid., 31.

10. Capt. Edward Moale, Headquarters, Fort Benton, to Lieut. William Krause, Third Infantry, February 5, 1880, microcopy 234, LR, OIA, roll 518, frames 049–051, RG 75, NARA.

11. Telegram, Henry Brooks to T. C. Power, January 6, 1880, LR (entry 2), Blackfeet Agency, RBA, RG 75, NARA-D. For reference to Brooks and the Judith Cattle Company, see Burlingame, *The Montana Frontier*, p. 267.

12. *Benton Weekly Record*, quoted in *Weekly Miner*, October 14, 1879, p. 4.

13. *Benton Weekly Record*, January 2, 1880.

14. T. C. Power to E. A. Hayt, Commissioner, OIA, telegram, January 7, 1880, microcopy 234, LR, OIA, 1824–81, roll 517, frame 0168-0169.

15. Ibid.

16. Ibid.

17. Alexander Ramsey, Secretary of War, to Secretary of Interior, February 6, 1880, microcopy 234, LR, OIA, roll 418, frames 0034–38, RG 75, NARA.

18. For the establishment of the "Common Hunting Ground," see Farr, "'When We Were First Paid,'" pp. 131–54.

19. Report of John C. Wood, Blackfeet Agency, M.T., September 25, 1875, in U.S. Commissioner of Indian Affairs, *Annual Report*, 1875, p. 300.

20. Col. N. A. Miles, Keogh, M.T., to E. D. Townsend, Adjutant General, Department of Dakota, St. Paul, November 8, 1879, copy of telegram, forwarded to Secretary of War and Secretary of Interior, microcopy 234, LR, OIA, roll 515, November 22, 1879, frames 0920–23, RG 75, NARA.

21. Blackfeet Agency, MR, November 1, 1879, entry 3A, vol. 2, p. 55, RG 75, NARA-D.

22. Ibid.

23. Ibid.

24. Ibid., November and December 1879, RG 75, NARA-D.

25. *Helena Weekly Herald*, October 16, 1879, p. 8.

26. Blackfeet Agent John Young to E. A. Hayt, Commissioner, OIA, January 14, 1880, microcopy 234, LR, OIA, roll 518, frames 0485–87, RG 75, NARA.

27. Ibid.

28. John Young to Col. Thomas H. Ruger, January 27, 1880, I-16, RBA, roll 56, frame or page 172, RG 75, NARA-D.

29. Ibid.

30. Ibid.

31. Blackfeet Agency, MR, January 1880, entry 3A, vol. 2, pp. 64–65, RG 75, NARA-D.

32. Thomas H. Ruger to John Young, February 1, 1880, I-16, RBA, roll 46, RG 75, NARA-D.

33. For a thoughtful discussion of the concept of "outbreak" as a new, post–Civil War form of Indian violence, rebellion, and warfare conducted by Indians seeking to escape confinement on reservations, see Deloria, *Indians in Unexpected Places*, pp. 21–22. For Deloria, the events at Wounded Knee in 1890 are illustrative; for the Piegan, however, their Wounded Knee had taken place

twenty years earlier, in 1870, at the Baker massacre. After their slaughter on the Marias, the Piegan simply did not entertain the thought of armed resistance, believing "that to attempt to provoke further war would only result in their total extermination." See Ewers, *The Blackfeet*, p. 252, where he quotes the 1878 *Annual Report* of the commissioner of Indian Affairs, p. 82.

34. John Young to E. A. Hayt, OIA, February 3, 1880, I-16, RBA, roll 56, pp. 179–80, RG 75, NARA-D.

35. Capt. Edward Moale to Lieut. William Krause, February 5, 1880 (see note 10).

36. Capt. J. M. J. Sanno to Lieutenant L. F. Burnett, A.A. Adjt., Department of Montana, October 7, 1877, microcopy 234, LR, OIA, roll 508, frame 960–68, RG 75, NARA.

37. *Helena Weekly Independent*, October 27, 1881.

38. *Fort Benton Record*, June 8, 1877.

39. Ibid.

40. Joel Overholser, *Fort Benton*, p. 94.

41. Schultz, Obituary for Joseph Kipp, *Great Falls Daily Tribune,* Sunday, July 5, 1914.

42. Schultz told his account of the events in White Calf's camp on at least five different occasions, recycling his indignant telling of their unjust removal over and over, in almost the exact same words, first in 1907, with *My Life as an Indian,* then in the obituary for his friend, Joe Kipp, that he wrote for the *Great Falls Daily Tribune,* appearing July 5, 1914. The third and fourth versions came from *Friends of My Life as an Indian* (1923, pp. 106–108) and *Signposts of Adventure: Glacier National Park as the Indians Know It,* published in 1926. Finally there was "The Last Trading Camp of the Pikunis (1879–80)," published in the *Great Falls Tribune,* April 7, 1935, and republished in Schultz's *Blackfeet and Buffalo.*

43. Schultz, *Signposts of Adventure,* p. 92.

44. Schultz, *My Life as an Indian,* p. 373.

45. Schultz, *Friends of My Life as an Indian,* p. 106.

46. Schultz, *Blackfeet and Buffalo,* p. 33.

47. Blackfeet Agency, MR, February 1880, entry 3A, vol. 2, RBA, RG 75, NARA-D.

48. Schultz, *Signposts of Adventure,* p. 95.

49. Senator G. G. Vest, Martin Maginnis, Council at Blackfeet Agency, September 15, 1883, in Report of the Subcommittee of the Special Committee of U.S. Senate, Serial Set 2174, Special Report 283, 48 Cong., 1 sess., p. 243.

50. Schultz, *Signposts of Adventure,* p. 95.

51. Ibid., p. 96.

52. Schultz, *Blackfeet and Buffalo,* p. 34.

53. For endorsement of the Treaty of Fort Benton, see William H. Fanton, Special Indian Agent, and R. F. May, Blackfeet Agent, to E. P. Smith, Commissioner of Indian Affairs, Washington, D.C., May 16, 1874, microcopy 234, LR, OIA, roll 499, frames 0730–34, RG 75, NARA.

54. Colonel Thos. H. Ruger, Eighteenth Infantry, to Headquarters, District of Montana, Helena, Montana, September 1, 1881, quoted in U.S. Commissioner of Indian Affairs, *Annual Report*, 1881, pp. 10–11.

55. *Benton Weekly Record*, February 17, 1880, p. 5.

56. Ibid., February 20, 1880, p. 3.

57. Ibid.

58. Schultz, *Blackfeet and Buffalo*, p. 36.

59. Ibid.

60. Lieut. William Krause to Capt. Edward Moale, Fort Benton, M.T., March 25, 1880, copy sent by Moale to Acting Adj. Gen., Headquarters, District of Montana, Helena, M.T., March 26, 1880, microcopy 234, LR, OIA, roll 518, frames 0231–0235, RG 75, NARA.

61. *Helena Daily Herald*, March 15, 1880, utilizing report from Fort Benton.

62. Col. Ruger, District Headquarters, Helena, Montana, to Assistant Adjutant General, Headquarters, Department of Dakota, May 10, 1880, microcopy 234, LR, OIA, roll 518, frame 0221, RG 75, NARA. For the estimate of the number of horses lost, see Schultz, *Blackfeet and Buffalo*, p. 36.

63. *Helena Daily Herald*, Monday, March 26, 1880, p. 3.

64. *Benton Weekly Record*, March 19, 1880, p. 3.

65. *Benton Record*, February 27, 1880, p. 3.

66. *Benton Record Weekly*, March 19, 1880, p. 3.

67. Col. Ruger to Agent Young, February 13, 1880, I-16, RBA, roll 56, RG 75, NARA-D.

68. John Young, Blackfeet Agent, to E. J. Brooks, Acting Commissioner of Indian Affairs, March 16, 1880, microcopy 234, LR, OIA, roll 518, frames 0521–23, RG 75, NARA.

69. Lieut. William Krause to Capt. Edward Moale, Fort Benton, M.T., March 25, 1880 (see note 60).

70. Schultz, *Blackfeet and Buffalo*, p. 3.

71. Captain Edward Moale to Acting Asst. Adj. General, Headquarters District of Montana, Helena, March 26, 1880, microcopy 234, LR, OIA, roll 518, frames 0226–30, RG 75, NARA.

72. Ibid., frame 0228.

73. Ibid.

74. Schultz, *Blackfeet and Buffalo*, p. 36.

75. Col. Thomas Ruger to John Young, April 17, 1880, microcopy 234, LR, OIA, MS, roll 518, frames 0241–42, RG 75, NARA.

76. John Young, Blackfeet Agent, to Col. Thomas H. Ruger, Commander District of Montana, Helena, Montana, April 20, 1880, I-16, RBA, roll 56, Letter Book, pp. 245–47, RG 75, NARA-D.

77. Ibid.

78. Ibid.

79. Telegram from Fort Missoula, Gibson commanding, to Asst. Adj. General, St. Paul, April 12, 1880, microcopy 234, LR, OIA, roll 518, RG 75, NARA.

80. *Benton Record*, October 14, 1880.

81. Report, Lieutenant Hannay to Post Adjutant, Fort Shaw, May 3, 1880, microcopy 234, LR, OIA, roll 518, frames 0178–91, RG 75, NARA.

82. Ibid.

83. See, for example, U.S. Commissioner of Indian Affairs, *Annual Report, 1858*, as quoted in Mark D. Spence, *Dispossessing the Wilderness*, p. 30.

84. See Stern, *Chiefs and Change*, p. 344. Stern relied on the recollection of Sarah I. McKinlay found in her letter to Eva Dye, January 23, 1892, E. E. Dye Collection, MSS 1089, Oregon Historical Society.

85. For one description of this attitude, see Deloria, *Indians in Unexpected Places*, p. 29n29.

86. Regarding those recommending "feed or fight," let this example present the case, made again and again by nearly everyone, from generals to local newspapers: "Again, as a matter of pure policy, leaving out of consideration higher motives, we ought to provide in some reasonable and proper way for the support of the Indian. It is cheaper to feed him than to fight him. For every dollar that has been spent to feed and clothe Indians we have spent ten to fight them." *Helena Weekly Herald*, August 12, 1880, p. 4.

87. *Helena Daily Independent*, December 25, 1880.

88. U.S. Commissioner of Indian Affairs, *Annual Report*, 1875, p. 527.

89. Ewers, *The Blackfeet*, p. 294.

CHAPTER 6

1. An illness, defined by words like "neurosis" and "depression," or "a state of mental depression, in which the misery is unreasonable." See George Henry Savage, *Insanity and the Allied Neuroses*, 1898, p. 151, as cited in Berrios, "Melancholia and Depression," p. 301.

2. Catherine M. MacLennan, Letter to President Woodrow Wilson, June 13, 1914, ROPA, pardon case files, 28-692, RG 204, NARA.

3. Millikan, "Wards of the Nation," p. 110.

4. Yanni, "Linear Plan for Insane Asylums," p. 24.

5. Millikan, "Wards of the Nation," pp. 52–56.

6. Yanni, "Linear Plan for Insane Asylums," p. 39.

7. Winfrid Overholser, "An Historical Sketch," p. 7.

8. Gamwell and Tomes, *Madness in America*, p. 93, quoting Thomas Kirkbride and Isaac Ray, Superintendent of Butler Hospital for the Insane in Providence, Rhode Island.

9. Winfrid Overholser, "An Historical Sketch," p. 7.

10. Yanni, "Linear Plan for Insane Asylums," p. 43.

11. Quoted in Winfrid Overholser, "An Historical Sketch," pp. 11–12.

12. Godding, "Our Insane Neighbor," p. 127, quoted in Milliken, p. 148.

13. Quoted in Winfrid Overholser, "An Historical Sketch," pp. 10–11.

14. Ibid.

15. Millikan, pp. 130–31, 133.

16. Gamwell and Tomes, *Madness in America*, p. 58.

17. Ibid.

18. This information comes from research done on my behalf by Dr. Jogues Prandoni, PhD (DMH), of St. Elizabeths Hospital. He investigated "Grey Ash," where records indicate that Spopee stayed, and determined that it was the name of a ward in West Lodge. Correspondence between author and Dr. Prandoni, June 9, 2011.

19. Linderman, *Plenty-Coups*, p. 311.

20. Nabokov, *Two Leggings*, p. 197.

21. Wissler, "Social Organization and Ritualistic Ceremonies," p. 47.

22. Rothman, *Discovery of the Asylum*, p. 266.

23. Nabokov, *Two Leggings*, p. 197.

24. Rothman, *Discovery of the Asylum*, pp. 129, 133.

25. Quoted in Sacks, "Lost Virtues of the Asylum," p. 50.

26. H. M. Teller, Secretary, Department of the Interior, OIA, to Dr. W. W. Godding, St. Elizabeths Medical Superintendent, August 1, 1882, RSEH, entry 66, case file 5445, RG 418, NARA.

27. Ibid., Synopsis of Record.

28. Ibid. In the Blackfeet agency census of August 1877, taken by Agent John Young, the head of the household given number 174 is named "One-goes-under-water," which is very close to "One-Who-Swims-Under-the-Water." See "Census of the Indians at the Agency, 1877," August 13, 1877, microcopy 234, LR, OIA, roll 506, 1877, frame 208, RG 75, NARA.

29. Conference Report, Case #5445, May 11, 1914, RSEH, entry 66, case file 5445, RG 418, NARA.

30. One-Who-Goes-Under-the-Water to Spopee, October 24, 1882, RSEH, entry 66, case file 5445, RG 418, NARA. The Big Lake referred to is not Chief Big Lake, who appeared in the 1840 accounts of Father Jean-Paul DeSmet and Nicolas Point, S.J., as they attempted to convert the Piegans to Christianity. Big-brave, or Mountain Chief, kept a winter count that is reproduced in Wissler, "Social Organization and Ritualistic Ceremonies," p. 48, where the second entry reads: "[I]n the fall of the year, Big-lake, chief of The-don't laugh band died." There is no indication as to the year, although it was probably 1874 because there was an election in 1875 to select a successor. See Ewers, *The Blackfeet*, pp. 273–74. As for Painted Wing, he was included in the 1907 Allotment Census as the father of Little Blaze and was still living in 1916. Enrollment records state that a "Painted Wings" died in May 1916 at age of eighty-five. See Indian Census Rolls taken by Superintendent C. H. Ellis: Probate record 35063-19 VDL, December 29, 1919, Blackfeet Tribe, Individual Records, Browning, Mont.

31. One-Who-Goes-Under-the-Water to W. W. Gooding, M.D., June 19, 1883, from Piegan, Choteau County, Montana, RSEH, entry 66, case file 5445, RG 418,

NARA. An "Antelope Woman" is listed in the "1877 Census of Indians at the Agency" as head of household number 175 with eighteen people in the lodge—located just next to "One goes under water." See John Young to J. W. Smith, August 13, 1877, microcopy 234, LR, OIA, roll 506, 1877, frame 208, RG 75, NARA.

32. One-Who-Goes-Under-the-Water to W. W. Gooding, M.D., June 19, 1883 (see note 31).

33. *Helena Daily Herald*, January 6, 1883, p. 3; and *Fort Benton River Press*, January 17, 1883, p. 7.

34. Spopee, Snake, to One-Who-Swims-Under-the-Water, June 27, 1884, RSEH, entry 66, case file 5445, RG 418, NARA. At his sentencing in the Helena courtroom, Spopee had signed his statement or final confession "Big Snake or O-much-sixXsic-a-nach-gaon." Like most men, Spopee had a number of names. For a discussion of "naming," see Wissler, "Social Organization and Ritualistic Ceremonies of the Blackfoot Indians," pp. 16–18. Perhaps the name Snake or Big Snake had special meaning to his wife. The doctor referred to as "Doctor Stocks" was Maurice J. Stack, M.D., second assistant physician. Dr. Stack died on October 17, 1909. See October 20, 1909, *New York Times* obituary, provided by Jogues Prandoni, Ph.D., St. Elizabeths Hospital.

35. Transfers, Spopee alias Turtle, RSEH, case file 5445, RG 418, NARA.

36. Superintendent William A. White to Secretary of the Interior, May 11, 1914, summarizing Spopee's tenure at the Government Hospital for the Insane, RSEH, case file 5445, RG 418, NARA.

37. Case history of Spopee presented by Dr. Bernard Glueck, May 11, 1914, RSEH, case file 5445, RG 418, NARA.

38. Ibid.

39. Ibid.

40. Ibid.

41. Spopee to John E. Toner, M.D. RSEH, case file 5445, RG 418, NARA, interpolation in original. Dr. Toner was listed as early as 1896 in the Annual Report of St. Elizabeths Hospital. By 1902 he was the fifth assistant physician in charge of Howard Hall and West Lodge and by 1905–06 he was senior assistant physician.

42. Conference Report (including case history of Spopee presented by Dr. Bernard Glueck), Officers of Hospital, 1908, RSEH, case file 5445, RG 418, NARA.

43. Ibid. Frank H. Dixon, M.D., was listed in the annual report as junior assistant physician for 1913–14 and resigned in 1915.

44. Conference Report, Officers of Hospital, 1910, RSEH, case file 5445, RG 418, NARA.

45. Gamwell and Tomes, *Madness in America*, p. 93.

46. Ward Notes, January 1, 1912, RSEH, case file 5445, RG 418, NARA.

47. Ibid., August, 1, 1912.

48. Ibid.

49. Ibid.

50. Conference Report, Officers of Hospital, 1914, RSEH, file 5445, p. 557, RG 418, NARA.

CHAPTER 7

1. Clarke, "The Story of Spo-Pee."

2. U.S. Commissioner of Indian Affairs, *Annual Report*, September 1914, p. 63.

3. Clarke, "The Story of Spo-Pee," p. 16.

4. Commissioner Sells to Mrs. Malcolm Clark, Browning, Montana, CCF, 41522-14-175.5, NARA. An alternative file within the CCF is Education-51948-1915, May 13, 1915.

5. U.S. Commissioner of Indian Affairs, *Annual Report*, 1914, p. 63.

6. Ibid.

7. Interestingly, Cato Sells in the 1920s became intimately involved in another strange and even more famous case, that of Jackson Barnett, a Creek Indian from Oklahoma, who became fabulously wealthy as a result of the discovery of oil on his property. Barnett, as with Spopee, was described by authorities as indifferent, eccentric, feeble minded, and incompetent. He became a pawn in a lengthy power struggle among many, including government authorities, over who should control his wealth and estate. This story is marvelously told by Tanis C. Thorne in *The World's Richest Indian*. But while Commissioner Sells may have succumbed to a patronizing concern for the weak and assailed in both cases, his altruism in the case if Jackson Barnett was both compromised and suspect.

8. Smith, *Reimagining Indians*, especially pp. 14–15.

9. *Washington Evening Star*, April 18, 1914.

10. *New York Sun*, Sunday, April 19, 1914, first section, p. 7.

11. Ibid.

12. *Washington Herald*, Sunday, April 19, 1914, p. 7. See also *Kalispell Daily Interlake*, April 24, 1914, p. 1, for Secretary Lane's support, and *Great Falls Tribune*, April 26, 1914.

13. Smith, *Reimagining Indians*, pp. 14–15.

14. Ewers, *The Blackfeet*, pp. 92–95.

15. Ibid., p. 304.

16. Malone and Roeder, *Montana*, pp. 124–25.

17. Wessel, "Agriculture on the Reservations," p. 18.

18. For a thorough discussion, see Rosier, *Rebirth of the Blackfeet Nation*, pp. 13–20.

19. From 1906, Indian reservations were no longer administered by "agents," subject to the old patronage system, but by "government school superintendents," who then came under Civil Service regulations. See Wessel, "Political Assimilation," p. 63.

20. Kvasnicka and Viola, eds., *Commissioners of Indian Affairs*, p. 244.

21. Ibid.

22. Arthur E. McFatridge, Superintendent, Blackfeet Agency, to Cato Sells, Commissioner of Indian Affairs, April 28, 1914, Blackfeet Agency, Copies of Official Letters Sent, vol. 27, entry 4, RG 75, NARA-D.

23. Ibid.

24. *Blackfeet Indian Reservation: Serial One,* Hearings before the Joint Commission of the Congress of the United States to Investigate Indian Affairs, 63rd Cong., 2nd sess., part 6, February 21, 1914.

25. E. B. Linnen, "A Digest of Charges against Arthur E. McFatridge as Superintendent of the Blackfeet School," CCF, 1907–39, Blackfeet Agency 154, RG 75, NARA.

26. E. B. Linnen, Chief Inspector, Memoranda for Commissioner Sells, April 3, 1914, CCF, 1907–39, Blackfeet Agency 154, RG 75, NARA.

27. Arthur E. McFatridge, Superintendent, Blackfeet Agency, to Cato Sells, Commissioner of Indian Affairs, April 28, 1914, Blackfeet Agency, Copies of Official Letters Sent, vol. 27, entry 4, pp. 248–52, RG 75, NARA.

28. Ibid.

29. Ibid.

30. Mrs. Takes Gun to Commissioner Sells, April 30, 1914, ROPA, enclosure 4451, received in the OIA May 9, 1914, and in the Dept. of Justice, Pardon Attorney's Office May 13, 1914, pardon case files, 28-692, RG 204, NARA.

31. Ibid.

32. See Arthur E. McFatridge to Cato Sells, May 4, 1914, I-16, RBA, roll 74, p. 272–73, RG 75, NARA-D.

33. Ibid.

34. One-Who-Goes-Under-the-Water to Spo-pe, October 24, 1882, RSEH, entry 66, case file 5445, RG 418, NARA.

35. Arthur E. McFatridge to Cato Sells, May 4, 1914 (see note 32).

36. Telegram, Cato Sells, Commissioner of Indian Affairs, to Arthur E. Mc-Fatridge, Superintendent, Blackfeet Agency, May 7, 1914, I-16, RBA, roll 74, p. 277, NARA-D.

37. Ibid., p. 278.

38. Rosier, *Rebirth of the Blackfeet Nation*, pp. 15–20.

39. For an excellent biographical sketch of Robert J. Hamilton, see Wessel, "Political Assimilation," p. 62.

40. *Blackfeet Indian Reservation: Serial One,* pp. 610–11 (see note 24).

41. Ibid.

42. Robert J. Hamilton to Cato Sells, Commissioner of Indian Affairs, May 1, 1914, Indian Delegations to Washington, University Publications, microfilm, reel 1 of 25, frame 0435, CCF, series A, RG 75, NARA.

43. Cato Sells, Commissioner of Indian Affairs, to Robert J. Hamilton, May 7, 1914, Indian Delegations to Washington, University Publications, microfilm, reel 1 of 25, frame 0446, CCF, series A, RG 75, NARA.

44. Indian Delegations to Washington, D.C. University Publications, microfilm, reel 1 of 25, frame 0444-0446.

45. Robert J. Hamilton to President of the United States, May 2, 1914, with note from Interior Department attached, May 5, 1914, signed by Adolph C. Miller, Asst. to the Secretary, ROPA, pardon case files, 28-692, RG 204, NARA.

46. William A. White to unknown, titled "In re: Spopee (alias Turtle)," May 13, 1914, RSEH, case file 5445, RG 418, NARA.

47. Conference Report, presented by Dr. Glueck, May 11, 1914, RSEH, case file 5445, RG 418, NARA.

48. William A. White to unknown, May 13, 1914 (see note 46).

49. Ibid.

50. Franklin K. Lane, Secretary of Interior, to Attorney General, Department of Justice, May 16, 1914, ROPA, pardon case files, 28-692, RG 204, NARA.

51. Ibid., p. 2.

52. Ibid., p. 4.

53. Ibid., p. 6.

54. Ibid., pp. 8–9.

55. William White to unknown recipient, May 11, 1914, RSEH, case file 5445, RG 418, NARA.

56. Catherine M. MacLennan to the President of the United States, June 13, 1914, ROPA, pardon case files, 28-692, RG 204, NARA. Born Catherine M. Kilbourne, Mrs. MacLennan had been in government service since 1896 and had resigned from her position as clerk to marry Dr. Gallagher in 1901. See "Order of March 10, 1903," p. 141.

57. *New York Evening Telegram,* June 15, 1914.

58. Catherine M. MacLennan to the President of the United States, June 13, 1914, ROPA, pardon case files, 28-692, RG 204, NARA.

59. James A. Finch, Pardon Attorney to Attorney General, James C. McReynolds, June 25, 1914, ROPA, pardon case files, 28-692, p. 4, RG 204, NARA.

60. Ibid., p. 5.

61. Ibid.

62. Ibid., p. 14.

63. Ibid.

64. Attorney General James C. McReynolds to President of the United States, no date (but cover of the envelope lists schedule, stating To President, June 6, 1914), ROPA, pardon case files, 28-692, RG 204, NARA.

65. Attorney General to William A. White, Superintendent, Government Hospital for the Insane, Washington, D.C., July 7, 1914, ROPA, pardon case files, 28-692, RG 204, NARA.

66. *Washington Times,* evening edition, July 7, 1914.

67. Ibid. See also "Spo Pee, Victim of Error," *Literary Digest,* August, 1, 1914, p. 207, quoting *Washington Times* and *New York World,* July 8, 1914, p. 10.

68. *Washington Herald,* July 8, 1914, and *New York World,* Sunday, July 12, second section, p. 5.

69. Catherine M. MacLennan to the President of the United States (see note 58).

70. *Washington Herald*, July 8, 1914.

71. *Washington Times*, July 8, 1914.

72. *Oakland Tribune*, July 8, 1914. For playing to the audience and the ensuing laughter, see *Washington Herald*, July 8, 1914, and *Los Angeles Times*, July 8, 1914, p. 1.

73. *Washington Herald*, July 8, 1914

74. *Washington Post*, July 10, 1914, p. 14.

75. *Los Angeles Times*, July 8, 1914, p. 1.

76. *New York Herald*, July 8, 1914, p. 8.

77. On July 12 the *New York World* reported, dateline Washington, July 11, 1914, that Spopee left on the train on the forenoon of Wednesday, July 8. The *New York Herald* said the same thing.

78. According to Earl Old Person, Piegan elder and hereditary chief of the Blackfeet, "When they [Piegans] won, it was said 'they came back eating berries.'" Author's interview with Earl Old Person, June 12, 2001, Missoula, Montana. See also Ewers, *The Horse in Blackfoot Indian Culture*, p. 177, where Weasel Tail, a principal informant, told of a favorite song sung by young men setting out on horse-raiding parties: "Girl don't worry about me. I'll be eating berries coming home." The diary of Willy Uhlenbeck (in Eggermont-Molenaar, *Montana 1911*, p. 47) related a story in which Bear Chief said, "Soon we will go home; then we will eat cherries and ride the horses we stole from our enemies." Undoubtedly, this is a mistranslation and "cherries" should be "berries."

CHAPTER 8

1. Herbert Quick, "What Shall We Do About Spo Pee's Lost Life," *St. Paul Daily News*, Saturday, July 25, 1914, p. 4.

2. *Detroit Free Press*, "Special to the Free Press," July 9, 1914.

3. *Minneapolis Journal*, Evening, July 9, 1914, p. 1.

4. Dempsey, *Big Bear*, pp. 150–62.

5. Dusenberry, *The Montana Cree*, p. 43.

6. For the trading at Carrol on the Missouri River, some 150 miles below Fort Benton, see Schultz, *My Life as an Indian*, pp. 376–79. Schultz estimated that "about two thousand Canadian Crees, under Chief Big Bear," traded there the winter of 1880–81.

7. *Great Falls Tribune*, July 12, 1914. See also *Kalispell Bee*, Tuesday, July 14, 1914, p. 6.

8. *Cut Bank Pioneer Press*, July 17, 1914, p. 1.

9. *Choteau Montanan*, July 10, 1914, p. 1.

10. James Upson Sanders to George Bird Grinnell, November 12, 1914, Grinnell papers, Scholarly Resources, series 2, subject files, Joe Kipp, 1885–1922, folder 180, reel 43, frames 0585–86.

11. Although there is no dateline, this syndicated story had a byline, William Atherton DuPuy, and it appeared in a number of newspapers under the heading "With Pen and Camera." It was a package with text and photographic halftones, sheets of metal that had been glued to blocks of wood, which were cut to size, called "cuts" and fitted to the text to form a page or part of a page. These were sent out by mail and could be used whenever. The story, "Spo-Pee. Sane Indian held Thirty-two Years Amid Maniacs," appeared, among other places, in the *Ogden Standard,* Ogden City, Utah, April 7, 1915, the *Edwardsville Intelligencer,* Edwardsville, Illinois, March 9, 1915, the *Fitchburg Daily Sentinel,* Fitchburg, Massachusetts, February 27, 1915, and the *Great Falls Daily Leader,* Great Falls, Montana, April 7, 1915.

12. *Great Falls Daily Leader,* April 7, 1915.

13. *Cut Bank Tribune,* July 16, 1914.

14. Ibid.

15. Indian Census Rolls, 1885–1940, Blackfeet Agency, 1914–19, reel 6, under "Takes Gun, 1914," microfilm publication 595, RG 75, NARA.

16. *Great Falls Daily Tribune,* July 11, 1914, p. 5.

17. Ibid.

18. Author's interview with Joe Bear Medicine, Star School.

19. *Great Falls Tribune,* July 9, 1914. For reference to legal complications, see Report of the Commissioner of Indian Affairs for 1914, September 21, 1914, p. 3.

20. Farr, "A Point of Entry," p. 69.

21. Arthur E. McFatridge to Cato Sells, Commissioner of Indian Affairs, July 24, 1914, I-16, RBA, roll 74, pp. 473–74, RG 75, NARA.

22. Ibid.

23. U.S. Commissioner of Indian Affairs, *Annual Report,* 1914, p. 3.

24. *Great Falls Daily Tribune,* July 22, 1914; and *Washington Post,* July 22, 1914, p. 14.

25. Harry Lane, Report to Joint Committee to Investigate Indian Affairs, January 23, 1915, in *Blackfeet Indian Reservation: Serial Two,* Hearings before the Joint Commission of the Congress of the United States to Investigate Indian Affairs, 63rd Cong., 3rd sess., part 6-A, February 11, 1915, pp. 653–58.

26. Ibid., p. 655.

27. John E. Daugherty, M.D., to Cato Sells, Commissioner of Indian Affairs, no date, received August 27, 1914, CCF, folder 92616-1914, Blackfeet 154, RG 75, NARA.

28. E. B. Linnen, "A Digest of Charges against Arthur E. McFatridge," CCF, box 38, 83592-1914-154 Blackfeet, RG 75, NARA.

29. *Washington Post,* August 30, 1914.

30. *Cut Bank Tribune,* July 23, 1914.

31. Arthur W. Brown (OIA Clerk), Report on Blackfeet Reservation, September 2, 1914, CCF, folder 126133-1914 Blackfeet Agency 154, RG 75, NARA.

32. Ibid.

33. E. B. Linnen, "Digest of Charges Against Arthur McFatridge, pp. 5–6 (see note 28).

34. Cato Sells to Arthur E. McFatridge, November 14, 1914, CCF, file 41522-14-Blackfeet 175.5, box 52, RG 75, NARA.

35. Superintendent A. E. McFatridge to Commissioner Cato Sells, December 18, 1914, CCF, 41522-14-175.5, box 52, RG 75, NARA.

36. Ibid.

37. There are many newspaper references to Spopee's supposed reason for adding "Purifies" to his name; for a representative, see *Spokesman-Review,* July 9, 1914, p. 3.

38. Spopee to Cato Sells, Commissioner of Indian Affairs, January 4, 1914, CCF, 41522-14-175.5, NARA.

39. Cato Sells to Spopee, January 19, 1915, CCF, 41522-14-175.5, RG 75, NARA.

40. Cato Sells to C. L. Ellis, Special Agent in Charge, Blackfeet School, January 19, 1915, CCF, 41522-14-175.5, RG 75, NARA.

41. Report of Investigation of Affairs on the Blackfeet Indian Reservation, Montana, E. B. Linnen, chief inspector, F. S. Cook, special agent, January 9, 1915, CCF, 1907–1939, Blackfeet Agency 150, Inspection Reports, RG 75, NARA. This report can also be found in *Blackfeet Indian Reservation: Serial Two,* Hearings before the Joint Commission of the Congress of the United States to Investigate Indian Affairs, 63rd Cong., 3rd sess., part 6-A, February 11, 1915.

42. Ibid.

43. C. L. Ellis to Commissioner Sells, February 2, 1915, CCF, 41522-14-175.5, RG 75, NARA.

44. Charles L. Ellis, Special Indian Agent in Charge, to Cato Salle, Commissioner of Indian Affairs, March 18, 1915, CCF, 1907–39, Blackfeet Agency 150, Inspection Reports, RG 75, NARA.

45. Cato Sells, Commissioner, to Spopee, May 13, 1915, CCF, 41522-194-175.5, RG 75, NARA.

46. C. L. Ellis to Cato Sells, Commissioner of Indian Affairs, May 30, 1915, CCF, 14522-14-175.5, RG 75, NARA.

47. *Great Falls Daily Tribune,* June 3, 1915, p. 3.

48. Ibid.

49. *Anaconda Standard,* June 4, 1915, p. 4.

50. Cato Sells, Commissioner, to Charles L. Ellis, Superintendent Blackfeet School, June 11, 1915, CCF, 41522-1914-Blackfeet 175.5, RG 75, NARA.

51. Commissioner Cato Sells to Mrs. Malcolm Clark, July 28, 1914, CCF, 41522-14-175, RG 75, NARA.

EPILOGUE

1. Author's interview with Charles Crow Chief, Great Falls, Montana, November 17, 2009.

2. *Helena Daily Herald,* January 6, 1883, p. 3; *Fort Benton River Press,* January 17, 1883, p. 7.

3. I-16, RBA, roll 56, Letter Press Book, p. 2, RG 75, NARA-D.

4. Chief Eustace interview, January 27, 1950, Claude Schaeffer papers (M-1100-88).

5. Ibid., folio 88.

6. Ben Sira (also called Sirach or Ecclesiasticus) 44:9. I was alerted to this passage, with its telling concern, by my friend Albert Borgmann. See Borgmann, *Holding On to Reality,* p. 229.

7. *Minneapolis Journal,* July 8, 1914, p. 9.

8. Borgmann, *Holding On to Reality,* p. 37.

References

ARCHIVES

1872 Laws of Montana Territory, Sec. 190.

Adney, Tappen. Papers. Montana Historical Society, Helena, Montana.

Canada. Parliament. Sessional Papers, 1880. Vol. 3. Paper no. 4, Report of the North-West Mounted Police for 1879 by Captain William Winder.

Canada. Parliament. Sessional Papers, 1880. Vol. 3. Second Session of the Fourth Parliament. Annual Reports for the Department of the NWMP.

Eli Guardipee's Story. Small collection 772. Montana Historical Society, Helena, Montana.

Grinnell, George Bird. Letters: private, business, editorial and private folders microfilmed for the Connecticut Audubon Society. Mansfield Library, University of Montana. Missoula, Montana.

Grinnell, George Bird. Papers. Huntington Library. San Marino, California.

Healy Reminiscences. Montana Historical Society, Helena, Montana.

Journal of Proceedings, Third Judicial District. Territorial Court, Helena, Montana. Records of U.S. District Courts. Record Group 21. National Archives and Records Administration, Pacific Alaska Region. Seattle, Washington.

Kennedy, Margaret A. "Whoop-Up Trail of Northcentral Montana." National Register of Historic Places, Montana State Historic Preservation Office. Helena, Montana.

Letters Received by the Attorney General, 1871–1884: Western Law and Order. Microfilm collection. University Publications of America.

Letters Received by the Montana Superintendency, 1824–81. Microcopy 234. Record Group 75. Rocky Mountain Region Archives – Denver. National Archives and Records Administration.

Pardon Case Files, 28-692. New Year's Day, 1881. Record Group 204. National Archives and Records Administration, Washington, D.C.

Records of St. Elizabeths Hospital. File 5445. Record Group 418. National Archives and Records Administration, Washington, D.C.

Records of the Bureau of Indian Affairs. RG 75. Rocky Mountain Region Archives, Denver. National Archives and Records Administration.

Report on Blackfeet Reservation, by Arthur W. Brown. September 2, 1914. Central Classified Files, File 41522-14-175.5 (pardons). National Archives and Records Administration.

Schaeffer, Claude. Papers. M-1100-88. Glenbow Archives, Calgary, Alberta.

United States v. Spo-pe alias Turtle. November/December 1880. District Courts, Territory of Montana, Third Judicial District. Case Files 1867–89. Box 28, Folder 425. Record Group 21. National Archives and Records Administration, Pacific Alaska Region, Seattle, Washington.

U.S. Army Corps of Engineers Map of Northern Montana, by John Wilson. 1881. Montana State Historical Preservation Office, Helena, Montana.

U.S. Congress. Joint Commission of the Congress of the United States to Investigate Indian Affairs. *Blackfeet Indian Reservation: Serial One.* 63rd Cong., 2nd sess, part 6, February 21, 1914.

U.S. Congress. Joint Commission of the Congress of the United States to Investigate Indian Affairs. *Blackfeet Indian Reservation: Serial Two.* 63rd Cong., 3rd sess., part 6-A, February 11, 1915.

BOOKS AND ARTICLES

Allen, Frederick. *A Decent Orderly Lynching: The Montana Vigilantes.* Norman: University of Oklahoma Press, 2004.

Berrios, G. E. "Melancholia and Depression during the Nineteenth Century: A Conceptual History." *British Journal of Psychiatry* 153, no. 3 (1988): 298–304.

Blackfoot Gallery Committee. *The Story of the Blackfoot People: Nitsitapiisinni.* Toronto: Key Porter Books, 2001.

Borgmann, Albert. *Holding On to Reality: The Nature of Information at the Turn of the Millennium.* Chicago: University of Chicago Press, 1999.

Brown, Alison K., and Laura Peers. *Pictures Bring Us Messages: Photographs and Histories from the Kainai Nation.* Toronto: University of Toronto Press, 2007.

Burlingame, Merle. *The Montana Frontier.* Helena: State Publishing Co., 1942.

Clarke, Ella. "The Story of Spo-Pee: From the New York World." *The Red Man* (September 1914): 10–18.

Commissioners of the North West Mounted Police. *Opening the West: Official Reports of the North West Mounted Police.* Toronto: Coles Canadiana Collection, 1973.

Daschuk, J. W., Paul Hackett, Scott Macneil. "Treaties and Tuberculosis: First Nations People in Late 19th-Century Western Canada, a Political and Economic Transformation." *Canadian Bulletin of Medical History* 23, no. 2 (2006): 307–30.

De Jong, Joselyn. *Blackfoot Texts.* Amsterdam: Johannes Mueller, 1914.

Deloria, Philip J. *Indians in Unexpected Places.* Lawrence: University Press of Kansas, 2004.

DeMarce, Roxanne. *Blackfeet Heritage, 1907–1908.* Browning, Mont.: Blackfeet Heritage Program, 1980. Now available in a revised edition: Hungry Wolf, Adolf. *Blackfeet Heritage Census Book, 1907–1908.* Browning, Mont.: Good Medicine Books. www.blackfootpapers.com/product/CEN.

Dempsey, Hugh A. *A Blackfoot Winter Count.* Occasional Paper No. 1. Calgary, Alberta: Glenbow-Alberta Institute, 1965.

———. *Jerry Potts: Plainsman.* Occasional Paper No. 2. Calgary, Alberta: Glenbow Museum, 1966.

———. *Crowfoot: Chief of the Blackfeet.* Norman: University of Oklahoma Press, 1972.

———. *Red Crow: Warrior Chief.* Saskatoon: Western Prairie Books, 1980.

———. *Big Bear: The End of Freedom.* Lincoln: University of Nebraska Press, 1984.

———. *Firewater: The Impact of the Whiskey Trade on the Blackfoot Nation.* Calgary, Alberta: Fifth House, 2002.

———. *The Vengeful Wife and Other Blackfoot Stories.* Norman: University of Oklahoma Press, 2003.

Dempsey, Hugh A., ed. "The Starvation Year: Edgar Dewdney's Diary for 1879: Part 1." *Alberta History* 31, no. 1 (Winter 1983).

———, ed. "The Starvation Year: Edgar Dewdney's Diary for 1879: Part 2." *Alberta History* 31, no. 2 (Spring 1983).

Dempsey, L. James. *Blackfoot War Art: Pictographs of the Reservation Period, 1880–2000.* Norman: University of Oklahoma Press, 2007.

Denny, C. E. *Riders of the Plains: A Reminiscence of the Early and Exciting Days in the North West.* Calgary, Canada: The Herald Company, 1905.

Dobak, William A. "Killing the Canadian Buffalo, 1821–1881." *Western Historical Quarterly* 27 (Spring 1996): 33–52.

Donovan, Tom. *Legal Hangings. Vol. 1* of *Hanging around the Big Sky: The Unofficial Guide to Lynching, Strangling and Legal Hangings of Montana.* Great Falls: Portage Meadows Publishing, 2007.

Dusenberry, Verne. *The Montana Cree: A Study in Religious Persistence.* Norman: University of Oklahoma Press, 1962.

Edgerton, Keith. *Montana Justice: Power, Punishment, and the Penitentiary.* Seattle: University of Washington Press, 2004.

Eggermont-Molenaar, Mary, ed. *Montana 1911: A Professor and His Wife among the Blackfeet.* Lincoln: University of Nebraska Press, 2005.

Ellis, Mark R. "Legal Culture and Community on the Great Plains: State of Nebraska v. John Burley." *Western Historical Quarterly* 36, no. 2 (Summer 2005): 179–99.

Ewers, John C. *The Horse in Blackfoot Indian Culture.* Smithsonian Institution, Bureau of American Ethnology Bulletin 159. Washington, D.C.: Government Printing Office, 1955.

———. *The Blackfeet: Raiders on the Northwestern Plains.* Civilization of the American Indian 49. Norman: University of Oklahoma Press, 1958.

Farr, William E. "'When We Were First Paid': The Blackfoot Treaty, the Western Tribes, and the Creation of the Common Hunting Territory, 1855." *Great Plains Quarterly* 21, no. 2 (Spring 2001): 131–54.

———. "Going to Buffalo: Indian Hunting Migrations across the Rocky Mountains." Part 2, "Civilian Permits, Army Escorts." *Montana The Magazine of Western History*, 54, no. 1 (Spring 2004): 26–44.

———. "A Point of Entry: The Blackfeet Adoption of Walter McClintock." In *Lanterns on the Prairie: The Blackfeet Photographs of Walter McClintock*, ed. Steven L. Grafe, 43–81. Norman: University of Oklahoma Press, 2009.

Flores, Dan. "The Great Contraction: Bison and Indians in the Northern Plains Environmental History." In *The Little Bighorn Legacy*, ed. Charles Rankin, 3–22. Helena: Montana Historical Society Press, 1996.

Friesen, Gerald. *The Canadian Prairies: A History*. Toronto: University of Toronto Press, 1987.

Gamwell, Lynn, and Nancy Tomes. *Madness in America: Cultural and Medical Perceptions of Mental Illness before 1914*. Ithaca, N.Y.: Cornell University Press, 1995.

Godding, W. W. "Our Insane Neighbor: His Rights and Ours." *American Psychology Journal*, 1883.

Grant, George M. *Ocean to Ocean: Sanford Fleming's Expedition through Canada in 1872*. Toronto: Coles, 1873.

Graybill, Andrew. *Policing the Great Plains*. Lincoln: University of Nebraska Press, 2007.

Greene, Jerome A. *Nez Perce Summer 1877: The U.S. Army and the Nee-Me-Poo Crisis*. Helena: Montana Historical Society Press, 2000.

Guice, John D. W. *The Rocky Mountain Bench: The Territorial Supreme Courts of Colorado, Montana, and Wyoming*. New Haven, Conn.: Yale University Press, 1972.

Hampton, Bruce. *Children of Grace: The Nez Perce War of 1877*. New York: Henry Hold, 1994.

Hogue, Michel. "Disputing the Medicine Line: The Plains Crees and the Canadian-American Border, 1876–1885." *Montana The Magazine of Western History* 52 (Winter 2002): 2–17.

Holmes, Oliver W., and James A. Garfield. "Peregrinations of a Politician: James A. Garfield's Diary of a Trip to Montana in 1872." *Montana The Magazine of Western History*, 6, no. 4 (Autumn, 1956): 34–45.

Hunt, William R. *Whiskey Peddler: Jonny Healy, North Frontier Trader*. Missoula, Mont.: Mountain Press, 1993.

Hutchinson, Elizabeth. *The Indian Craze: Primitivism, Modernism, and Transculturation in American Art, 1890–1915*. Durham, N.C.: Duke University Press, 2009.

Keve, Paul W. "Building a Better Prison: The First Three Decades of the Detroit House of Correction." *Michigan Historical Review* (Fall 1999): 1–28.

Kirkbride, Thomas S. *On the Construction, Organization, and General Arrangements of Hospitals for the Insane*. Philadelphia: Lindsay & Blakiston, 1854.

Kluger, Richard. *The Bitter Waters of Medicine Creek: A Tragic Clash between White and Native America*. New York: Alfred A. Knopf, 2011.

Kvasnicka, Robert M., and Herman J. Viola, eds. *The Commissioners of Indian Affairs, 1824–1977*. Lincoln: University of Nebraska Press, 1979.

LaDow, Beth. *The Medicine Line: Life and Death on a North American Borderland*. New York: Routledge, 2001.

Linderman, Frank B. *Plenty-Coups: Chief of the Crows*. Lincoln: University of Nebraska Press, 1962.

MacEwan, Grant. *Sitting Bull: The Years in Canada*. Edmonton: Hurtig, 1973.

Malone, Michael P., Richard B. Roeder, and William L. Lang. *Montana: A History of Two Centuries*. Seattle: University of Washington Press, 1976.

Mathes, Valerie Sherer, and Richard Lowitt. *The Standing Bear Controversy: Prelude to Indian Reform*. Urbana and Chicago: University of Illinois Press, 2003.

McClure, A. C. "Wilber Fisk Sanders." *Contributions to the Historical Society of Montana*, 8 (1917): 25–35.

McCrady, David G. *Living with Strangers: The Nineteenth-Century Sioux and the Canadian-American Borderlands*. Lincoln: University of Nebraska Press, 2006.

McKanna, Clare V., Jr. *The Trial of "Indian Joe": Race and Justice in the Nineteenth-Century West*. Lincoln: University of Nebraska Press, 2003.

McManus, Sheila. *The Line Which Separates*. Lincoln: University of Nebraska Press, 2005.

Millikan, Frank Rives. "Wards of the Nation: The Making of St. Elizabeths Hospital, 1852–1920." Ph.D. diss., George Washington University, 1990.

Morris, Alexander. *The Treaties of Canada with the Indians of Manitoba and the North-West Territories Including the Negotiations on Which They Were Based and Other Information Relating Thereto*. 1880. Reprint, Saskatoon, Saskatchewan: Fifth House Publishers, 1991.

Morriss, Andrew P. "Judicial Removal in Western States and Territories." In *Law in the Western United States*, ed. Gordon Morriss Baaken. Norman: University of Oklahoma Press, 2000.

Nabokov, Peter. *Two Leggings: The Making of a Crow Warrior*. New York: Thomas Y. Crowell Company, 1967.

"Order of March 10, 1903," *Good Government: Official Journal of the National Civil Service Reform League*, 20 (January 1903–December 1903).

Overholser, Joel. *Fort Benton: World's Innermost Port*. Fort Benton, Mont.: J. Overholser, 1987.

Overholser, Winfrid. "An Historical Sketch of Saint Elizabeths Hospital." In *Centennial Papers Saint Elizabeths Hospital, 1855–1955*. Baltimore: Waverly Press, 1956.

Palmer, Howard, with Tamara Palmer. *Alberta: A New History*. Edmonton: Hurtig Publishers, 1990.

Pemberton, W. Y. "Montana's Pioneer Courts." *Contributions to the Historical Society of Montana*, 8 (1917): 99–104.

Prucha, Francis Paul. *American Indian Treaties: The History of a Political Anomaly.* Berkeley and Los Angeles: University of California Press, 1997.

Racska, Paul M. *Winter Count: A History of the Blackfoot People.* Calgary, Alberta: Friesen Printers, 1979.

Reeves, Brian, and Sandra Peacock. "Our Mountains Are Our Pillows: An Ethnographic Overview of Glacier National Park." Unpublished manuscript. Final Report 2006. On file at the National Park Service, Rocky Mountain Regional Office, Denver, Colo.

Reid, John Phillip. *Law for the Elephant: Property and Social Behavior on the Overland Trail.* 1980. Reprint, San Marino, Calif.: Huntington Library Press, 1996.

———. *Policing the Elephant: Crime, Punishment, and Social Behavior on the Overland Trail.* San Marino, Calif.: Huntington Library Press, 1997.

Revised Statutes of the United States, Second Edition, 1873–1874. Washington: GPO, 1878.

Rosier, Paul C. *Rebirth of the Blackfeet Nation, 1912–1954.* Lincoln: University of Nebraska Press, 2001.

Rothman, David J. *The Discovery of the Asylum.* Boston: Little, Brown and Company, 1971.

Sackman, Douglas Cazaux. *Wild Men: Ishi and Kroeber in the Wilderness of Modern America.* New York: Oxford University Press, 2010.

Sacks, Oliver. "The Lost Virtues of the Asylum." *New York Review of Books.* September 24, 2009: 50–52.

Schultz, James Willard. *My Life as an Indian.* New York: Houghton-Mifflin, 1914.

———. *Friends of My Life as an Indian.* Boston: Houghton Mifflin, 1923.

———. *Signposts of Adventure: Glacier National Park as the Indians Know It.* Boston: Houghton Mifflin, 1926.

———. Edited by Keith C. Seele. *Blackfeet and Buffalo: Memories of Life among the Indians.* Norman: University of Oklahoma Press, 1981.

Sharp, Paul F. *Whoop-Up Country: The Canadian-American West, 1865–1885.* 2nd ed. Helena: Historical Society of Montana, 1955.

Smith, Sherry L. *Reimagining Indians: Native Americans through Anglo Eyes, 1880–1940.* New York: Oxford University Press, 2000.

Spaulding, John M. "The Canton Asylum for Insane Indians: An Example of Institutional Neglect." *Hospital and Community Psychiatry* 37, no. 10 (October 1986): 1007–11.

Spence, Clark C. "The Territorial Bench in Montana: 1864–1889." *Montana The Magazine of Western History* 13 (1963): 32.

———. *Territorial Politics and Government in Montana 1864–89.* Urbana: University of Illinois Press, 1975.

———. "We Want a Judge: Montana Territorial Justice and Politics." *Journal of the West* 20, no. 1 (January 1981): 7–13.

Spence, Mark D. *Dispossessing the Wilderness: Indian Removal and the Making of National Parks*. New York: Oxford University Press, 1999.

Stern, Theodore. *Chiefs and Chief Traders: Indian Relations at Fort Nez Perces, 1818–1855*. Corvallis: Oregon State University Press, 1993.

———. *Chiefs and Change in the Oregon Country: Indian Relations at Fort Nez Perces, 1818–1855*. Corvallis: Oregon State University Press, 1996.

Thorne, Tanis C. *The World's Richest Indian: The Scandal over Jackson Barnett's Oil Fortune*. Oxford: Oxford University Press, 2005.

Tobias, John L. "Canada's Subjugation of the Plains Cree, 1879–1883." In *Sweet Promises: A Reader on Indian-White Relations in Canada*, ed. James R. Miller. Toronto: University of Toronto Press, 1991.

Treaty 7 Elders and Tribal Council, with Walter Hildebrandt, Sarah Carter, and Dorothy First Rider. *The True Spirit and Original Intent of Treaty 7*. Montreal; McGill-Queen's University Press, 1996.

U.S. Commissioner of Indian Affairs. *Annual Report*. Washington, D.C.: U.S. Government Printing Office, various years.

Viola, Herman J. *Diplomats in Buckskins: A History of Indian Delegations in Washington City*. Washington, D.C.: Smithsonian Institution Press, 1981.

Wessel, Thomas R. "Agriculture on the Reservations: the Case of the Blackfeet, 1885–1935." *Journal of the West* 43 (October 1979): 17–24.

———. "Political Assimilation on the Blackfoot Indian Reservation, 1887–1934: A Study in Survival." In *Plains Indian Studies: A Collection in Honor of John C. Ewers and Waldo R. Wedel*, ed. Douglas H. Ubelaker and Herman J. Viola. Washington, D.C.: Smithsonian Institution Press, 1982.

West, Elliott. *The Last Indian War: The Nez Perce Story*. New York: Oxford University Press, 2009.

Wilkinson, Charles F. *American Indians, Time, and the Law: Native Societies in a Modern Constitutional Democracy*. New Haven, Conn.: Yale University Press, 1987.

Wischmann, Lesley. *Frontier Diplomats: The Life and Times of Alexander Culbertson and Natoyist-Siksina'*. Spokane: Arthur H. Clark, 2000.

Wissler, Clark. "Social Organization and Ritualistic Ceremonies of the Blackfoot Indians." *Anthropological Papers of the American Museum of Natural History* 7 (1912).

Woodford, Frank B., and Arthur M. Woodford. *All Our Yesterdays: A Brief History of Detroit*. Detroit: Wayne State University Press, 1969.

Wright, Dennis A., Guy L. Dorius, David L. Innes, and H. Dale Lowry. "Mapping the Alberta Route of the 1887 Mormon Trek from Utah to Cardston." *Alberta History*, June 22, 2003: 2–11.

Wunder, John. "Persistence and Adaptation: The Emergence of a Legal Culture in the Northern Tier Territories, 1853–1890." In *Centennial West: Essays on the Northern Tier States*, ed. William L. Lang. Seattle: University of Washington Press, 1991.

Yanni, Carla. "The Linear Plan for Insane Asylums in the United States before 1866." *Journal of the Society of Architectural Historians* 62, no. 1 (March 2003): 24–49.

NEWSPAPERS

Unless otherwise noted or indicated by name, all newspapers listed here are (or were) published in Montana.

Anaconda Standard
Benton Record
Benton Weekly Record
Calgary Herald (Alberta, Can.)
Choteau Montanan
Cut Bank Pioneer Press
Cut Bank Tribune
Daily Missoulian
Detroit Free Press
Dillon Tribune
Edwardsville (Ill.) Intelligencer
Fitchburg (Mass.) Daily Sentinel
Fort Benton River Press
Fort Benton Weekly Record
Great Falls Tribune
Great Falls Daily Tribune
Great Falls Daily Leader
Great Falls Daily Tribune
Helena Daily Herald
Helena Daily Independent
Helena Independent
Helena Weekly Independent
Helena Weekly Herald
Kalispell Bee
Lethbridge Herald (Alberta, Can.)
Literary Digest (New York)
Los Angeles Times
Madisonian (Virginia City, Mont.)
Minneapolis Journal
Montanian
New North-West (Deer Lodge, Mont.)
New York Evening Telegram
New York Herald
New York Sun

New York World
Oakland (Calif.) Tribune
Ogden (Utah) Standard
Saskatchewan Herald (Regina, Can.)
Spokesman-Review (Spokane, Wash.)
St. Paul Daily News
Washington (D.C.) Herald
Washington (D.C.) Evening Star
Washington (D.C.) Post
Washington (D.C.) Times
Weekly Miner (Butte, Mont.)

INDEX

CPSIA information can be obtained at www.ICGtesting.com
Printed in the USA
LVOW06s0422110614

389509LV00002B/3/P